D0895432

THE RELIGIONS OF THE WORLD

THE RELIGIONS OF THE WORLD

JAN 9 1970

UNIVERSITY OF THE PACIFIC

By

GEORGE A. BARTON

*Professor of Semitic Languages and History of Religions, University
of Pennsylvania, and New Testament Literature and
Language, Philadelphia Divinity School*

GREENWOOD PRESS, PUBLISHERS
NEW YORK

LIBRARY

JAN 29 1970

UNIVERSITY OF THE PACIFIC

211287

Copyright © 1917 and 1919
by the University of Chicago Press

Reprinted with the permission
of Provident National Bank

First Greenwood Reprinting 1969

Library of Congress Catalogue Card Number 74-90469

SBN 8371-2216-3

PRINTED IN UNITED STATES OF AMERICA

TO

THE MEMORY OF

MORRIS JASTROW, JR.

COLLEAGUE, FRIEND

MASTERLY INVESTIGATOR

OF THE

BABYLONIAN-ASSYRIAN RELIGION

PREFACE

In attempting a study of the religions of the world, one is confronted with the problem of the order in which they should be taken up. The order in which they are presented in the following pages is that which the writer has found most advantageous in his own classroom: (1) an outline of primitive religions; (2) the religions of Babylonia and Egypt, which approach most closely to the primitive type; (3) the other religions which have sprung from the Hamito-Semitic stock, the religion of the Hebrews, Judaism, and Mohammedanism; (4) passing eastward to Persia, the study of Zoroastrianism; (5) the religions of India, China, and Japan; (6) the religions of Greece and Rome; and (7) the study of Christianity.

To some it may seem unnecessary to treat the religion of the Hebrews, Judaism, and Christianity in a textbook which forms a part of an educational series in which whole volumes are devoted to these subjects, but no book on the religions of the world would be complete from which a treatment of these great religions was absent, and it often gives the student a new sense of the value of these religions to study them briefly in comparison with the other religions of the world. If the time devoted to the course is too brief to permit the study of so many religions, and if the religions of Israel and Christianity are studied in other parts of the curriculum, chapters iv, v, and xv may be omitted from the course.

It is believed that teachers will find it useful to have their pupils master the outline of each religion given here, and then make it the basis of wider reading. As the library facilities of colleges differ greatly, two lists of reading are given at the end of each chapter. If considerable time can be given to the course, and the library contains the necessary material, the student should be required to look up the references cited under "Class A." If the library facilities are meager, or the time allotted to the course is brief, then those cited under "Class B" should be used. If the teacher deems it wiser to direct the student who has mastered the text of this book to investigate special topics, such topics are suggested in Appendix I, where a list of books that will be of use in such investigation will also be found.

A student who works by himself should make himself familiar with the text of this volume as already suggested, and, after doing such other reading as the works available may permit, should write a brief book on the subject for himself. For his guidance an outline of such a book will be found in Appendix II. Those who take the course under a teacher will find this exercise of writing their own books most helpful.

The writer's thanks are due to Professor A. V. Williams Jackson of Columbia for reading and criticizing the chapter on Zoroastrianism, to Professor Franklin Edgerton of the University of Pennsylvania for like help in the chapters on the religions of India, and to his colleagues Professors Tenney Frank and James F. Ferguson for rendering a similar service for the chapters on Rome and Greece.

GEORGE A. BARTON

BRYN MAWR, PA.
May, 1917

PREFACE TO THE SECOND EDITION

By the insertion in the present edition of a chapter devoted to the religion of the Celts and Teutons, a defect of the first edition of this little book has been corrected. A chapter has also been added on the unfolding of the idea of God in the religions of the world. This chapter will, in part, serve as a review of the student's previous work and, it is hoped, direct his mind to a kind of comparative study of religion that is profitable and inspiring. Minor errors have been corrected here and there throughout the book. It is hoped that in its new form the volume may continue to meet the needs of the body of students whose use of the first edition made a second possible.

GEORGE A. BARTON

July, 1919

PREFACE TO THE THIRD EDITION

In the present edition the writer has made a few corrections in the text of the book and has endeavored to bring the bibliography up to date. During the last ten years publications in the field covered by this volume have been especially numerous and more than a hundred and twenty-five new titles have been added to the list of reference books, without including those published in foreign languages. It is the writer's hope that in its new form the book may continue to merit the confidence that teachers and students have reposed in it.

GEORGE A. BARTON

PHILADELPHIA, PA.
June, 1929

TABLE OF CONTENTS

CHAPTER I

THE RELIGIONS OF PRIMITIVE PEOPLES

And yet he left not himself without witness.—Acts 14:17.

1. **Primitive peoples,** as the term is here employed, are the peoples who have never developed sufficiently to embody their ideas in literature. They are the savage and barbarous tribes of ancient and modern times. According to the generally accepted theory of evolution, all the civilized peoples of the world have arisen from a savage ancestry. The primitive peoples of antiquity may be known to some extent through survivals of their ideas and customs among their civilized descendants, as well as through occasional descriptions of their institutions by ancient writers; those of modern times, from the descriptions of travelers and missionaries and from the investigations of anthropologists.

Between the lowest and the highest savages there are many gradations. Anthropologists, however, recognize four well-defined classes of peoples: those of the early Stone Age, often called Paleolithic; those of the later Stone Age, also called Neolithic; those of the Copper Age; and those of the Bronze Age. This classification is based on the degree of intelligence manifested in making implements. Paleolithic man did not shape the stones employed for tools. He found, for example, one shaped roughly like an ax and used it as an ax. Neolithic man made flint implements and often became very skilful in their manufacture.

Men of the Copper Age learned to employ copper. The passage from the Copper Age to the Bronze Age was slow, as men learned with difficulty to employ tin and antimony as alloys. Social and religious institutions varied with the people's advancement.

2. **The method** of studying the religions of uncivilized peoples necessarily differs from the method of studying the religions of civilized races. In the latter case we turn, not only to institutions, but to religious literatures; in the former we can study only their institutions and such myths and ideas as travelers, ancient or modern, have collected from them. Myths were the hypotheses of prescientific men. By means of them they explained, in ways satisfactory to themselves, the world and their religious institutions. Myths accordingly often aid us in ascertaining fundamental religious conceptions.

3. **The psychological unity of man** is one of the most striking results of modern investigation. There are, of course, details in which the religion of any people differs from that of every other people. Indeed, in some respects the religion of every individual is peculiarly his own; it differs in some details from the religion of everyone else, for the facts of the universe impress each mind differently. Nevertheless the variations are far less than one would expect. The surprising fact is that in all parts of the world the minds of men, as they react to the fundamental facts of existence, work in so nearly the same way. This likeness of the psychological processes of man is one of the most striking discoveries of modern times. One writer declares:

The laws of human thought are frightfully rigid, are indeed automatic and inflexible. The human mind seems to be a machine; give it the same materials, and it will infallibly grind out the same product.[1] . . . . Under ordinary conditions of human life there are many more impressions on the senses which are everywhere the same or similar than the reverse. Hence the ideas, both primary and secondary, drawn from them are much more likely to resemble than to differ.[2]

While, then, early religions differ in innumerable minor details, in the great fundamental conceptions they are the same. Of many secondary conceptions too it may be said that they are all but universal. It is not the purpose of this book to follow out the details in which the religions of primitive peoples differ, but rather to glance at the fundamental ideas and institutions which they have in common. Such a survey is necessary because these fundamental ideas form the basis of the religions of civilized peoples, and many of these institutions have persisted for centuries in civilized religions, often producing far-reaching consequences.

4. **The universality of religion** is now generally conceded. Man is a worshiping animal; he is "incurably religious." Certain Australian tribes, reported on by Spencer and Gillen, appear at first sight to be exceptions to this rule, but a closer study of the facts leads one to believe that religion is not entirely absent.[3] "Religion is man's attitude toward the universe regarded as a social and ethical force," and there is no satisfactory historical evidence that since man was man there have been peoples who did not

[1] D. G. Brinton, *Religions of Primitive Peoples* (New York, 1897), p. 6.

[2] *Ibid.*, p. 7.

[3] C. H. Toy, *Introduction to the History of Religions* (New York, 1913), §§ 10–12.

attempt to enter into social relations with the extra-human powers of the universe.

5. The nature of religion.—Among primitive peoples the essential part of religion is not belief, but practice. The primary aim is to avert the anger of supernatural beings and to secure their aid in the struggle for existence. As among men anger is aroused by improper conduct, so it is believed to be with the gods. One must be careful to *do* the things that are pleasing to them. The gods are supposed to be pleased, not with what men think of them, but by the service that is rendered them. Religion is the proper manners to be observed in approaching the gods. Carelessness as to the ritual which embodies the proper etiquette toward them is thought to arouse the anger of deities and spirits. The emphasis in early religions is quite different from that in the so-called positive religions. Nevertheless we can trace in early religions certain beliefs.

6. The soul is among all men intimately connected with religion. All tribes, even the lowest, observe that a human being is made up of two parts, the body of flesh and bones, and an impalpable something that lives within. This impalpable something, or soul, is called by various names, but belief in it is universal. Among the lowest Australian tribes. it is not as well defined as among more advanced peoples, but the belief is still there, and a man's *Murup* or soul may, when he sleeps, go off and talk even with the *Murups* of the dead.[1] Among savage peoples the soul is thought to have a material form. They cannot otherwise conceive of it.

[1] See A. W. Howitt, *The Native Tribes of South-East Australia* (New York, 1904), pp. 434–42.

Perhaps a man's shadow, which, in his ignorance of optics, is to the savage inexplicable, contributed originally to this belief. Souls were not, however, always thought of as existing in human form; sometimes they were conceived in animal shapes. Early men generally identified the soul with the breath, since they noticed that a dead man no longer breathed. They seem not to have thought, however, of any one part of the body as the home of the soul.

7. **Life after death** is another of man's universal beliefs. It is only among a few modern thinkers, in whom the elemental intuitions are "sicklied o'er with the pale cast of thought," that it has ever been doubted. The universality of man's faith in the survival of the soul after death is attested in part by the universality of the belief in ghosts, and in the uniform practice of placing food in the tombs of the departed. Among all peoples, whether in the two Americas, in Central Africa, in Australia, or among the ancient inhabitants of Egypt or Palestine, not only food and drink, but the utensils that the departed had used in life were buried with him. Along with quantities of delicacies Queen Tai, of Egypt's Eighteenth Dynasty, placed in the tomb of her parents splendid easy chairs, a bed, chests of clothing, and even a chariot in which they might ride! Similarly the Indians bury with their brave his bow and arrows for use in the happy hunting-grounds beyond the setting sun.

8. **The underworld**, while not universally believed in, plays an important part among many peoples. Except where the bodies of the dead are burned, or where, as in Northern Alaska, the earth is continuously frozen, they

are buried in the ground. Where some are deposited for a time in trees, as in Australia, they are ultimately buried in the earth.[1] Naturally it was inferred that the soul descended into the earth with the body. In many parts of the world, accordingly, there is supposed to be a great cavern in the heart of the earth in which the dead abide. Such was the Aralu of the Babylonians, the Sheol of the Hebrews, the Hades of the Greeks, and the Hel of the Scandinavians. This underworld was generally thought to be a dark and cheerless place. The dead longed for the free life of the upper air where the sun shone. Among some races, as civilization advanced, this underworld was divided into Elysian fields in which the good passed cheerful and happy lives, and places of punishment in which the wicked received the reward of their deeds. Belief in an underworld is not, however, universal. Peoples living near the sea have sometimes thought of the dead as dwelling beyond the deep; others have thought of them as living in high mountains; still others have thought of them as living in the sun, moon, or stars.[2] Several peoples who have begun by thinking of the dead as in an underworld have, as they advanced, transferred that dwelling to the sky or to a heaven above the sky. Such a change can be traced among the Egyptians.

9. Animism.—As early man was conscious that he himself possessed a spirit or soul, so he attributed a similar spirit to everything about him, not only to animals, in whom the presence of a spirit was manifested

[1] Spencer and Gillen, *The Northern Tribes of Central Australia* (London, 1904), pp. 505–56.

[2] See Toy, *Introduction to the History of Religions*, § 65.

in action, but to trees, rocks, springs, plants, weapons, heavenly bodies, etc. This general belief of men is called *animism*. These spirits might be weak or powerful, kind or unkind, helpful or hurtful, but in their midst man was compelled to live. He must, accordingly, come into relationship with them. In course of time the good and more powerful spirits developed into gods.

10. Transmigration.—One of the earliest and most persistent beliefs is that souls are reborn or reincarnated as human beings, beasts, plants, or inanimate things. The rise of such a belief is natural. If at the moment of a child's birth a person dies, it is natural to infer that the spirit has passed from one body to the other. Such a belief has been held among savages in America, Africa, Asia, and Oceania, as well as by the Brahmins, Buddhists, and Plato.[1]

11. Gods are powerful and fully personified spirits with whom clans or tribes are believed to have established friendly relations. It is not always easy to distinguish a god from a spirit or ghost. The spirit or ghost may be regarded as just as powerful in his sphere as Ashur or Jupiter in his, but the sphere of the god is larger and his functions are more varied. In the earliest times the gods appear to have been the spirits of springs or of fertile localities. As man was dependent on their blessings, it was easy to regard them as powerful and beneficent. If the god was the god of a locality, it might be thought to dwell in a tree or a rock. Later the sun, moon, certain stars, the wind, rain, and even the sky were personified as gods, i.e., their spirits were thought to be influential in human life, so that man for

[1] See Toy, *op. cit.*, §§ 55 ff.

his own good should cultivate friendly relations with them. At times the local spirit of a tribe's dwelling-place became associated with the tribe as its god, and was gradually detached from its original locality. Thus tribal gods arose. As human society is constituted of men and women, so the gods were thought to be male and female.

12. Fetishism.—In many parts of the world a power akin to that of man is supposed to reside in certain inanimate things. When such objects are parts of an animal, such as bones, claws, tails, feet, etc., or of vegetables, they are probably thought to retain something of the power of the living thing to which they belonged. Fetish objects in West Africa are believed to be inhabited by spirits. In Australia an object called a *churinga* is regarded as the abode of the soul of an ancestor endowed with marvelous power.

13. Idols.—Closely related to fetishism is the practice of making images of the gods, although idolatry is a step higher in the process of evolution. An idol is an image or an object consciously made by man to represent his god. It is a distinct advance when it is supposed that a spirit which originally dwelt in a spring, or a rock, or a tree, can be persuaded to make its dwelling in an object of man's own manufacture, so that he may carry its presence with him continually.

14. Social organization has everywhere affected the conceptions entertained of the gods. It is natural for men to think of the earth as a goddess—as the great mother of inexhaustible fertility. It is also natural for them to think of the rain-deity, who enables the earth to bear and whose thunderbolts are like a warrior's darts,

as masculine. But whether the god or the goddess is regarded as the head of the divine family is determined by the social organization of human society. In matriarchal communities a goddess is the superior deity, in patriarchal communities, a god.[1]

15. Environment and economic conditions also had their influence upon the conceptions of the gods. In regions like Arabia, where by far the larger part of the land is utterly barren and the fertile oases are the rare exception, the struggle for existence is severe. Deities of fertility were accordingly there given great prominence. Such deities have been worshiped in all parts of the world, but in these desert regions they have been given special importance.

16. Ceremonies.—Early religious expression consists largely of ceremonies. These are of social and economic significance. They consist of harvest festivals, or, among pastoral peoples, festivals of the yeaning time, at which the gladness of the populace finds expression as a tribute to deity. Among uncivilized peoples these feasts are often orgies of a bestial nature. When, as among the Semites, the feast was held in honor of a deity of fertility, sexual license was thought to be pleasing to such deities.[2] But similar license was granted at such times in many other parts of the world.[3] At such feasts wives were often selected and marriages

[1] See G. A. Barton, *A Sketch of Semitic Origins, Social and Religious* (New York, 1902), pp. 119–21.

[2] See the article "Hierodouloi" in Hastings' *Encyclopaedia of Religion and Ethics*, VI; and Barton, *Semitic Origins*, pp. 110 f.

[3] See, for example, J. Dowd, *The Negro Races* (New York, 1907), p. 137; and for the Fiji Islanders, J. G. Frazer, *The Belief in Immortality* (London, 1913), pp. 433 f.

consummated. As religion covered the whole of life, marriage feasts had a certain religious significance.

Birth, too, was attended with certain other ceremonies. But most important of all were the ceremonies through which young men, and in parts of the world young women, must pass at the age of puberty. These initiated the young people into the full life of the tribe as adult members; as adults they also came into full relationship with the god of the tribe. The ceremonies were usually such as to try the courage of the initiate, especially of the male, and to predispose the mind to religious impressions. Often the men of a tribe have for long periods been organized into secret societies which had a religious or magical significance.[1]

17. Taboo.—Uncivilized men conceive of the supernatural as a kind of divine electricity with which many things in the world are charged. If things so charged are not handled in certain ways, the holiness, or supernatural power, will discharge itself and harm the individual. From this general conception many prohibitions have arisen. These are found among all peoples in early stages of development, though they vary in different tribes. The word "taboo" is taken from a Polynesian dialect, where the phenomenon was first studied. Of course many taboos prevent activities the harmfulness of which are purely imaginary. Taboos have had an important influence in the development of ethics. Taboos control the actions of men, not only in daily life, but during their religious festivals and ceremonies, though the taboos that are in force at such times often differ from those that control daily life.

[1] See H. Webster, *Primitive Secret Societies* (New York, 1908).

18. **Totemism** is the name given to the system of tribal subdivision denoted by totems. Totems are natural objects, usually animals, though they are sometimes plants, assumed as the emblem of a clan or family. The name is derived from the languages of the American Indians, among whom totemism was first studied. The totem is sometimes regarded as the ancestor of the tribe and is often closely associated in one way or another with its deity. Totemism exists in many parts of the world among tribes in a low stage of development, though there is no evidence that it has been universal. A number of the highly civilized nations of antiquity appear, however, to have passed through a totemistic stage of development.

Totemism was a kind of imaginary social alliance, offensive and defensive, between a group of human beings and the class of animals or plants to which the totem belonged. The clan and its totem were usually supposed to be akin to one another. In many parts of the world exogamous marriage was controlled by the totem. If the totem of one tribe would eat the totem of another, the two could not intermarry. Among many tribes it was forbidden to eat the flesh of the totem. Sometimes the animal totem was regarded as especially valuable for sacrifices. In totemistic groups gods, men, and animals, or plants are thought to be embraced in one social organization. Totemism is, therefore, intimately connected with religion.

19. **Sacrifice.**—In all parts of the world men have offered to the gods gifts of food. They have assumed that the gods needed sustenance as much as they themselves. These gifts have, however, not consisted

merely of grain or bloodless offerings, but of animal life
as well, and, among many peoples, even of human
victims. Only a few of the higher religions have
reached a stage of evolution in which animal sacrifice
is discarded, although human sacrifice survives only
among the lowest savages. At times the entire victim
has been burned as an offering to the deity; at times
the flesh has been consumed by the worshipers, while
only the bones, the entrails, and the blood were offered
to the deity. In some rituals the blood has been poured
out on the earth; in others, care is taken to prevent
this, lest the earth become surcharged with its sacred
power.

The reason why animal sacrifice is a part of all
early religion is obscure. It is regarded by some as
a gift to the gods of the most costly kind of food;[1] by
others, as a meal in which the kinship or social bond
between gods and men is renewed by both partaking of
the flesh of a totemic victim akin to both;[2] by still
others its significance is found in the bursting forth of
the victim's blood, the sight of which is supposed to
appease the offended god.[3] Whatever the explanation
of the practice of animal sacrifice may be, it is clear
that all men have, at a certain stage of religious development, believed that through it they entered into renewed
communion with their gods. When great danger has
threatened a community, so that the deity has been

[1] So F. B. Jevons, *Comparative Religion* (Cambridge, 1913), p. 35.

[2] So W. R. Smith, *Religion of the Semites* (London, 1904), Lectures
VI–XI.

[3] So S. I. Curtiss, *Primitive Semitic Religion Today* (New York,
1902), p. 216.

thought to be estranged, the most costly victims have been offered in order to regain the aid of the god.   Under such circumstances human sacrifices have been offered by peoples who had generally discarded the practice. Such was the case when at Marseilles a man was sacrificed to avert a pestilence;[1] among the Aztecs, when in the fifteenth century human sacrifices were offered to avert a famine;[2] and among the ancient Moabites, when the king sacrificed his son to gain victory in war (II Kings, chap. 3).

20. Circumcision is a rite practiced in many parts of the world, though not by all peoples.   It was employed by the ancient Egyptians, by the Semites, by many African tribes, by peoples of Australasia and Polynesia. Among some peoples both men and women were subjected to it.   At times great religious significance is attached to it.   For example, among the Hebrews it was interpreted as the sign of the covenant between the people and Yahweh (Jehovah).   The reason for the origin of the practice of circumcision is obscure.   At times it has been explained as a sacrifice of a portion of the generative organs to the goddess of fertility in order to insure fertility; others have seen in the rite the sacrifice of a part of the individual instead of the whole; while others explain it as a simple device to facilitate procreation.

21. Magic.—Side by side with early religions one finds magical practices, and there has been much discussion as to whether magic originated before religion or whether it is a degenerate form of religion.   In

[1] Jevons, *Comparative Religion*, p. 32.
[2] *Ibid.*, p. 33.

religion men appeal to higher powers to be gracious; they seek to gain the good will of gods by offerings and prayer; in magic they seek to force supernatural powers to do their will. There is in magic no reverence, but compulsion only. It is believed that the utterance of certain words or the performance of certain ceremonies compels spirits to do what men desire. It is impossible to tell whether religion or magic is the older; they may have been coeval. At all events, they have existed side by side in history. Possibly religion was the spontaneous attitude of the earliest men toward spirits sufficiently powerful to excite fear, while magic was the contemporaneous human attitude toward lesser spirits.

22. Importance of primitive religion.—The religions of all the civilized nations had their root in the religion of an uncivilized people. As some of the material of a tree comes from the earth through its roots, though more comes from the air through the leaves, so civilized religions, however much they owe to the inspiration of great souls after the rise of civilization, owe something to the inheritance of the remote, uncivilized past. The beliefs of primitive men are often unintelligent and their practices often revolting, but through them the way outward to the infinite was opened just a little. Each god represented to his worshipers in shadow, however faint, some rudimentary conception of the All-Father, and we need not doubt that through his worship there came to the worshiper in some degree the inspiration and courage that come from communion with God. The universal presence among uncivilized men of religion of some sort is evidence that in no part of the world has God "left himself without a witness."

SUPPLEMENTARY READING

CLASS A

On sec. 1: A. H. Keane, *Man Past and Present* (Cambridge, 1899), pp. 8–23; A. L. Kroeber, *Anthropology* (New York, 1923); H. F. Osborne. *Men of the Old Stone Age* (New York, 1925).

On secs. 2, 5: W. R. Smith, *Religion of the Semites*, 2d ed. (London, 1894), pp. 15–20.

On sec. 3: D. G. Brinton, *The Religion of Primitive Peoples* (New York, 1897), pp. 1–11.

On sec. 4: C. H. Toy, *Introduction to the History of Religions* (New York, 1913), §§ 1–12.

On secs. 6, 10: C. H. Toy, *ibid.*, §§ 18–45.

On secs. 7, 8: C. H. Toy, *ibid.*, §§ 45–70.

On sec. 9: The article "Animism" in Hastings' *Encyclopaedia of Religion and Ethics*, I, 535–37.

On sec. 11: Toy, *op. cit.*, §§ 635–70; or W. R. Smith, *op. cit.*, pp. 28–48.

On sec. 12: "Fetishism" in Hastings' *Encyclopaedia of Religion and Ethics*, V, 894–903.

On sec. 13: Toy, *op. cit.*, §§ 1091–94.

On secs. 14, 15: G. A. Barton, *A Sketch of Semitic Origins, Social and Religious* (New York, 1902), chap. iii, or chaps. ii and iii.

On sec. 16: Toy, *op. cit.*, §§ 101–52.

On sec. 17: Toy, *op. cit.*, §§ 581–624.

On sec. 18: Toy, *op. cit.*, §§ 542–59, or 422–559.

On sec. 19: Toy, *op. cit.*, §§ 1027–84; or Jevons, *op. cit.*, chaps. xi and xii.

On sec. 20: The article "Circumcision," in Hastings' *Encyclopaedia of Religion and Ethics*, III, 659–80.

On sec. 21: Toy, *op. cit.*, §§ 883–904.

CLASS B

D. G. Brinton, *The Religions of Primitive Peoples* (New York, 1897).

CHAPTER II

THE RELIGION OF BABYLONIA AND ASSYRIA

The holy Tigris, the holy Euphrates,
The holy scepter of Enlil
Establish Kharsag;
They give abundance.

. . . .

O lord of darkness, protect man!
O lord of light, protect man!
O lord of the field, protect man!
O lord of the sanctuary, protect man!

. . . .

O divine lord, protect the little habitation!
O well of the mighty abyss, give protection!

. . . .

To Ninkharsag belongs demon-enchantment;
Brilliant enchantment her hand created;
Bada opposed to her his word.
"The house is bright," may she say!
"The house is good," may she say!
"A thing lofty, brightest of all," may she say!
"Unspeakable with the brightness
Of many cedar fires," may she say!

. . . .

O mother, brilliant goddess, come!   The flour withhold not
May thy might man's garden restore!
O my mother, divine lady, is there no might with thee?
To expel the sickness from the land I cry mightily!
In the fold may there be no demon!
Sickness, fever, expel!

—From the oldest known Babylonian religious text.[1]

[1] Written about 2800 B.C. See G. A. Barton, *Miscellaneous Babylonian Inscriptions* (New Haven, 1918), Part I, No. 1.

O lady, with outpouring of heart I earnestly raise to thee
    my voice!   How long?
O lady, to thy servant speak pardon, let thy heart be
    pacified!
To thy servant who suffers pain grant favor!
Thy neck turn to him!   Receive his entreaty!
Unto thy servant with whom thou art angry be favorable!
              —From a prayer to Ishtar of Agade.

Unto the land of No-return, the land of darkness,
  . . . .
To the house of darkness, the dwelling of Irkalla,
Unto the house whose entrance has no exit.
Along the way whose going has no return,
To the house whose entrance is deprived of light,
Where dust is their food, their sustenance clay,
Light they do not see, in darkness they dwell.
    —From "Ishtar's Descent to the Lower World."[1]

23. **Babylonia** lay in the southern extremity of the
Tigris-Euphrates Valley, just north of the Persian Gulf.
In it there developed one of the two oldest civilizations
of the world.   This civilization was produced by the
mingling of two races, Semites from Arabia and the
Sumerians from the mountains of the East.   The racial
affinities of the Sumerians have not yet been determined.
The Semites wore long beards;   the Sumerians shaved
both their faces and their heads.[2]   Gods in ancient
times were believed to be attached to the soil, and,
when a new people entered the country, they felt compelled to seek the favor of the gods of the land.[3]   From

---

[1] See G. A. Barton, *Archaeology and the Bible* (5th ed., Philadelphia,
1927), Part II, chap. xxvi, § 4, for the whole poem.

[2] See Eduard Meyer, *Sumerier und Semiten in Babylonien* (Berlin,
1896).

[3] An example of this occurs in the Old Testament: II Kings
17: 24–34.

these customs, reflected in their art, it is proved that the Semites were in the land before the coming of the Sumerians, for the beardless Sumerians picture their gods with Semitic beards! While the Semites were first in the land, the Sumerians were the inventors of Babylonian writing,[1] and, apparently, of the higher elements of the civilization.

24. The Semitic background of the Babylonian religion is of fundamental importance. The Semites in Arabia, their cradle land, were compelled by the struggle for existence in that barren country to advance somewhat beyond most savages of that far-off time. They were nevertheless still savages. The world was to them animistic; they had, apparently, their totems, and their lives were controlled by many taboos. On account of the poverty of the country, their social organization was matriarchal, and they imagined that the relations of their gods to one another resembled their own. Their chief deity was, therefore, a goddess, whom they called Athtar, or Ishtar, or Attar, or Astar, or Ashtar, or Ashtart, according to their various dialects.[2] This name probably meant "the self-waterer"[3] and was given to her because she was the spirit of the springs in the oases. This goddess had a son, who was the spirit of the vegetation that grew by the spring; or, more particularly, he was the spirit of the date palm. The early Semitic name of this god has not survived. He is

---

[1] See G. A. Barton, *The Origin and Development of Babylonian Writing* (Leipzig, 1913).

[2] See G. A. Barton, *A Sketch of Semitic Origins, Social and Religious*, chap. iii.

[3] See G. A. Barton, "The Etymology of Ishtar," *Journal of the American Oriental Society*, XXXI, 355-58.

generally known as Tammuz, a late form of one of his Babylonian names. It is probable that along with this mother and son other spirits were more vaguely worshiped as her husbands—the spirit of the wind, of the moon, of the sun, etc.

25. The prehistoric period, ca. 5000–ca. 3200 B.C.—This period began with the infiltration of Semites into Babylonia. They came, apparently, from the south, settling first at Eridu, which was then at the head of the Persian Gulf, afterward founding Ur, Erech, and a group of four towns, Girsu, Ninâ, Erim,[1] and *Alu-ellu*, "the bright city," which the Sumerians, translating into their language, called Uru-azagga. These four were afterward united into the city-state of Lagash. Each of these cities was at first the fortified residence of a tribe or part of a tribe. In the productive soil of Babylonia the matriarchal organization gave place to a patriarchal, and in course of time in many centers the goddess was superseded by a god. In some cases the god was the goddess herself masculinized. Such, for example, was Ningirsu, the chief deity of Lagash, whose name means "Lady of Girsu." At other times the son of the mother-goddess or one of her husbands was exalted to the chief place. This was the case at Erech, where Anu, the god of the sky, became her father, though in reality he never displaced the goddess in the affections of the people. Sometimes, probably, she was displaced by a Sumerian deity, for the Sumerians moved into Babylonia long before the dawn of history, and it is impossible in most cases to disentangle the Sumerian and Semitic strands.

[1] See G. A. Barton, *Semitic Origins*, pp. 184–201.

The Sumerians founded Nippur, and perhaps Adab and Umma. They also overran the Semitic settlements. Perhaps there had been a Semitic settlement at Nippur, for Enlil, its god, whose name means "lord of spirits," is pictured with a beard, but the chief importance of that city was gained from the Sumerians. During the long prehistoric period these cities often fought and conquered one another. When a city ruled the land, homage was paid to its god by all conquered cities. Meantime the local god was not neglected. It thus happened that, when written history begins, Enlil of Nippur, Enki (Ea) of Eridu, Anu and Ishtar (often called Nana) of Erech, were worshiped throughout the country. Each of these cities had for a time held sway.

Before the end of this period another wave of Semitic migration had entered Northern Babylonia. The new immigrants occupied the cities of Agade and Kish, the gods of which were respectively Shamash (the sun-god) and Zamama. Either from this source or from some other the worship of the sun-god had spread over the country before written history begins.

26. The early Sumerian period, ca. 3200–ca. 2800 B.C.—During this period the chief rivalry was between kings of Lagash and kings of Kish, though other cities entered into the struggle also. At times Lagash was in the ascendant; at times Kish. Many local gods were worshiped and many demons feared. Enlil of Nippur (contracted later to Ellil; also called Bel by Semites) was, however, worshiped by all. Kings of the south as well as kings of the north maintained that he gave them lordship over the land. Nippur must have been dominant over the whole land in prehistoric time long

enough for Enlil to become recognized as the divine
suzerain of the whole country. Enlil had a spouse,
Ninlil, who is also called the goddess Sir, or the serpent-
goddess.

Most of our inscriptions for this period come from
Lagash; more is therefore known of its religion. From
the reigns of the last two rulers of Lagash before the
close of this period extensive lists of viands for consumption at the festivals of various gods have come
down. In addition to Enlil and Enki (of Eridu) these
rulers worshiped the deities[1] of their own fourfold city.

There were, too, a number of other deities. Whether
these were originally different, or whether they were
different epithets of those just mentioned, it is often
difficult to say. There was a tendency, however, to
multiply gods by applying to known deities new names.
In time the new name and the old were thought to
designate different beings. At all events, the documents
of this period present a bewildering perplexity of divine
names. While we cannot explain all of these, it is
clear that there were many deities, and that the number
of these was increasing. Ninkharsag, "the lady of the
mountain," a name brought from the East, was an
epithet of Ninlil. Ningirsu, however, received the
chief homage, and the government of the state was
carried on as a theocracy in his name. At the sacrificial festivals, which seem to have been conducted
mainly in the interest of the worshipers, large quantities

[1] Chief of these was Ningirsu, called in one inscription the *Patesi*,
or priest-king, of the gods. Bau, goddess of Uru-azagga, Ninâ, goddess
of the city Ninâ, Ininni, goddess of Erim, and Lugal-Erim, her masculine counterpart, were also especially honored.

of beer, black beer, oil, milk, flour, fish, some kind of vegetable wine, and sheep were consumed.

Lagash was a simple agricultural community. Its calendar was purely agricultural. The names of the months were derived in part from the feasts of the gods and in part from the agricultural work that fell in each month. Most of the months had more than one name; the month March-April, in which the largest number of agricultural activities were carried on, had as many as fifteen different names! Only one month-name was connected with a heavenly body. This month was named from the rising of a star, probably Sirius.[1] The heavenly bodies played as yet little part in Babylonian life and thought. As early as 2900 B.C. Enki was regarded as the giver of intelligence—the god of wisdom. The religious life of Lagash is probably typical of that in other Babylonian cities in this period. Similarly organized worship was carried on at Eridu with the god Enki at its head; in Ur, where Nannar was the supreme deity; at Erech, where Nana-Ishtar and Anu were worshiped; at Nippur, the home of Enlil; at Kutha, whose chief god was Nergal; at Kish, the shrine of Zamama, and at other centers.

27. The first Akkadian period ca. 2800–ca. 2400 B.C. —After Lugalzaggisi of Umma, who overthrew Urkagina of Lagash, had enjoyed a brief period of supremacy, Sargon of Agade took the country. The chief deities of Umma were Shara and Nidaba; that of Agade,

---

[1] On the calendar of this period, see G. A. Barton, "Recent Research in the Sumerian Calendar," *Journal of the American Oriental Society*, XXXIII, 1–9, and "Kugler's Criterion for Determining the Order of the Months in the Earliest Babylonian Calendar," *ibid.*, pp. 297–305.

Shamash, the sun-god. During this period Babylonian armies reached the Mediterranean. After Agade had ruled for nearly two hundred years, a foreign dynasty from Gutium on the east held the land for 159 years. Each new dynasty brought in new gods, but the general features of the religion remained the same. With the domination of Agade the worship of Shamash, the sun-god, became more general. His consort, the water-goddess Ai, later known as Malkatu or "the Queen," emerged in this period. The moon-god, Enzu, also became prominent. The dynasty of Agade was a part of that branch of the Semitic race known as Amurru, or Amorites, whom we find in Syria and Palestine. It is not surprising, therefore, that under this dynasty two gods, afterward worshiped on the Mediterranean coast, appear in Babylonia. These are Adda, or Hadad, the god of wind and storms, and Dagon, the corn-god.

Another new feature of the religion of this period is the deification of certain kings during their lifetime. Rimush and Naram-Sin were both honored as gods. Babylonian kings did not usually pretend to be divine. Why these two were so honored we cannot tell.

Toward the end of this period, probably under the dynasty of Gutium, Ur-Bau and Gudea flourished as priest-kings at Lagash. Gudea built a palace, and both repaired the temple. Gudea placed a brazen sea in the temple as Solomon did at Jerusalem (I Kings 7:23–26). Both Ur-Bau and Gudea left inscriptions from which we discover the names of the gods of Lagash worshiped in their time. Some of the divine names of the earlier period have vanished, and several new ones appear, but none of these became permanently important. We learn from the inscriptions of Gudea that *Anu*, Enlil (Bel), and Enki (Ea, who was regarded as the god of the deep) had been grouped in a triad. These gods represented respectively the sky, the earth, and the sea.

28. The dynasties of Ur and Nisin, ca. 2400–ca. 2100 B.C., after a brief interval, followed the dynasty Gutium. The triumph of Ur was a triumph of the Sumerians. We begin in this period to meet the name Sumer for Southern Babylonia. North Babylonia was called Akkad, a corruption of Agade. With the triumph of Ur its god Nannar became prominent. A large number of new deities appear in the inscriptions of this period. Gula (derived from Bau by the use of an epithet) is one of these. Most of them are not important; Dungi, the second monarch of the dynasty of Ur, was deified and extensively worshiped in his lifetime. Bur-Sin and Gimil-Sin, his successors, were also regarded as gods.

29. The first dynasty of Babylon, about 2100 B.C., made the city of Babylon mistress of the country. This dynasty had arisen out of a new wave of Amoritic immigrants who had come into the country. The chief god of Babylon was Marduk, whose worship now became prominent, but the older deities were all honored too, especially the triad Anu, Bel, and Ea. Among the bewildering number of new divine names that came into use in this period there is one that was destined to play a great rôle in the later religion of Babylonia and Assyria. This was Nabu, god of Borsippa, opposite Babylon, who later became the god of eloquence and of writing. Frequent mention is made of the spirits of heaven and the spirits of earth. By this time greater knowledge of the stars had also been attained. The goddess Ishtar had been identified with Dilbad, the star Venus, and apparently some rudimentary knowledge of the signs of the zodiac had been gained.

30. **The Kassite dynasty**, about 1750 B.C., came in from the East and occupied the throne of Babylon for 576 years. Barbarians at first, the Kassites soon assimilated Babylonian culture. They added little to Babylonian religion except a few barbarous divine names like that of their war-god, Shukamuna. Early in the Kassite period Sin, Shamash, and Ishtar, representing the moon, sun, and Venus, were grouped together as a triad. By this time the city of Lagash had been destroyed and its god, Ningirsu, known now as Ninib, was detached from his local origin and worshiped as a sun-god.

31. **Assyria** emerges from obscurity about 2100–2000 B.C. The dominant strain in its population was Semitic, derived partly from Babylonia and partly from the West. Recent discovery shows that Babylonian immigrants went thither as early as 3000–2800 B.C.

The national god of Assyria was Ashur, the deity of the city of Ashur, but from early times Anu and Adda were also worshiped there with him. Nineveh, later the capital, was founded by immigrants from Ninâ, a part of Lagash. They brought their goddess Ninâ with them, later calling her by her Semitic name Ishtar. Ishtar was also the chief deity of Arbela, another Assyrian city. The Ishtar of Arbela became a warrior goddess—the goddess of the bow. Assyria was the most warlike and ruthless of the ancient nations. Her kings boasted of impaling men and flaying them alive.

Their deities Ashur and Ishtar were accordingly cruel. The Assyrian kingdom lasted until 606 B.C. Throughout its history many Babylonian deities were worshiped, since Assyrians always looked up to the ancient divinities of their mother-country.

32. The neo-Babylonian empire, 625–538 B.C., added little to the religion of the country. In this period we find the triad Sin, Shamash, and Adad (the moon-, sun-, and the weather-god), as well as the triad Sin, Shamash, and Ishtar. The worship of a multitude of deities was maintained, but Marduk, Nabu, Ishtar, Shamash, and Sin were the most popular. After Babylon lost her independence the worship of local deities was in some places continued down to the Christian era.

33. Monotheism was never attained or even approached by the Babylonians. In the early time the nearest approach to a conception of unity was the formation of the triads, Anu, Bel, and Ea; and Sin, Shamash, and Ishtar. Perhaps in the latest period some priests went farther, for a neo-Babylonian litany reads:

> Ninib is the Marduk of might,
> Nergal is the Marduk of fight,
> Zamama is the Marduk of battle,
> Enlil is the Marduk of dominion,
> Nabu is the Marduk of superintendence (?)
> Sin is the Marduk of nocturnal light,
> Shamash is the Marduk of decisions,
> Adad is the Marduk of rain [etc.].

The author of this litany saw in the activities of these gods Marduk performing different functions, but there is no evidence that his view was shared by any considerable number of people. Some of the gods kept many functions till the end. Some were gradually assigned more and more to special functions. Thus Ea (Enki) became in very early times the god of wisdom, a rôle that he maintained till the end. Shamash, the god of light, naturally became the god of justice, and Hammurapi before 2000 B.C. professes to have received from him the great code of laws.

34. Creation-myths.—In Babylonia and Assyria various creation myths were developed. One of the oldest assumes the existence of the earth and narrates the building of cities and the development of agriculture. Another, which is known only through a broken tablet written about 2100 B.C., attributes the creation of the world to the triad Anu, Bel, and Ea, together with the goddess Ninkharsag, while Nintu or Ishtar created mankind. The best known of these myths was in late Assyrian and Babylonian times developed into an epic in seven tablets or cantos. The essence of this story is that Tiamat, the great mother-dragon of the sea, determined to destroy the gods whom she had borne. They then chose one of their number, Marduk, to fight her; he overcame her, split her in two, and formed of one part of her the heavens and of the other the earth. There is evidence that in substance this myth is very old and that, in earlier forms of it, Enlil of Nippur and Ea of Eridu had stood in place of Marduk. In still another creation-myth the god Ashur is the chief actor. Such a myth was the natural product of lower Babylonia, where, on account of the annual overflow of the rivers, the sea seems to come and try to overwhelm the land.

35. **Gilgamesh** is a name around which another cycle of myths and legends clusters. These now form an epic in twelve tablets or cantos. Some of the myths come from that very early time when gods and men were thought to mingle freely together, others embody apparently bits of history, while still others reflect comparatively advanced thoughts on death. One interesting passage tells of the creation of a primitive man by the goddess Aruru from a bit of clay taken from the ground. It is strikingly like the creation of man in Gen. 2:7. The whole epic is now arranged in twelve parts according to the signs of the zodiac, and is thought by some to be at bottom a sun-myth. The eleventh canto contains an account of the flood almost identical with that in the Bible.[1]

36. **Ishtar's Descent** is the name of another mythical poem, which describes the underworld.[1] A quotation from it stands at the head of this chapter. The myth, so far as it relates to the goddess, undoubtedly had its origin in the annual death of vegetation in the burning sun of a Babylonian summer. The picture which it affords of life after death is most gloomy, but is not unlike that found in Isa. 14:9-11 and Ezek. 32:22-32.

37. **Other myths** relate to various matters. Two are concerned with the acquisition of knowledge on the part of man. According to one of these, preserved to us by Berossos, Oannes (a late name for Ea) was a fish-god who lived in the water at night, but came up by day and

---

[1] The tablets on which the Gilgamesh Epic and Ishtar's Descent are written come from the seventh century B.C., but both poems are probably much older.

taught men agriculture, horticulture, the art of building houses, and how to make laws. According to another, called the Adapa-myth, Ea feared lest man, who had become intelligent, should partake of the food of the gods and become immortal. At a time when Ea knew that other gods would offer Adapa such food he warned Adapa not to partake of it, lest it destroy him. Adapa obeyed Ea and thus missed immortality. These myths reflect the feeling that, while the gods are willing to help man up to a certain point, they are jealous of his too great advancement.

Another myth relates how Etana, a shepherd king, after various adventures with a serpent and an eagle, essayed at last to mount to heaven on the back of an eagle. Still another myth relates how the *zu*-bird broke the wing of the south wind.

38. **Temples,** built generally of brick, the common Babylonian building material, existed in Babylonia from the dawn of history. From the walls of some of them which have been discovered, it appears that they were elaborate structures built on brick terraces. They contained, besides the sanctuary for the chief deity, minor sanctuaries for other deities and extensive apartments for priests and temple attendants. To each temple was attached a *ziggurat*, or staged tower. This represented a mountain peak as Gudea's brazen sea represented the deep. The deities were represented by idols, and on festal days were carried in procession in "ships." It was a pious deed for a king to present a god with one of these "ships."

39. **Priesthoods** had developed in the prehistoric period. Later, elaborate liturgies were developed. As

time advanced, the duties of the priests were differentiated; some gave themselves to the ordinary duties of a priest, while others were set apart for the observance of omens, and still others for the recitation of the incantations which were supposed to drive out the demons of sickness. In connection with the temples there also existed men and women who represented the life-giving functions of the deity. It was their duty to have commerce with those who resorted to the temple for the cure of sterility.[1]

The Babylonian priesthood was the learned class. Among them the art of writing was kept alive. Schools of instruction existed in the temples, from which some of the students' exercises have survived. Here men were trained, not only in mathematics and bookkeeping, which were necessary for the administration of the large temple estates, but in the religious literature. In the temples the hymns and myths were copied and preserved.

40. **Divination** as a means of ascertaining the future was practiced throughout Babylonian history. The earliest method mentioned was by pouring oil upon water. Skilled diviners were supposed to read the future in the shapes assumed by the oil. King Urkagina, before 2800 B.C., found it necessary to regulate the charges for such divination. A form of divination that became prominent under Sargon of Agade was the inspection of the markings on the liver of a sheep. In later time this developed into an extensive pseudo-science. From Babylonia it extended to the Etruscans and the West. Augury was practiced by watching the

[1] See G. A. Barton, "Hierodouloi (Semitic and Egyptian)" in Hastings' *Encyclopaedia of Religion and Ethics*, VI, 672–76.

flight of birds. Omens were also derived from unnatural
and deformed births, both of animals and of human
beings. In the late Assyrian and neo-Babylonian
periods omens were drawn from the stars, and the
pseudo-science of astrology was formed. It also spread
to other countries, and is practiced to the present day
even in our own land. It is difficult to tell whether
some of these practices were more closely related to
religion or to magic.

41. **Incantations** were extensively employed throughout Babylonian history for the cure of sickness. This
is the more remarkable since medical knowledge had so
far advanced before 2000 B.C. that the Code of Hammurapi contained laws relating to medical practice.
To the end, however, disease was regarded by the masses
as a kind of demoniacal possession, and it was thought
that by reciting incantations the demon could be driven
out. A number of these incantations have survived.

42. **Prayers and hymns** employed in the temple
service and in private devotions have also been preserved. Some of them are beautiful in form, and
touchingly present the suppliant's sense of need and his
cry for help. Some of the appeals remind one of parts
of the Hebrew Psalter.

43. **Sin and atonement.**—The Babylonian sense of
sin seems to have been simply a consciousness, brought
on by misfortune, that some god or gods were angry
and estranged. It does not appear to have had a
marked ethical content. The main effort was to appease
the divine anger, so as to remove the affliction. From
the earliest times sacrifices were thought to accomplish
this, but sacrifice was reinforced by pathetic personal

appeal and by intercession. In the penitential psalms
one god or a group of gods is frequently called upon to
intercede with the deity who is angry. About 2400
B.C. this intercessory idea found expression in a proper
name. A man called his son *Ningirsu-zidda-šagišše-
Ninâ-ta*, i.e., "Ningirsu brings the blessing from Ninâ."

44. Ethics.—The Babylonians developed at an early
time a highly organized social and commercial life,
which, as the Code of Hammurapi shows, was controlled
on well-formulated principles of justice. All the con-
tingencies of such a society, even those of commercial
travelers, are provided for in a way that denotes a high
degree of ethical feeling. The gods, although in the
myths they sometimes lie to men and deceive them,
were believed to demand ethical conduct of their worshipers, for in the code provision is frequently made for
the employment of oaths as guaranties of obligations.
In the general ethics of ordinary life the Babylonians
were fully abreast of other nations. The Assyrians
were more backward. Perhaps in private life they did
not fall behind the Babylonians, but in war they were
the most cruel of all the great nations of antiquity.

45. In general, the spirit of the Babylonian and
Assyrian religion is well summed up by the quotations
at the head of this chapter. Their pantheon was a
highly developed polydemonism. They lived in constant fear of the demons of floods, pestilence, and
darkness. Some of their gods were good; they gave
life and could protect it if they would; but sickness and
misfortune, which were all too frequent, made the
worshiper realize poignantly their estrangement. Hence
the frequent and pathetic appeals for mercy. Then at

the end came death, inscrutable mystery, and ruthlessly swept man into a most cheerless underworld!

Acute as the Babylonians were in working out the initial problems of agriculture, social organization, mathematics, and astronomy, they produced in the entire course of their history no great prophetic or philosophic soul. Their religion remained, therefore, to the end, in many respects, a religion of grown-up children. They did, however, amid many primitive conceptions, develop a keen appreciation of ethical values and of responsibility to the gods for failure to lead ethical lives.

SUPPLEMENTARY READING

CLASS A

On sec. 24: either L. B. Paton, "Ishtar" in Hastings' *Encyclopaedia of Religion and Ethics*, VII, 428–34; or G. A. Barton, *Sketch of Semitic Origins*, chap. iii.

On secs. 25–33: R. W. Rogers, *Religion of Babylonia and Assyria* (New York, 1908), pp. 49–98; or M. Jastrow, Jr., *Religion of Babylonia and Assyria* (New York, 1898), pp. 48–234, or *Aspects of Religious Belief in Babylonia and Assyria* (New York, 1911), pp. 143–206.

On sec. 34: either L. W. King, *The Seven Tablets of Creation* (London, 1902), pp. 1–155; or R. W. Rogers, *Cuneiform Parallels to the Old Testament* (New York, 1912), pp. 1–60, or *Religion of Babylonia and Assyria* (New York, 1908), chap. iii; or R. F. Harper, *Assyrian and Babylonian Literature* (New York, 1901), pp. 282–303; or G. A. Barton, *Archaeology and the Bible* (5th ed., Philadelphia, 1927), Part II, chaps. i–viii. Chapter viii of the last-mentioned work contains material not found in the other books.

On sec. 35: R. F. Harper, *op. cit.*, 324–68; or M. Jastrow, Jr., *Religion of Babylonia and Assyria* (New York, 1898), pp. 467–517.

On sec. 36: R. W. Rogers, *Cuneiform Parallels to the Old Testament*, pp. 121–31; or G. A. Barton, *Archaeology and the Bible*, Part II, chap. xxvi, § 5; M. Jastrow, Jr., *Religion of Babylonia and Assyria*, pp. 556–611; or E. Hershey Sneath, *Religion and the Future Life*, chap. iv.

On sec. 37: R. F. Harper, *op. cit.*, pp. 304–23.

On secs. 38, 39: Jastrow, *Religion*, etc., pp. 612–89, or *Aspects of Religious Belief*, etc., pp. 265–350.

On sec. 40: L. W. King, *History of Sumer and Akkad* (London, 1910), pp. 183 ff.; Jastrow, *Aspects of Religious Belief*, etc., pp. 143–255, and *Babylonian-Assyrian Birth-Omens and Their Cultural Significance* (Giessen, 1914), pp. 1–141.

On sec. 41: Jastrow, *Religion*, etc., pp. 253–93.

On secs. 42, 43: R. W. Rogers, *Religion*, etc., pp. 142–84; or Jastrow, *Religion*, etc., pp. 294–327.

On sec. 44: Jastrow, *Aspects of Religious Belief*, etc., pp. 351–418, and in E. Hershey Sneath, *Evolution of Ethics* (New York, 1927), chap. iii.

CLASS B

G. F. Moore, *History of Religions*, I (New York, 1913), chap. x.

CHAPTER III

THE RELIGION OF EGYPT

King Unis is one who eats men and lives on gods.

. . . .

It is "Punisher-of-all-evil-doers"
Who stabs them for king Unis;
He takes out for him their entrails.

. . . .

Shemsu cuts them up for king Unis
And cooks for him a portion of them.

. . . .

He has taken the hearts of the gods;
He has eaten the Red,
He has swallowed the Green.
King Unis is nourished on satisfied organs,
He is satisfied, living on their hearts and their charms.

. . . .

He hath swallowed the knowledge of every god.[1]

   —From a pyramid text of the Fifth Dynasty.

If thou art the son of a man of the council . . . . be not partial.

If thou becomest great after thou wert little, and gettest possessions after thou wert formerly poor in the city, ... be not proud-hearted because of thy wealth. It has come to thee as the gift of the god.

If thou searchest the character of a friend, ... transact the matter with him when he is alone.

Let thy face be bright as long as thou livest.

   —From the precepts of Ptahhotep.[2]

---

[1] Breasted, *Development of Religion and Thought in Ancient Eygpt* (New York, 1912), pp. 127 f.

[2] Breasted, *ibid.*, pp. 234 f.

Thou, O Amon, art lord of the silent,
Who cometh at the cry of the poor.
When I cry to thee in my affliction,
Then thou comest and savest me.
That thou mayest give breath to him who is bowed down,
And mayest save me lying in bondage.
Thou, Amon-Re, lord of Thebes, art he,
Who saveth him that is in the Nether World,
.   .   .   .
When men cry unto thee,
Thou art he that cometh from afar.
—From a hymn of the Empire period.[1]

46. **Egypt** is unique among the countries of the world for its form and its isolation. Created by the river Nile as a narrow strip of green out of the barren and almost trackless deserts which bound it on either side, Egypt was long isolated. Here she worked out alone the problems of civilization centuries before she was drawn by the impact of foreign invasion into the whirlpool of world-affairs.

We have no positive knowledge concerning the savages who may have occupied the Nile Valley before it was settled by the ancestors of the Egyptians. We only know that about 5000 B.C. or earlier forty-two tribes, most of whom seem to have belonged to the Hamitic branch of the Hamito-Semitic race, settled there.[2]

47. **The prehistoric period, ca. 5000–ca. 3400[3] B.C.—** During the first part of this period each tribe seems to

[1] Breasted, *Development of Religion and Thought in Ancient Egypt*, p. 351.

[2] See G. A. Barton, *A Sketch of Semitic Origins, Social and Religious*, chap. i; "Tammuz and Osiris," *Journal of the American Oriental Society*, XXXV, 213–23.

[3] For a discussion of Egyptian chronology, see Breasted, *Ancient Records, Egypt*, I, 25 ff.; or Barton, *Archaeology and the Bible*, chap. i, § 5.

have been independent. Each had its separate god, and, like many other early tribes, they appear to have been henotheists. At this period there seems to have been a different totem for each tribe, although the relation of animals to their religious and social organization does not conform altogether to the laws of totemism as formulated from the study of its features in other parts of the world.[1] Nevertheless in each Egyptian nome[2] or tribe an animal or a bird was so closely associated with the god that it was thought to be sacred to the deity, and the god was often represented in the form of the totem. Thus Amen of Thebes was represented by the ram, Ptah of Memphis by the bull, Atum of Heliopolis by the lion, Bastet of Bubastis by the cat, Har-khent-kheti of Athribis by the serpent, Harshef of Akhnas by a ram, Hathor of Denderah by the cow, Khnum of Elephantine by the goat, Khons of Thebes by the sparrow hawk, Min of Koptos by an ithyphallic man, Mut of Thebes by the vulture, Nekhbet of El-Kab by the vulture, Opet, a goddess of childbirth in Thebes, by a pregnant hippopotamus, Osiris of Busiris and Abydos by a peculiar post which seems to have been a conventionalized palm tree, Horus of Edfu by the sparrow hawk, Set of Ombos by the ass, Shu of Leontopolis by the lion, Sobk of the Fayum by the crocodile, Thoth of Hermopolis by the ibis and baboon, Wto of Buto by the serpent, and Wep-wat of Siut by the wolf. Such information as we have comes from

[1] Cf. C. H. Toy, *Introduction to the History of Religions*, §§ 515–21.

[2] "Nome" is the word applied by Greek writers to the different divisions or "counties" of ancient Egypt, each one of which was originally occupied by a different tribe.

later times, and while we cannot trace the animal which was sacred in every nome, we can trace so many that the inference is justified that every tribe had its sacred animal or plant. In some nomes more than one animal was sacred. This may indicate that in the lapse of centuries war and invasion created in such cases a mixture of different tribes. This association of animals with Egyptian gods was so long continued, and their civilization crystallized sacred customs at a time so early, that the animal representations of the deities continued down to Roman times.

The physical environment of the Hamitic tribes in North Africa was so similar to that of the Semitic tribes in Asia that the power to produce life appeared to these tribes, as to the Semites, to be an especially divine quality. There is reason to believe that the larger number of Egyptian gods were at the beginning gods of fertility. The most popular of these deities of fertility in later times was Osiris and his sister-wife, Isis. Isis was a mother-goddess and is pictured nursing a child-god in the reed lands.[1] Though the myths of Osiris make her prominent, she seems herself to have become popular in actual worship only in late times.

On some of the pottery found in pre-dynastic tombs it appears that standards were attached to different boats, some of which were in animal form. Whether these were private emblems or were the banners of

---

[1] See Erman, *Aegyptische Religion*, 2te Aufl. (Berlin, 1909), p. 40. The writer has stated above his own view of the god Osiris, but opinions differ. According to some scholars he is Tammuz or Marduk, borrowed from Babylonia or from the Semites, and given another name. According to Frazer, *Adonis, Attis, Osiris* (London, 1914), he is a corn-god.

different tribes, we have no means of knowing.[1] Little by little through many wars these tribes were united into two kingdoms. The territory from near the first cataract to the apex of the Delta formed the kingdom of Upper Egypt, the region of the Delta formed that of Lower Egypt. These two kingdoms existed side by side for several centuries, or at all events for a time so long that to the end of Egyptian history Egypt was called the two kingdoms or the two Egypts. Like Austria-Hungary it was a dual monarchy. The names of a few kings who reigned before the union of these two kingdoms have survived on the Palermo stone.[2]

As in Babylonia, the victory of one city over another led to some measure of worship being given by the conquered to the god of the conquerors. The deity of the nome whose chieftain ruled the kingdom was worshiped in all the nomes composing the realm along with the local gods. Thus the worship of some gods tended to become universal in the country, and a syncretism began which in the end created pantheons. At some time, while the two kingdoms were separate, Set, the god of Ombos, was regarded as the god of Upper Egypt, and Horus of Behdet the god of Lower Egypt. A war occurred between the two realms in which Lower Egypt was victorious. Horus was said to have triumphed over Set. In later generations the political circumstances were forgotten, though the myth of the strife remained, and the priests of later centuries, assigning to

[1] See E. A. W. Budge, *History of Egypt* (Oxford University Press, 1902), I, 78.

[2] See Breasted, *Ancient Records, Egypt*, I, 57.

Horus the functions of light and to Set those of darkness, read deeper meanings into the myth of this conflict.[1]

48. The archaic period, ca. 3400–ca. 3000 B.C.— About 3400 B.C. the kingdoms of Upper and Lower Egypt were united into one monarchy by Mena, or Menes, and that period began which Manetho covered in his chronicle. This writer divided the time from Mena to Alexander the Great into thirty-one dynasties. The archaic period covers the time of the first two dynasties, both of which came from the nome of This in Upper Egypt, the chief city of which was Abydos. The original god of This was Enhor, but in some way that is now obscure the worship of Osiris, the god of Busiris in the Delta, had become popular at Abydos. Perhaps a colony from Busiris had settled in Abydos. The long supremacy of the nome of This under the first two dynasties gave to the worship of Osiris as the most popular god of This a vogue in all parts of Egypt which the theories of later ages tended to heighten. Mena chose the city of Memphis, near the borders of the two kingdoms that he had united, as an administrative center. This fact tended to bring into prominence Ptah, the god of Memphis. During this period a great advance in the conception of the divine appears to have been made. Images of the gods began to be represented in human form. This was a distinct advance over the animal forms of the earlier time. The older ideas were still expressed, however, by giving to the statue of the god the head of the animal that represented that particular deity. Thus originated

[1] Cf. G. Steindorf, *Religion of the Ancient Egyptians* (New York, 1905), p. 30.

divine images, the bodies of which were in human form, while the heads were those of animals or birds.

During this period and the preceding the king, through the evolution of an absolute government, came to stand entirely apart from the people. In an animistic stage of society any man who rises above his fellows by the exercise of superior ability is supposed to be possessed of a more divine spirit than the common crowd. It thus came about very naturally that the kings were now regarded as gods.

49. The Old Kingdom, ca. 3000–ca. 2475 B.C.— This includes Dynasties III, IV, V, and VI. It is the period in which the long processes through which Egypt's civilization had been developing reached their first culmination. It was the age of pyramid-builders. In it the great pyramids came into existence. Dynasties III and IV were attached to Memphis, and Memphis was the capital of the country throughout the period. The political supremacy of his city tended to increase the importance of the worship of the god Ptah in all parts of Egypt. The Fifth Dynasty came from the family of the priesthood of On (Gen. 41:45), called Heliopolis by the Greeks. At On, Atum had by this time been identified with the sun and was often called Re, the Egyptian word for the sun. The ascendency of this priestly family in the Fifth Dynasty gave Re a degree of universal homage in all parts of Egypt that he never afterward lost.

In this period the sky was sometimes represented as a gigantic cow, whose legs stood upon either horizon, and whose belly was studded with stars. Sometimes the sky was pictured as a woman, whose feet stood upon one horizon, and who stooped so that her fingers touched the other.[1] It was thus that the mother-goddesses of the earlier time began to be transferred to the sky.

The long-continued existence of Egypt under one ruler produced in this period in the minds of the more thoughtful a sense of the unity of the world. It began to seem anomalous that there should be so many deities. This difficulty was met in part by the assignment of different functions to different deities—Nut became a sky-god; Geb, the earth-goddess; Shu, the god of the air, etc. To some degree the end was also sought by grouping the gods in families of father, mother, and son. At On the priesthood had, before the end of the Old Kingdom, taken another step and formed a group of nine affiliated gods, called by the Greeks an ennead. The scheme of this ennead was as follows:

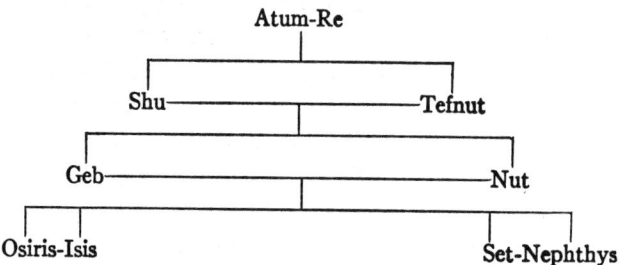

This ennead was imitated all over Egypt, but ancient conceptions were too deeply ingrained and the gods were too numerous to permit the movement toward a unitary conception to make much progress.

In the tomb of Unis, the last king of the Fifth Dynasty, and in the tombs of the kings of the Sixth

[1] See Breasted, *History of Egypt*, 2d ed., p. 55.

Dynasty, religious texts were inscribed. These texts are the oldest literary remains which we have from Egypt. They consist of sentences which depict in various forms the fortunes of the king after death. These fortunes are described in the terms of fortunes of the god Osiris.[1] It is assumed that the king will become an Osiris. Osiris was a vegetation god (originally a palm-tree god?) like the Semitic Tammuz. Like Tammuz he had a mother, Isis. As Ishtar later became the wife of Tammuz, so Isis became the wife of Osiris. As a god of vegetation Osiris, like Tammuz, died, and Isis, like Ishtar, mourned for him. The myth, as time passed, took on many features, but the feature of importance here is that Osiris rose from the dead, and before the pyramid texts were written it was supposed that he was translated after the resurrection to a place in the sky along with the sun and other heavenly bodies. Ordinarily the dead were supposed to pass a miserable existence in an underworld, but the king, as a god, was to escape from this and, like Osiris, to be translated to a heavenly paradise.

The paradise portrayed in these texts was of a peculiarly material sort. Although at times the king is represented as soaring through the heavens like the god Re, his paradise has a tree of life growing in its midst, from which at times the king feeds. This tree of life is probably a survival from the date palm of the primitive North African and Arabian desert, which furnished to both Semites and Hamites their conception

[1] See Breasted, *Development of Religion and Thought in Ancient Egypt*, Lecture V.

of the tree of life.[1]   But the king is not always confined
to this.   Upon his arrival in paradise he was thought
to be an infant in the heavenly realm, so the sky-goddess
extended to him her breasts to suckle him.[2]   Later he
was provided with a feast which consisted of viands
such as men were fond of on earth—a thousand of
bread, a thousand of beer, a thousand of oxen, a thousand
of geese, a thousand of everything whereon the god
lives.[3]   He was also provided with a mistress, and is
described as the man who takes women from their
husbands whither he wills, and when his heart[4] desires.
He is even represented as pursuing those cannibal
practices which the savage Egyptians of an earlier
time had employed, by which they hoped to absorb the
brave qualities of their enemies.   He is said to eat
other gods, so as to swallow the knowledge and power
of every god.[5]

50. The Middle Kingdom.—Strictly speaking, the
Middle Kingdom comprises the Eleventh and Twelfth
dynasties, 2160–1792 B.C., but in classifying the stages
of religious development it may be said to begin with
the fall of the Sixth Dynasty in 2475 B.C.   From the
accession of the Fifth Dynasty onward the tendency of
social evolution was away from the absolutism that had
culminated in the power of the pyramid-builders.   The
organization of the Sixth Dynasty was thoroughly
feudal, and upon its fall Egypt appears for a time to

[1] Barton, *Semitic Origins*, pp. 88–96.
[2] Breasted, *op cit.*, p. 130.
[3] *Ibid.*, p. 132.
[4] *Ibid.*, p. 177.
[5] See quotation at the beginning of this chapter.

have fallen into its original parts. The later organization of society under Dynasties IX, X, XI, and XII was thoroughly feudal, and this change left its mark upon the religious conceptions of the time.

With the accession of the Eleventh Dynasty the nome of Thebes became the dominant nome in Egypt, a position which it held for more than a thousand years. This gave to Amon, the god of that nome, a position of reverence in all parts of Egypt similar to that attained at an earlier time by Osiris, Ptah, and Re, though none of the others ever attained the popularity of Osiris.

The most striking religious development of the Middle Kingdom was the emergence into prominence of the common man. A series of writings from this period shows the development of a sensitive social conscience and of an advanced system of ethics. The social conscience appears in such compositions as the popular story of the "Eloquent Peasant,"[1] in which the grievances and rights of a poor man are so effectively set forth that a noble and a king do justice to him, and in the admonitions of a sage, Ipuwer, who mourns the unjust social conditions of his age, and, in the opinion of some, refers to an ideal king, a kind of Messiah, who was to come.[2] Of a similar social nature is a work

[1] Students who read German should consult F. Vogelsang and Alan H. Gardiner, *Die Klagen des Bauern* (Leipzig, 1908), which contains the best translation of it into a modern language. Those who do not should consult Breasted, *Development of Religion and Thought in Ancient Egypt*, pp. 217 ff.; G. A. Barton, *Archaeology and the Bible*, Part II, chap. xxiv; or Petrie, *Egyptian Tales*, First Series, pp. 61 ff.

[2] See Breasted, *Development of Religion and Thought in Ancient Egypt*, pp. 203 ff., especially p. 212, note. The whole work is translated in Alan H. Gardiner's *Admonitions of an Egyptian Sage* (Leipzig, 1909).

embodying instructions to a vizier.[1] The ethical ideals
of the time are set forth in the Wisdom of Ptahhotep,
who gave instruction that in many respects reminds one
of the Book of Proverbs.[2]

The age was one of reflection. The glad childhood
of Egypt had passed. Skepticism and misanthropy had
begun to prevail in some circles as "The Dialogue of a
Misanthrope with His Own Soul" proves.[3] Another
testimony to the importance now attached to the
common people is shown in the changed conceptions of
the life after death. In the old kingdom it was only
the kings who ascended to heaven like Osiris; now it
was thought to be the destiny of the common man as
well.[4]

51. The Early Empire period, 1580–1375 B.C.—In
the period between the Middle Kingdom and the
Empire, Egypt was subject for a hundred years to conquerors from Asia, commonly known as the Hyksos.
The effort to expel these, and so to conquer Asia as to
keep them out of Egypt, led to the building up of the
Empire. In this struggle the local nobility, who had
for several hundred years restrained the power of the
king, were killed off, and the king emerged with
power as absolute as of old. Nevertheless the literary
products of the earlier period, in which the social conscience of that time found expression, were read and

[1] See Breasted, *Development of Religion and Thought in Ancient
Egypt*, pp. 240–43.

[2] Breasted, *ibid.*, pp. 227–37; and Barton, *Archaeology and the
Bible*, Part II, chap. xxii.

[3] Breasted, *Development of Religion and Thought in Ancient Egypt*,
pp. 188–98.

[4] Breasted, *ibid.*, Lecture VIII.

treasured. The victories of the kings in Asia tended to increase the glory of Amon, god of Thebes. Beginning with Thothmes III large quantities of booty were contributed to his temple. This increased the weatlh and importance of his priesthood. Indeed Thothmes III had been a member of the priesthood of Amon before he came to the throne and had secured the throne through a coup planned and executed by that priesthood. He accordingly paid his political debts by making the high priest of Amon primate of Egypt—a step which resulted in long making Thebes the religious capital of the country. The new imperial power was accompanied by a new tendency toward a unitary conception of the universe. In the reign of Amenophis III two brothers, architects, inscribed in a tomb a hymn to Amon as the sun-god, that speaks of him as the only lord of the world. He is called:

> Sole lord taking captive all lands every day,
>
> . . . .
> When he enfolds them
> Every land is in rejoicing
> At his rising every day, in order to praise him.[1]

52. The reform of Ikhnaton, 1375–1350 B.C.—This monotheistic tendency culminated in the reign of Amenophis IV, who preferred to be called Ikhnaton, or "Spirit of Aton." This king was a religious enthusiast rather than a politician. He looked about for some deity that alone could be worshiped. The time had not come in the development of the human mind when men could get away from material things and think of a

[1] See Breasted, *Development of Religion and Thought in Ancient Egypt*, pp. 315 ff., for the entire hymn.

really spiritual deity. Ikhnaton accordingly selected the sun disk as his one god. Amon, as we have just seen, was identified with the sun, but the name of Amon was really bound up with the old polytheism. Re of On was also a sun-deity who had long been worshiped throughout Egypt, but Ikhnaton felt the same objection to him. He selected a different name, Aton, for his god, and employed all his imperial power to compel men to worship him. The priesthoods of the old cults were, however, strong, and the priests of Amon at Thebes so thwarted the king's power that he soon left Thebes and founded a new city as his capital. This city was about midway between Thebes and Memphis on the site of the modern Tell-el-Amarna. The new city was called Akhetaton, or "Horizon of Aton." Here a temple to Aton was constructed and the whole city given over to his worship, and here the king composed hymns to Aton, the one god, some of the strains of which remind one of the Hebrew Psalter.[1] Ikhnaton used his regal power to extend the worship of Aton and the new monotheism. Temples of this deity were planted in distant Nubia and elsewhere. So absorbed was Ikhnaton in this work that he permitted the dominions of Egypt in Asia to fall into a state of anarchy and ultimately to become separated from Egypt. Egypt was not prepared for such a reform as Ikhnaton's, and one of the early successors of Ikhnaton was compelled to abandon it, return the royal residence to Thebes, and restore the god Amon to his old place.

[1] See Breasted, *Development of Religion and Thought in Ancient Egypt*, pp. 324 ff.

53. The Later Empire period, 1350–1167 B.C.—A reform that fails leaves matters in worse condition than before, and after Ikhnaton the religion of Egypt as a whole settled down to a repetition of ancient ceremonies and the acceptance of old ideas. In the inscriptions from the tombs of Thebes, where the common people now received such burial as had formerly been accorded to kings, and where they died in hope of a resurrection like that of Osiris, we can trace for a century or two a development of marked personal piety.[1] Under Seti I and Ramses II the Asiatic empire was renewed, and before the end of this period contact with Asia led to the introduction here and there of Asiatic deities, such as Baal, Resheph, Anath, and Ashtart. These foreign cults, however, made no deep impression upon the religion of Egypt as a whole.

54. Period of decadence and foreign control, 1167–31 B.C.—The centuries that followed the Empire were centuries of decadence. Various changes occurred, but they could hardly be called advances. In this period great attention was given to old and obscure forms. Care was taken to preserve the bodies of the sacred animals. We hear of tombs for the Apis bulls at Memphis as early as the Eighteenth Dynasty, but in the Persian and Hellenic periods extensive cemeteries of other sacred animals were supported. The Serapeum at Memphis contained the mummies of more than sixty bulls, the last one found having been buried after 100 B.C. Similar cemeteries for bulls existed at On and Hermonthis, for rams at Mendes, for cats at Bubastis and Beni Hasan, for crocodiles at Lake Moeris, for

[1] See Breasted, *ibid.*, Lecture X.

falcons at Buto, and for ibises at Eshmunen. Such numbers of mummified cats have been found at Beni Hasan that modern enterprise has employed them as fertilizer!

At the beginning of this period we learn from the Papyrus Harris that about one person in every fifty in Egypt was a slave to some temple. In other words, the temples owned about 2 per cent of the population. They also owned about $14\frac{1}{2}$ per cent of the cultivatable land of the country, and enormous flocks and herds and treasure in proportion.[1] By far the larger share of these vast possessions was in the hands of the priesthood of Amon. The immense power thus acquired by this priesthood led before the end of the Twentieth Dynasty to an assumption of authority on the part of the high priest of Amon almost equal to that of the king, and at the beginning of the Twenty-first Dynasty the high priest Hrihor seized the crown.

During the reigns that followed the king usually resided at Tanis in the Delta, and the high priest was a son or brother of the monarch and viceroy of the southern third of Egypt. Under the Nubian kings of the Twenty-fifth Dynasty the sisters and daughters of the monarch filled this office. Apparently these kings thought that the best means of controlling the powerful priesthood of Thebes was to have a woman at its head!

From 663 to 525 B.C., after three centuries of control by foreign dynasties, Egypt once more enjoyed the rule of native kings. This period was accompanied by a great revival of national feeling, but in religion it was not a creative period. The ceremonies and texts of

[1] See Breasted, *History of Egypt*, p. 491.

the Old Kingdom were revived, assiduously studied, and an attempt was made to galvanize them into life, but it was not a religious revival in the deeper sense of the word. Under the Hellenic kings after 306 B.C. the god Osiris as Osiris-Apis or Serapis triumphed over the solar gods Re and Amon and became the most popular deity of Egypt. This position he retained until overwhelmed by Christianity. Isis also received in this period a greater degree of adoration than ever, and in Roman times became the center of a cult practiced by many non-Egyptians.

55. **Priesthood and cult.**—The priesthood of the Egyptian temples was, as in other countries, gradually evolved from the chieftains and medicine men of the earlier time. The stages of the evolution are involved in obscurity. As finally organized the priesthoods consisted of various classes of priests, prophets, etc., to whom different duties were assigned. These derived their whole living from the temple and its revenues. They were subject to many minute rules of ceremonial purity, which prescribed how they should bathe, shave, dress, and what they should eat. To some were assigned the duties of awakening the god, making his toilet, and feeding him. Greek writers tell of festivals at which priests acted out the myths of the gods. At some of the temples (probably at all) schools existed for the instruction of candidates for the priesthood in the mysteries of their work and the culture of their time.

56. **Sacrifice.**—In the earliest times the sacrifices consisted mainly of gazelles, antelopes, and wild goats, the flesh of which was most often employed by men as food

The meat was offered partly raw and partly cooked.[1]
When cooked, it was brought forward on metal braziers.
Probably the use of fire is of later development than the
uncooked offering. Herodotus bears witness to the
continuance of the burnt offerings down to the fifth
century B.C. According to him the head of the victim
was cut off and imprecations were pronounced over it,
after which it was thrown into the river or sold to
Greeks. The ritual in other respects varied in different
places, but the sacrifice to one of the principal goddesses
consisted, he says, of bullocks. These were flayed, the
intestines removed, though the vitals and fat were left
in the body. The priests then cut off the legs, the
extremity of the hips, the shoulders, and neck, after
which they filled the trunk with fine bread, honey,
raisins, figs, incense, myrrh, and other perfumes.
Having poured oil over the whole, they burned it.[2]

Apart from such offerings the priests prepared for
the gods at meal-time food consisting of bread, meat,
cakes, and pastry.[3] At their festivals great quantities
of food and wine were also consumed.[4]

57. Magic.—As in other ancient countries magic
developed in Egypt at an early date. It appears to
have been fairly well advanced by the time of the Old
Kingdom. As in Babylonia it attached itself to the
cure of disease. In later time it connected itself with
the burial of the dead, and magic formulae, often
sentences from the book of the dead, were written on

---

[1] See Erman, *Aegyptische Religion*, 2te Aufl. (Berlin, 1909),
pp. 58 ff.

[2] Herodotus ii. 39.

Erman, *op. cit.*, pp. 60 ff.   [4] Herodotus ii. 60.

the inside of the coffins in order to ward off from the departed evil spirits which would block their way. When these became too numerous for the inside of the coffin, they were inscribed on rolls of papyrus. Such superstitions hindered the best development of religion, and Ikhnaton prohibited them during his reign. After him they were again revived.[1]

58. **The ka and the soul.**—According to Egyptian belief each person possessed a *ka* given to him by a god at his birth. As long as he was master of this *ka* he lived. The *ka* was invisible, but it was assumed to have an appearance exactly like the body in which it dwelt. At death the *ka* left the body, but it was hoped that it would occasionally visit and reanimate the form in which it had dwelt so long. It was for the *ka* that food was so carefully placed in the tomb, and that such care was taken to preserve the body.[2] Besides the *ka* each person was thought to have a *bai* or soul, which could be seen, and which also left the body at death. This was often conceived to exist in the form of a bird, and it was thought that, while the mourners were lamenting the departed, he might be sitting among the birds of a neighboring tree watching them. This conception continued into Christian times, for in Christian cemeteries in Nubia the souls of the departed in the form of stone birds are found perched on the gravestones.

59. **Life after death.**—Interest in the life after death was developed among the Egyptians to a higher degree

---

[1] See Breasted, *History of Egypt*, pp. 101 ff., 175, 249 ff., 369 ff., 390, 459, and 498.

[2] Professor Breasted thinks the *ka* simply awaited a man in the hereafter. *Development of Religion and Thought in Ancient Egypt*, p. 52.

than among any other ancient people. Probably it is in part due to the development of their civilization at a time so early that the mind of man could not disentangle its thoughts from the physical that the preservation of the body was considered essential to the life after death. Every effort was accordingly made to preserve the body, and the art of mummification was evolved. As to the life after death itself, it is probable that at the beginning different conceptions prevailed in different parts of Egypt. At the beginning, however, all Egyptians thought of the dead as having an earthly abode. As time passed this abode was, in the thought of many, through the influence of the Osiris-myths, transferred to the sky. Side by side with this last conception some of the older ones survived. The life of the departed was, according to the most widely accepted view, but a continuance of the life on earth. The child remained a child and the old man remained an old man. The same social organization existed, and the same joys and physical needs of food. In the earliest time the dwelling-place of the dead was supposed to be the sands of the desert, generally to the west of the cities, where the cemeteries were situated.[1] According to another conception, which apparently originated in some particular part of Egypt, the dead lived in a lower world, which, like Egypt, was a narrow land bounded by deserts through which a river flowed. This land was dark by day, but was visited by the sun at night.[2] The conception that the dead were taken up to

[1] See Steindorf, *Religion of the Ancient Egyptians* (New York, 1905), pp. 116–19.

[2] Steindorf, *ibid.*, pp. 126 ff.

heaven became the popular one in later times. The earliest literary witnesses to it are the pyramid texts, where its blessings are confined to kings. As in later time it became more democratic, other expressions of faith in it were committed to writing, sometimes on coffins, sometimes on papyri. In the Empire period and the revival of the Twenty-sixth Dynasty efforts were made to collect these, but no collection embraces them all. This body of literature is known as the Book of the Dead.[1] While it is mainly devoted to the Osirian conception of the hereafter, older views also often find expression. It is a confused and repetitive mass of material, but is a powerful witness to the ancient Egyptian yearning for immortality.

60. **Myths.**—The Egyptians appear to have had a considerable number of myths about their gods. There are in the Book of the Dead and other religious texts many allusions to such myths. Comparatively few of these have survived. The most popular of those which we know was the myth of the death and resurrection of Osiris, which played such an important part in the development of the conception of the hereafter, and of which some description has already been given.[2] Another popular myth told how the goddess Isis learned the secret name of Re. This myth seems to have circulated among magicians. Still another told how, when Re had grown old and feeble, his authority was despised. Men conspired against him as they might against an old Pharaoh who had outlived his vigor. Re

[1] See E. A. W. Budge, *The Book of the Dead*, II (London, 1898). This volume contains a translation of the various texts. Vol. I is occupied with the Egyptian text, and Vol. III with an Egyptian glossary.

[2] See above, sec. 50.

in anger sent the fierce lion-headed goddess Sekhmet to devour them, and she executed her task so well that mankind was in danger of complete destruction. The problem then became how to induce the goddess, who had once tasted blood, to desist. This Re accomplished by making seven thousand jars of beer look like blood, so that the goddess drank herself drunk on these, and the remnant of the human race escaped. Egypt had no story of the flood. The overflow of the Nile was there not an evil, but the greatest blessing.

61. Ethics.—The thought of the Egyptian people, though in some domains always of a peculiarly elementary character, achieved its greatest triumphs in the realm of ethics. Civilization developed at too early a date to permit the acceptance of an advanced system of religious thought. To the end animal-worship, together with a confused mass of gods and myths about the hereafter, perpetuated certain primitive conceptions. The realm of religious theory was in Egypt always occupied by a chaos of contradictory views. The Egyptians, like the Babylonians and Chinese, were an exceedingly practical people. They worked out for the human race, as did the Babylonians, many of the initial problems of civilization. In ethical thought, too, they did yeoman service. The precepts of Ptah-hotep and the admonitions of Ipuwer take high rank. Ptahhotep's precepts are, like the biblical Book of Proverbs, eminently practical, but they also betray deep insight into human nature and the exigencies of practical life. The expressions of a social conscience which come from the Middle Kingdom are also evidence of advanced ethical thought. No doubt practice lagged

behind theory, but it is to Egypt's credit that her sages were able to formulate such lofty theories of conduct.

SUPPLEMENTARY READING

CLASS A

On Egyptian history: cf. Barton, *Archaeology and the Bible*, chap. i; or better, Breasted, *A History of the Ancient Egyptians* (New York, 1908); or better still, Breasted, *History of Egypt*, 2d ed. (New York, 1909); or Arthur Weigall's *History of the Pharaohs* (New York, 1925–27).

On secs. 47, 48: cf. Barton, "Tammuz and Osiris," *Journal of the American Oriental Society*, XXXV, 213–23; and Breasted, *History of Egypt*, 2d ed., chap. iii, or *Development of Religion and Thought in Ancient Egypt*, Lecture I.

On sec. 49: cf. Breasted, *Development of Religion and Thought in Ancient Egypt* (New York, 1912), Lectures II–V.

On sec. 50: cf. Breasted, *op. cit.*, Lecture VIII.

On secs. 51–54: cf. Breasted, *ibid.*, Lectures IX and X.

On sec. 55: cf. Herodotus, Book ii. 37; and Breasted, *History of Egypt*, 2d ed., pp. 62–63, 171, 241, 247, 249 ff., 272, 362, 401–3, 475, 489–97, 506 ff., 520–28, 574–96.

On sec. 56: cf. Herodotus, Book ii. 39–41; and Erman, *Handbook of Egyptian Religion*, 1907, chap. vi.

On sec. 58: cf. Steindorf, *Religion of the Ancient Egyptians*, pp. 106–13.

On sec. 59: cf. Breasted, *Development of Religion and Thought in Ancient Egypt*, Lectures II–VIII; and E. A. W. Budge, *The Book of the Dead*, II, *passim;* also Steindorf, *Religion of the Ancient Egyptians*, pp. 114–37.

On sec. 59: cf. D. A. Mackenzie, *The Myths of Egypt* (London, 1914), *passim;* Petrie, *Religion and Conscience in Ancient Egypt*, Lecture IV and Breasted in E. Hershey Sneath's, *Religion and the Future Life*, chap. ii.

On sec. 60: cf. Breasted, *Development of Religion and Thought in Ancient Egypt*, Lectures VI and VII; and Petrie, *Religion and Conscience in Ancient Egypt*, Lecture VI.

CLASS B

G. F. Moore, *History of Religions* (New York, 1913), chaps. viii and ix.

CHAPTER IV

THE RELIGION OF THE ANCIENT HEBREWS

Yahweh is a man of war:
Yahweh is his name.
                    —Exod. 15:3.

I Yahweh thy God am a jealous God.
                    —Exod. 20:5.

Hear, O Israel, Yahweh our God is one Yahweh.
                    —Deut. 5:4.

When Israel was a child, then I loved him,
And called my son out of Egypt.
                    —Hos. 11:1.

But he was wounded for our transgressions,
He was bruised for our iniquities.
The chastisement of our peace was upon him;
And with his stripes we are healed.

                    —Isa. 53:5.

62. The land.—Palestine consists of a strip of fertility, varying in width from 70 to 125 miles, between the Mediterranean Sea and the Arabian Desert. The fertility is caused by the rain from moisture-laden clouds which are driven in from the Mediterranean during the winter months, and extends eastward until the moisture of the clouds is exhausted. This strip of land formed in ancient times a bridge of fertility between the Nile and the Mesopotamian valleys. The whole country is about the size of the states of Rhode Island and Con-

necticut. On the west is the maritime plain, bordered
on its southeastern part by the Shephelah or low hills;
east of this is the central range of Palestinian hills, cleft
in parts by many deep valleys, the chief of which is the
great valley of Esdraelon or Jezreel; east of this again
is the Jordan Valley, in many respects the most remarkable valley in the world. From the Huleh southward
it is altogether below the level of the Mediterranean Sea,
and at the Dead Sea reaches a depression of about 1,300
feet. East of this is a great tableland which rises, in
parts, to a height of 3,500 feet above sea-level. At its
northern extremity Mount Hermon rises 9,166 feet,
and from November to July or August is capped with
snow. In no other part of the earth's surface is such
a variety of flora and fauna found within such narrow
limits. The land and its climate no doubt played some
part in the birth of that religion which has so influenced
the world for good.[1]

63. **Value of the patriarchal narratives.**—The historical study of the early books of the Bible has shown
that they were written much later than was formerly
supposed, and that the traditions of the Hebrew patriarchs collected in the Book of Genesis consist largely of
traditions of later tribal history, which are in some cases
attached to the names of tribes represented as persons,
and in some cases to immigrants from Babylonia whose
names had been attached to localities in which the
Hebrew tribes settled.[2]

[1] For a fuller statement, see George Adam Smith, *Historical Geography of the Holy Land*, pp. 43–61.

[2] For a more extensive discussion of these narratives, see G. A.
Barton, in the *Proceedings of the American Philosophical Society*, LII,
185–200, or *The Religion of Israel* (in press), chap. ii.

64. The formation of the Hebrew nation.—The
traditions indicate that the Hebrew nation is composed
of four groups of tribes, which are said to be descended
from four mothers. Of these groups the most important
are the Leah tribes and the Rachel tribes. Leah means
"wild cow" and Rachel, "ewe." Opinions differ as
to whether these were totems or economic symbols or
both. The Rachel tribes may have been sheep-raisers
and the Leah tribes cattle-raisers. There is considerable evidence, both archaeological and biblical, to show
that the Leah tribes entered Palestine and secured a
footing there about 1375–1350 B.C., and that the Rachel
tribes did not enter the country until 1200 B.C. or
later. The evidence indicates that the Leah tribes
entered the land from the south, the Rachel tribes
from the east. The probability is that the Rachel
tribes only were in Egypt, that it was they who were
led out by Moses, and that it was with them that the
covenant was made at the burning mountain called
Horeb.[1]

65. The early religion.—Analogy makes it probable
that the religion of these tribes before they entered
Palestine did not differ materially from that of other
nomadic tribes about them. Since the primitive
Semitic pillars and *asheras* (or wooden posts), circumcision, the *herem* or ban, and law of blood-revenge were
perpetuated by them into much later times, it is probable
that in other respects their religion was similar to that
of other nomadic Semites. Each tribe may have had its

[1] For full discussion of the evidence, see L. B. Paton, *Biblical World*,
XLVI, 82–88, 173–80; also *Journal of Biblical Literature*, XXXII, 1–54;
and G. A. Barton, *Religion of Israel*, chap. iii.

deity; at least we hear of a god Gad[1] (Isa. 65:11) which was probably originally the god of the tribe Gad, and there is reason to believe that the tribe of Asher worshiped the goddess Ashera. In the tribe of Judah some Kenites settled. The Kenite god was Yahweh (Jehovah), and the J document written in Judah reflects the belief that the worship of Yahweh went back to the earliest times (Gen. 4:26). We cannot now determine the date of this fusion. It is possible that it began before the settlement of the Leah tribes in Palestine.

66. Yahweh before Moses.—A theory that has in recent years won the assent of the majority of the writers on the religion of Israel is that Yahweh was the god of the Midianite-Kenites before he became the God of Israel. This tribe was nomadic and wandered from the borders of Egypt as far eastward as the volcanic lands to the north of Medina, in Arabia. Their god, like most Semitic gods, was a god of fertility. The epithet Yahweh, by which he was called, probably meant "he who causes passionate love." They attributed all activity to him. Volcanic eruptions were his appearance on the burning mountain, the showers of the peninsula of Sinai were given by him, their victories over their enemies were won by him. There are indications that Yahweh may have been a divine name in North Arabia for a thousand years before Moses, and that emigrants from this region to Babylonia and Palestine had carried the name to those countries.[2]

[1] Rendered "Fortune" in the Revised Version.

[2] For a fuller discussion of this point, see G. A. Barton, "Yahweh before Moses," *Studies in the History of Religion Presented to Crawford Howell Toy by Pupils, Colleagues, and Friends* (New York, 1912), pp. 187–204.

Possibly some of the Leah tribes other than Judah had learned before they came to Palestine to apply this epithet to their god, but of this we have no definite information.

67. The work of Moses.—Moses, fleeing from Egypt, married the daughter of Jethro, Yahweh's priest among the Midianite-Kenites. At the burning bush on Yahweh's volcanic mountain he was so impressed with the power and majesty of Yahweh that it marked an epoch in his life. He returned to Egypt to preach to his enslaved kinsmen the hope of escape through the power of Yahweh. The escape was effected, and at the burning mountain the Rachel tribes entered into covenant with Yahweh to make him their God and to serve him (see Exod., chaps. 1–24). At the first sacrifice offered after the Hebrews reached Yahweh's mountain Jethro officiated (Exod. 18:1–12); but later the covenant was consummated at a sacrificial feast at which Moses and Aaron officiated (Exod. 24:1–11). The E document holds that the name "Yahweh" first became known to Israel at this time (Exod. 3:1–14), and this is probably true for the Rachel tribes.

A box or ark, which could be easily carried from place to place, and which, perhaps, contained a sacred stone, became the symbol of Yahweh's presence with them. The sum of his requirements of his new worshipers, as nearly as we can now ascertain them, consisted of ten commands which could be easily numbered off on the fingers and remembered. They are now embedded in Exod., chap. 34, where later agricultural regulations have in two or three instances overlaid their originally nomadic character. They appear to have been the following:

1. Thou shalt worship no other god.
2. Thou shalt make thee no molten gods.
3. The feast of the Passover thou shalt keep.
4. The firstling of an ass thou shalt redeem with a lamb; all the first-born of thy sons thou shalt redeem.
5. None shall appear before me empty.
6. Six days thou shalt work, but on the seventh thou shalt rest.
7. Thou shalt observe the feast of ingathering [of dates].
8. Thou shalt not offer the blood of my sacrifice with leavened bread, neither shall the sacrifice of the Passover remain until the morning.
9. The firstlings of thy flocks thou shalt bring unto Yahweh, thy God.
10. Thou shalt not seethe a kid in its mother's milk.

There is much reason to believe that these commands were not written down, but were committed to tradition. This fact made it easier for later prophets to reinterpret the covenant and to make its basis ethical. In the fact of the covenant, the possibility of such ethical reinterpretation, and the belief in Yahweh's intolerance of other gods lay the germs of future progress.

68. Yahweh an agricultural God.—The entrance of the Rachel tribes into Palestine led to their union with the other tribes of Israel. Yahweh was already known to some of these, and by silent processes of assimilation which are now obscure to us he was accepted more or less definitely by all the tribes as their God. The political and religious life of the early time was in no sense organized. Until the time of Saul and David there was no national consciousness. In the early days there was no organized priesthood (cf. Judg., chaps. 17, 18). In the union of the tribes the vivid memories which the Rachel tribes entertained of their experiences triumphed over all other traditions of Yahweh. Spread by the omnipresent oriental story-teller, they were so much more vivid than the tamer experiences of the other tribes that in time they became the common inheritance of all.

When Palestine was conquered the shrines of the agricultural gods were taken over and became shrines of Yahweh. This happened at Schechem, Bethel, Hebron, Gezer, and at many other places. Stories of how it occurred at Dan and Jerusalem have survived in the Bible (Judg., chaps. 17, 18; II Sam., chap. 24) The stories which at these shrines were told of the old gods were now told of Yahweh. Yahweh was now believed to send the rain and to give the crops. The old gods had been called *baals*, i.e., owners of the soil, and in time the name was applied to Yahweh also (see Hos. 2:16). To Yahweh's feasts new agricultural feasts were added, and agricultural elements were introduced into the old ones. The sensual orgies of Semitic religion became more reprehensible when practiced by a wealthy population. These orgies as they had been practiced by the Canaanites were taken over into Yahweh's religion.

During all this time the orthodox type of sanctuary for Yahweh was a high place open to the sky. We hear of one small temple at Shiloh (I Sam., chaps. 1–5), with doors and apparently a roof—a temple in the holiest place of which Samuel slept! The open-air high place was nevertheless the normal type of sanctuary. Solomon's temple was an innovation. It was constructed on the general plan of the temples of Israel's more civilized neighbors. It contained an altar of bronze, whereas an altar of earth or unhewn stone was regarded long after this as the only proper altar (Exod. 20:24–26). Centuries later the temple of Solomon was revered as the ideal dwelling-place of Yahweh, but for a considerable time it was thought to be of a heretical type.

69. Elijah and after.—In the reign of Ahab there began a religious and social ferment which led to the transformation of Israel's religion. Ahab's Tyrian wife, Jezebel, had brought with her the worship of the Tyrian god Melkart. She and her husband in the case of Naboth (I Kings, chap. 21) outraged Hebrew popular rights. At this juncture Elijah came from Gilead, proclaiming the old nomadic ideal of Yahweh and linking his religious ideals to the rights of the people as against the king. To Elijah and his followers, not only was the worship of the Tyrian Melkart wrong, but the worship of the agriculturized Yahweh of the west Jordan lands was little better. It was, he thought, also the worship of Baal. In the person and work of the prophet Elisha the ideals of Elijah, though somewhat obscured, were to some degree cherished. In the circles of Elijah's disciples stress was laid on ethics rather than upon ritual as the essence of Yahweh's covenant with his people.

It is not surprising, accordingly, that in the E document, written in the Northern Kingdom, where the ministry of these prophets was spent, ethical requirements were substituted for the ritualistic requirements in the ten "words" or commands, which were supposed to sum up what Yahweh required of his people when he made his covenant with them. This substitution was the easier because at the beginning the commands had not been written, but committed to oral tradition. Such substitution involved no conscious fraud. It was but an expression of the feeling we all have that, if properly transmitted, the fundamental religious document of our faith must teach the highest religion and ethics of which we know. The ethical decalogue which resulted was as follows:

1. Thou shalt have no other gods before me.
2. Thou shalt not make unto thee a graven image.
3. Thou shalt not lift up the name of Yahweh to a vanity [i.e., thou shalt not swear to a lie].
4. Remember the Sabbath day to keep it holy.
5. Honor thy father and thy mother.
6. Thou shalt do no murder.
7. Thou shalt not commit adultery.
8. Thou shalt not steal.
9. Thou shalt not bear false witness against thy neighbor.
10. Thou shalt not covet thy neighbor's house.

This decalogue sums up the religious advance which Elijah and his followers had achieved, though some of the commands clearly go back to the early days. It is tempting to think that the commands against coveting, swearing to a lie, and bearing false witness were suggested by the experience of Naboth. It should be noted that Israel was not yet in theory monotheistic. The first of these commands presupposes the reality of the existence of other gods.

70. The eighth-century prophets.—The insight of four great men, Amos, Hosea, Isaiah, and Micah, who lived and preached between 755 and 690 B.C., carried

the work begun by Elijah to much higher levels. While
they presented no philosophical theory of monotheism,
each one of them was a practical monotheist. They
assumed that Yahweh controlled all nations. Amos
was the first to proclaim this (Amos 9:7), and it became
an axiom with the others. Their monotheism was one-
sided in its conception of Yahweh's attitude toward
the world. They thought him chiefly interested in
Israel, and as dealing with the other nations as such
dealing was necessary for the discipline of Israel. They
all represented Yahweh as a God whose one desire was
his passion for social justice. His chief demand was
righteousness between man and man. In their earlier
ministry they maintained that this was the sum-total
of his religion. They declared that he demanded no
sacrifices; that he was disgusted with ritual (Amos 5:
21, 25; Isa. 1:12–14); that the essence of his religion
was that "justice roll down as waters and righteousness
as an ever-flowing stream" (Amos 5:24). Amos held
out as a motive for righteousness only the fear of punishment. Hosea, the first prophet of the love of Yahweh,
urged as a motive his great love. Hosea interpreted the
covenant at Horeb as a marriage contract. Yahweh
had chosen Israel as his bride, and her faithlessness
was base ingratitude to him and deeply grieved his
heart.

71. Beginning of the messianic hope.—Isaiah was,
in the opinion of the writer, the first prophet of the
messianic hope. There has been a tendency in the last
thirty years to believe that all messianic prophecy was
written after the exile. Against this view the writer
has elsewhere protested. There is no adequate reason

for denying to Isaiah the authorship of the two oracles in Isa. 9:2–6 and 11:1–9.[1]   The first of these visions dates from the Syro-Ephraimitish war of 735 B.C., and represents the ideals of a young man whose blood is hot. He looked for a king to come who should surpass in all kingly qualities Tiglath-pileser IV of Assyria. He was to be

> a wonder-counselor,
> a god of a warrior,
> a father of booty,
> a prince of peace.

The vision recorded in Isa. 11:1–9 is a vision of his old age, dating from the time of Sennacherib's second invasion of Judah in 691 or after.[2]   In this vision the figure of the king fell into the background, and in imagery of unsurpassed beauty the prophet set forth the unsullied righteousness that should then prevail. Here is crystallized the essence of the ethical teaching of the prophets of the eighth century.

72. Isaiah's compromise with ritual.—Apparently in his old age Isaiah saw that the world was not ready for a religion without ritual and persuaded King Hezekiah to try to reduce ritual to such limits that it could be purified of those agricultural and primitive elements which the prophets now identified with the worship of the Canaanitish Baals. Hezekiah accordingly attempted to suppress all the outdoor shrines of the land and to center

---

[1] For a more extended discussion, see G. A. Barton, *Journal of Biblical Literature*, XXXIII, 68–74; *Religion of Israel* (in press), chap. vi.

[2] See the argument of Fullerton in *Bibliotheca Sacra*, LXIII, 577–634; and Rogers, *Cuneiform Parallels to the Old Testament*, pp. 332–40.

the worship in the temple at Jerusalem (II Kings 18:
1–6 and 22). This movement naturally met with
much opposition.

73. Jerusalem the dwelling of Yahweh.—When
Sennacherib came against Jerusalem the second time
and all looked hopeless, Isaiah, in accordance with the
principles of Hezekiah's reform, conceived Jerusalem
to be necessary to the worship of Yahweh, and declared
that Yahweh would protect it (Isa. 31:5). The army
of Sennacherib was decimated by bubonic plague, which
the people of Jerusalem believed to be inflicted by the
angel of Yahweh (II Kings 19:36),[1] the Assyrian
withdrew and Jerusalem was spared. This providential
vindication of the prophet's word gave to Jerusalem
a new significance in the minds of many Hebrews, and
was the beginning of the belief that Yahweh dwelt on
Zion rather than at Horeb.

74. The writing of Deuteronomy.—Under King
Manasseh, 686–641 B.C., there was a violent reaction
against the prophetic reforms. The country shrines
were restored, and the people, led by their king, revived
heathen Semitic customs that had been discarded.
During this period, while the disciples of the great
eighth-century prophets could do nothing openly, they
cherished their ideals in secret and made plans for the
future. In these circles about 650 B.C. the Deuteronomic law was composed. Its basis was the "Book of
the Covenant," Exod. 20:24—23:19, the legal kernel
of the E document, but the law of the altar, Exod.
20:24–26, was changed so as to limit the sanctuary to

---

[1] See G. A. Smith, *Historical Geography of the Holy Land*, pp. 158 ff.,
or Hastings' *Dictionary of the Bible.* One-volume ed., p. 403.

the "place which Yahweh should choose," and other features of the code, which presupposed a multiplicity of sanctuaries, were modified .to conform to this. The striking deliverance from Sennacherib was held to show that Yahweh had chosen Jerusalem, and there was never a question that Jerusalem was the one place of worship. Some of the social features of the older code were softened, so that the law as it appears in Deuteronomy embodies something of the social emphasis of the preaching of the eighth-century prophets.

75. Josiah's reform.—Josiah, the grandson of Manasseh, was friendly to the prophetic ideals, and by the eighteenth year of his reign the advocates of those ideals found a favorable opportunity to secure public action. Repairs upon the temple were in progress, and it was so arranged that a copy of the Deuteronomic law was found while the temple was being cleared out. When it was read to the king, he appealed to the prophetess Huldah to know whether it was really the law of Moses. It corresponded with her conception of what religious law ought to be, so she declared it genuine. Thereupon Josiah undertook to reform the religion of his kingdom, so as to bring it into conformity to this law. The country shrines were abolished, the cult was centralized in Jerusalem, while pillars, *asheras*, the ministers of social impurity, and other survivals of primitive Semitic religion were removed. The people of Judah did not acquiesce in this reform much more readily than in the time of Hezekiah and Manasseh, and a long spiritual struggle ensued.

76. Jeremiah.—About six years before the finding of the Deuteronomic law, Jeremiah, a very young man, began to prophesy, and his prophetic activity continued for forty years during the period of Judah's decline and fall. The form in which the Book of Jeremiah has come down to us is forbidding, so that few realize how great a prophet Jeremiah was. He contributed four great ideas to Israel's religion which became potent in after-time and which tended greatly to its purification and advancement. The first of these ideas was theoretical monotheism. Earlier prophets had been practical monotheists; it remained for Jeremiah to declare that the gods of the heathen were "vanities"—mere figments of the imagination (Jer. 10:15; 14:22). As a corollary of this conception he also taught that Yahweh was willing to become the God of the nations as well as of the Jews; that, if they were repentant, he would receive them (Jer. 16:17–21). His third contribution was the doctrine of the inwardness of religion. The heart must be changed, not the outward life only (Jer. 31:31–34). To these great doctrines Jeremiah added that of individual responsibility (Jer. 31:29, 30). Down to his time the nation or family had been the moral unit (see Josh., chap. 7), but on that basis no great progress could be made in personal religion or in ethics. The teaching of Jeremiah set religion free from many time-worn shackles.

In addition to these doctrines, Jeremiah revived Hosea's conception of the covenant of Yahweh, enforcing the view that it was a covenant of marriage and that Yahweh was a God of love. His view of the inwardness of religion enabled him to declare, when invaders threatened Jerusalem, that its preservation was no longer necessary to the worship of Yahweh. For the time of Jeremiah that was true. The Deuteronomic law had supplied religion with a tangible form from which the temple could be temporarily omitted, and the teaching of Jeremiah had given it an inward significance, which for the more choice spirits made it independent of outward forms.

77. **Ezekiel, a** young priest who had been taken to Babylonia with those first deported by Nebuchadrezzar in 597, began to prophesy five years later. His prophetic activity continued until about 570 B.C. Until the fall of Jerusalem in 586 B.C., Ezekiel in Babylonia reinforced the teaching which Jeremiah was giving in Palestine. He was animated by the same lofty ethical ideals, as is shown by the seventeenth and eighteenth chapters of his prophecy. In 586 B.C. Jerusalem was again captured by Nebuchadrezzar, the temple was destroyed, and another considerable number of the more prominent inhabitants were transported to Babylonia. The poorer peasantry were left behind to drag out their existence among the ruins. After this event Ezekiel, who was a priest as well as a prophet, in brooding over the fortunes of his people felt certain that at some time Yahweh would rehabilitate a Hebrew state in Palestine, and he drew up a form of organization and of law for the regulation of such a state and its worship; see Ezek., chaps. 40–48. The plan outlined by Ezekiel advances a step farther than the law of Deuteronomy in blending prophetic ideals with the ritual law. Details are laid down for the measurements of temple and altar and for various details of the ritual. Ezekiel first called into existence a class of Levites as distinct from the priests. In Deuteronomy every Levite had been a potential priest. Before the exile,

so Ezekiel informs us, the menial work of the temple, such as the slaying of the sacrifices and the cleansing of the implements, had been performed by foreign slaves (see Ezek., 44:8–13). This Ezekiel prohibited, and ordained that such work should in the future be done by the priests, who had formerly officiated in the high places which were now abolished.

78. Second Isaiah.—After the death of Ezekiel no great Hebrew voice was heard for twenty years. The great Nebuchadrezzar died in 562 B.C., and, after the rapid succession of three weak kings, in 555 the religious devotee Nabonidus gained the throne. In 553 B.C. Cyrus the Persian overthrew the Median kingdom and inaugurated that series of conquests which created the Persian empire. In 546 he overcame Croesus, king of Lydia. Cyrus revoked the policy of transportation practiced by the later Assyrian and Babylonian kings, and permitted peoples who had been transported to dominions which he now conquered to return to their respective lands and revive their national institutions. His deeds during these years seem to have been fairly well known in Babylon, which he did not conquer until 538 B.C. About 550 there arose, many believe, a new prophet, whose utterances are now summed up in chapters 40–55 of the Book of Isaiah. We do not know his name, but call him the second Isaiah because by some literary accident or misconception his prophecies were attached to the book containing those of Isaiah.

In the first half of his prophecies (Isa., chaps. 40–48), which were uttered before 538 B.C., he asserted that Cyrus was conquering for Yahweh and for Israel, declared that the opportunity for Hebrews to return to

Palestine was approaching, sought to impress his hearers with the might and majesty of Yahweh, the only real God, and to prepare them to return to their land when the opportunity came. When Babylon fell and the opportunity occurred, but few Judaeans embraced it, in spite of the prophet's impassioned appeals. He accordingly uttered another series of discourses (Isa., chaps. 49–55) to encourage them to return. All through his preaching he had addressed Israel as the "servant of Yahweh." When it was necessary to reprove her slowness, she was the unfaithful servant; when he thought of her possible service in the world, he portrayed her as the ideal servant. This ideal he embodied in four poems, the greatest of which constitutes Isa. 52:13—53:12. Here he pictured Israel as by her sufferings making Yahweh known to the world. It was thus that he found a philosophy of the national misfortunes. Israel's sufferings had been double the amount that her own sins deserved (Isa. 40:2). A part of this suffering had been incurred because she received the chastisement due to the nations. When the nations beheld, they would repent, the prophet declared, and turn to Yahweh (see Isa. 52:15; 53:1–5). An ideal was thus called into existence which no nation could really fulfil. One only, Jesus of Nazareth, has fulfilled it.

79. The Code of Holiness.—About 500 B.C. or earlier (perhaps during the time of the second Isaiah) a priest imbued with the prophetic spirit drew up the so-called Code of Holiness, which, excluding later additions,[1]

---

[1] See J. E. Carpenter and G. Harford-Battersby, *Hexateuch*, II, 166–81; or S. R. Driver, "Leviticus," in Haupt's *Sacred Books of the Old Testament*, pp. 33–53.

now constitutes Lev., chaps. 17–26. This writer felt the influence of Ezekiel strongly, as his laws and style prove. These laws were another step toward a religion which should attain by law what the great prophets had attempted to attain by loyalty to Yahweh.

80. The rebuilding of the temple.—About 520 B.C. two prophets, Haggai and Zechariah, who had apparently recently returned to Jerusalem from Babylonia, persuaded the Judaeans that a lack of rain and its consequent famine were evidences of Yahweh's displeasure because the temple had not been rebuilt. The voices of these prophets were so persuasive that its rebuilding was undertaken, and by 516 B.C. the temple was completed, though in a fashion far inferior to its former splendor.

81. The third Isaiah.—It has been thought that the second Isaiah lived about 549–529 as indicated in §78, and that Isa., chaps. 56–66 were in the main the work of a third Isaiah who wrote about 450 B.C. It has recently been made probable, however, that Isa., chaps. 40–66 is the work of one man—the greatest of the prophets—who lived in Jerusalem shortly before 400 B.C.[1]

82. The priestly law.—Meantime priestly circles, probably in Babylonia, were busy making a further codification of the priestly law. In order to give that law and its requirements a proper perspective, an account of the creation was written, as well as brief narratives of the chief crises of the earlier history. The whole constituted the P document.[2] In this law Ezekiel's plan for

[1] See Charles C. Torrey, *The Second Isaiah*, New York, 1928.

[2] For the sections comprising the P document see J. E. Carpenter and G. Harford-Battersby, *Hexateuch*, II; or W. E. Addis, *Documents of the Hexateuch* (London, 1898), II, 195–406.

Levites to perform the menial services of the sanctuary was adopted. Of course these Levites were descended from the priesthoods of the cities that in the old days had possessed the most flourishing high places. Later followers of the codifiers of the P document drew from this conclusion that all such cities must have been assigned by Joshua to Levitical clans—an inference that resulted in the distortion of historical perspective on a gigantic scale.

83. Adoption of the priestly law.—During the administration of Nehemiah, which began in 444 B.C., a great convocation of Judaeans was held in the temple court at Jerusalem at which the new law was read to them and they bound themselves to keep it (see Neh., chaps. 8–10). The adoption of this law as the fundamental law of religion marked the complete transformation of the religion. The old nature religion was discarded and Judaism was born. While Judaism was the result of the transformation begun by the prophets, it differed in many respects from the prophetic ideals of the eighth century. To them Yahweh was a present God, whose voice still spoke in the hearts of his prophets. From the priestly point of view Yahweh was a distant, exalted God, who long ago spoke to Moses. The prophets had little use for ritual; to the priests ritual was of the utmost importance.

84. Life after death.—To all Hebrews up to this time the dealings of Yahweh with his people were confined to life on the earth. He rewarded his faithful here; he punished the wicked in this life. The pictures of the life after death drawn in Isa. 14:9 ff. and Ezek. 32:22–32 present the same gloomy non-religious conception as that held by the Babylonians and as that reflected in the eleventh book of Homer's *Odyssey*.

85. Spirits and demons.—The ancient Hebrews thought that the world was filled with spirits. These spirits were non-ethical. They were subject to Yahweh, and might be sent by him on missions either of blessing to man or of harm (see I Kings, chap. 22; Job, chaps. 1 and 2). In the prophetic period no need was felt for a belief in Satan. Yahweh was thought to do everything both good and evil (see Amos 3:6; Isa. 45:7). It was only after the exile that the figure of Satan began to emerge, and he was then only an adversary (Zech. 3:1), not the full-fledged prince of evil that he afterward became.

86. Importance of the Hebrew religion.—The development of Israel's religion through the influence of the prophets from its primitive Semitic beginnings to the formation of Judaism is one of the most significant chapters in the history of the human race. In other countries, as in Egypt, monotheism was grasped by a few; in Israel alone was it made the possession of the people. Others conceived it as a great idea; the prophets linked it with human rights and common justice. Perhaps even here it would have failed but for the misfortunes of the Jewish state. These constituted a sifting process by which the devotees of the higher religion were separated from the reactionaries and formed into a community in which it was an axiom to men, women, and children that there is but one God and that he demands a righteous life. In this achievement were the seeds of the best religious experience of mankind. It was on account of this that the Hebrew religion became

the mother of the three great monotheistic religions of the world, Judaism, Mohammedanism, and Christianity.

SUPPLEMENTARY READING

CLASS A

On sec. 62: G. A. Smith, *Historical Geography of the Holy Land*, pp. 43–61.

On sec. 63: G. A. Barton, *The Religion of Israel* (New York, 1918), chap. iii.

On secs. 64, 65: L. B. Paton in the *Biblical World*, XLVI, 82–88, 173–80, and in the *Journal of Biblical Literature*, XXXII, 1–54; also G. A. Barton, *The Religion of Israel*, chap. iii, or "The Historical Value of the Patriarchal Narratives," *Proceedings of the American Philosophical Society*, LII, 185–200.

On. sec. 66: G. A. Barton, "Yahweh before Moses," *Studies in the History of Religion Presented to Crawford Howell Toy by Pupils, Colleagues, and Friends* (New York, 1912), pp. 187–204.

On sec. 67: G. A. Barton, *Religion of Israel*, chap. iv.

On secs. 68–86: G. A. Barton, *Religion of Israel*, chaps. v–ix; or K. Budde, *The Religion of Israel to the Exile*, Lectures II–VI; W. E. Addis, *Hebrew Religion* (New York, 1906), chaps. iv–ix; or K. Marti, *The Religion of the Old Testament* (New York, 1907), chaps. ii–iv.

On secs. 78 and 81, C. C. Torrey, *The Second Isaiah*, New York, 1928.

CLASS B

H. T. Fowler, *The Origin and Growth of the Hebrew Religion* (Chicago: The University of Chicago Press, 1916); J. M. P. Smith, *The Prophet and His Problems* (New York, 1914).

CHAPTER V

JUDAISM

The law of Yahweh is perfect, restoring the soul.
$$\text{—Ps. 19:7.}$$

Oh how love I thy law!
It is my meditation all the day.
$$\text{—Ps. 119:97.}$$

Behold the fear of Yahweh, that is wisdom;
And to depart from evil is understanding.
$$\text{—Job 28:28.}$$

But the saints of the Most High shall receive the kingdom, and possess the kingdom for ever, even for ever and ever.—Dan. 7:18.

Simon the Just was one of the last of the great synagogue, He used to say: "The world rests upon three things—upon the law, upon the service, and upon the charity of the pious."—Pirqe Aboth i, 2.

Until what time do they recite the *Shema*[1] in the evening? . . . . The wise say: "until midnight." Rabban Gamaliel says: "until the dawn of morning."—Berakoth i, 1.

87. The Persian period.—The adoption of the Law in the time of Nehemiah led, as pointed out in the last chapter, to the establishment of Judaism. Not all the Jews were resident in Palestine. Most of those who had been settled in Babylonia did not return, but continued to live there. Babylonian business documents of the Persian period contain a large number of Jewish

---

[1] *Shema* ("hear") is the Jewish name for the great confession of faith found in Deut. 6:4 f., beginning "Hear, O Israel: Yahweh our God is one Yahweh."

names. This colony, known as the Goliouth, or "Captivity," continued for fifteen hundred years to be an important colony in Babylonia. Like their brethren in Palestine, the Babylonian Jews accepted the priestly law. Indeed, it is the belief of most scholars that it had been compiled among them by disciples of Ezekiel. From Babylonia Jews had spread eastward to Media and Persia. A considerable Jewish colony existed at Elephantine in Egypt also. They possessed a temple, and apparently did not receive the new law at once.[1]

When the temple was rebuilt at Jerusalem and the worship was reorganized, an appropriate hymn book was necessary, hence the first portion of the Psalter (Pss. 3–41) was compiled. Enthusiasm for the Law and the high hopes it awakened in many pious souls are reflected in some of these psalms, as in Ps. 19:7–11.

Extensive as was the influence of the Law it did not, however, enlist the affections of all. The sages appear to have been almost untouched by it. About 400 B.C. one of these composed the great poem which is now the Book of Job. He was a devout Israelite and a believer in Yahweh, but he investigated and discussed the problems of life with a freedom entirely untrammeled by the Law. In his poem the problem of suffering is treated in a way that proves the inadequacy of the popular theology and portrays the growth that may come to a soul in the crucible of suffering.[2]

Josephus informs us[3] that about 350 B.C. the Persian general Bagoses dealt very harshly with the Jews for

[1] See G. A. Barton, *Archaeology and the Bible* (5th ed., 1927), Part II chap. xxi.

[2] See G. A. Barton, "Job," *Bible for Home and School* (New York, 1911), pp. 7–12.

[3] *Antiquities of the Jews*, XI, vii, 1.

seven years. Many scholars think that the cause of this
was an attempt on the part of the Jews to gain their
independence. This attempt is believed to have called
forth much national and religious enthusiasm, and to
have been the occasion of the compilation of two more
books of the Psalter, Pss. 42–73, to which Pss. 84–89
were later added as an appendix.

88. The Samaritans.—The Book of Nehemiah shows
that friction between the Jews and the Samaritans
existed as early as the fifth century. The Samaritans
wished to be counted as Jews; the Jews looked on them
with suspicion because of their mixed descent (see
II Kings 17:24–34). Before the time of Alexander the
Great the friction had become so acute that the schism
was complete. The Samaritans built a temple on
Mount Gerizim and became a separate sect (see John
4:20), which has persisted, though with greatly dimin-
ished numbers, to the present day.[1] They took as their
Bible the Pentateuch and the Book of Joshua, though
they have transformed Joshua so freely that it is hardly
recognizable.

89. The Greek period.—With the conquest of
Palestine by Alexander in 332 Palestine passed under
Hellenic control. After his death both the Ptolemies
of Egypt and the Seleucidae of Antioch offered Jews
inducements to settle in various cities of their dominions.
The settlements thus made tended to scatter the Diaspora, as the Jews outside of Palestine were called, more
widely, and to bring them into contact with the varied
life of the world. So many of them settled at Alexandria

[1] For the character and history of the Samaritan sect, see J. A
Montgomery, *The Samaritans* (Philadelphia, 1907).

in Egypt that it became a little Judaea. There about 250 B.C. the translation of the Jewish Scriptures into Greek, known as the Septuagint, was begun. Meantime Palestine, subject at first to the Ptolemies, then a bone of contention between them and the Seleucidae, passed in 199 B.C. under the dominion of the Syrian monarchs. It felt the influence of the various currents of life and thought that swayed the world, although the Jews resident in it were far more sheltered than their brethren of the Diaspora.

In Judaea the variety of thought manifested in the Persian period continued. The sages were active. The book of Proverbs, the collection of which was, perhaps, begun under the Persians, was brought to completion.[1] An unknown sage composed, about 200 B.C., the Book of Ecclesiastes in which the skeptical influences generated by Greek thought are clearly apparent.[2] About twenty years later Joshua, son of Sirach, composed the book commonly called Ecclesiasticus. Devotees of the Law were not, however, wanting. Its precepts were cherished by many, and its priestly regulations were not only pondered, but supplemented.

90. The rise of apocalyptic literature.—Before the organization of Judaism the voice of prophecy had nearly ceased. After that time there were but few to prophesy, and their voices were not strong. Such were Joel, the author of Isa., chaps. 24–27, and of Zech., chaps. 9–14. This last prophet lived in the Greek period, perhaps as

---

[1] See Cornill, *Introduction to the Canonical Literature of the Old Testament*, pp. 437–47.

[2] See the introduction to G. A. Barton, "Commentary on Ecclesiastes," *International Critical Commentary*.

late as 250 B.C., and predicted that there should be no more prophets after him (see Zech. 13:2-5). After this time no one dared to speak in his own name as a mouth-piece of Yahweh. Struggling humanity could not rest satisfied without religious guidance, so after 200 B.C. there arose a succession of apocalyptists, who couched the teaching the age needed in the form of visions which were attributed to some famous person of ancient times.

Six such apocalypses were attributed to Enoch, one to Noah, one to Moses, one to Isaiah, six to Baruch, one to Shealtiel, two to Ezra, one to Daniel, one to each of Jacob's sons, not to mention apocalyptic frag-ments attributed to Solomon and the Sibyl. The earliest of these, written between 200 and 170 B.C., was attributed to Enoch and is now embodied in Enoch, chaps. 1–36. The sources of apocalyptic visions were unfulfilled prophecy and the Babylonian creation-myth. The Babylonian myth gave the apocalyptists their philosophy of the universe. Evil was personified as a great world-power, and, they thought, that just as in the myth there had been a great struggle before the present heavens and earth could be created— a struggle in which the dragon had been overcome—so there would be a great conflict before the new heaven and new earth could be created. Under the influ-ences of this apocalyptic material the messianic hope was eventually transformed from the 'expectation of an earthly king of the Davidic dynasty to the expecta-tion of a heavenly Messiah who should come on the clouds of heaven.

91. The Maccabean revolt.—The readiness with which certain Jews accepted Hellenic ideas led Antiochus IV

of Syria to attempt in 168 B.C. to suppress the Jewish
religion and forcibly to establish Hellenic religion in its
place. This led to the so-called Maccabean uprising,
which was supported by the most ardent devotees of the
Law. After a struggle of twenty-five years, through
various vicissitudes, military, political, and religious,
the Jews won their independence, emerging from the
struggle with Simon the Maccabee as their high priest
and prince—two offices which they made hereditary in
his house.[1] This successful uprising called forth the
greatest national and religious enthusiasm. The hopes
and fears of its early stages are reflected in the Book of
Daniel, written between 168 and 165 B.C.; the religious
aspirations and enthusiasm are mirrored in Books IV
and V of the Psalter (Pss. 90–150), which were compiled
just at the close of this period.

92. The synagogue.—The origin of the synagogue
is shrouded in obscurity. When it is first mentioned in
religious literature it was an institution already old.
It apparently arose before the Maccabean revolt, as
the burning of synagogues is one of the atrocities laid
to the Syrians in Ps. 74:8—a psalm which was probably
re-edited in the Maccabean period. Perhaps the synagogue originated in Babylonia. In any case it was
intended to be a place for the public reading and interpretation of the Law and for united prayer. It was
introduced into Palestine, not only into the country
villages far from the temple, but into Jerusalem itself.
Little by little the synagogue became the center of the
religious life of Judaism, especially after the destruction of the temple. Its democratic services are elastic

[1] See I Macc. 13:35–41.

and have adapted themselves to all the forms of Jewish life.[1]

93. Rise of the Pharisees and Sadducees.—Under the descendants of Simon, who are often called Asmonaeans, the Jews were independent for eighty years. These princes soon assumed the title of king and conquered practically all the territory over which David had ruled. The pious devotees of the Law did not relish having a worldly high priest who played politics and engaged in wars. Little by little they developed their ideas into a tolerably consistent system and took the name "Pharisees," or separated ones, to signify their idea that the Jews should be separate from the world. They came into particular prominence as an opposition party in the reign of Alexander Jannaeus, 104–79 B.C., and were so strong that upon his death Alexander advised his wife to make her peace with them. During her reign, therefore, they were the dominant party and continued to exert a paramount influence in Judaism. With reference to legal customs they were conservative, insisting upon the rigid fulfilment of the Law; in thought they were in some respects more advanced, accepting, for example, the newer conception of the resurrection of the dead (see Dan. 12:2–4). The Sadducees were more conservative in thought, adhering to the older Hebrew non-belief in a resurrection, while in practice they were less rigid, and did not insist so strictly upon all the details of the Law.

Another somewhat obscure sect that developed before the Christian era was the Essenes, who mingled with the observance of the Jewish law some elements of

[1] See "Synagogue" in the *Jewish Encyclopedia.*

Persian thought. They were not very numerous and lived in coenobitic communities.

94. The oral law.—The desire of the Pharisees to give strict adherence to the Pentateuch in all the details of life led to a careful study of its requirements and to definite interpretations of them. These interpretations led to the formulation of traditional rules as to what was and what was not allowed by the Law. These traditions were ultimately written down in the Mishnah, but for two centuries or more they were passed from rabbi to pupil as traditions and constituted the oral law.

In the reign of Herod the Great (37–4 B.C.) the first schools for the conservation and transmission of this oral law were organized in Jerusalem. Shammai was the head of the school of strictly literal interpretation; Hillel, who had been born in Babylonia, was the head of the school of more liberal interpretation. Hillel, for example, so interpreted the law against taking interest in Deut. 23:19, 20 that it was practically set aside and the Jews were permitted to become a commercial people. Shammai and Hillel had their successors in Judaism for many centuries. In interpreting the Law and applying it to the details of the life of a continuous community, these rabbis naturally developed the Law. The oral law, like the Pharisaic movement out of which it sprang, is evidence of an intense desire to do the will of God and to order the earthly life according to the expressed will of heaven. God had, however, become to these men remote. His voice, once heard, was thought to have been long silent. The best that religion could do was to treasure the words uttered long ago.

95. Philo.—While in Jerusalem and Babylonia Pharisaism was developing, in some of the western settlements of the Diaspora Judaism was being broadened by contact with philosophic thought. This was notably the case in Alexandria, where Philo Judaeus, born about 20 B.C., lived and wrote. He died before 40 A.D. and was accordingly a contemporary of Jesus of Nazareth. Philo was the successor of the sages of the earlier time. A thorough monotheist, he approached the problems of life from the standpoint of reason rather than from that of the Law. He was profoundly affected by Greek philosophy, and developed a doctrine of the *Logos*, or Word, as an emanation from God which in some respects resembles that in the Gospel of John, though in some of its phases it is quite different from that.

96. Judaism in the time of Paul.—Jewish life in the first century of the Christian era presented great variety, nevertheless it was all bound together by the doctrine of monotheism and by the congregational life of the synagogue. The ideals of the Pharisees were very influential far beyond the borders of Palestine. Paul, for example, born at Tarsus of a family that had apparently been resident there for nearly two centuries,[1] was sent to Jerusalem to be educated under Gamaliel, Hillel's great successor. Paul, though of the Diaspora, was a Pharisee. No doubt his case is typical of many. Paul's missionary journeys afford glimpses, even if prejudiced glimpses, into many synagogues. Distinguished strangers, if Jews, were invited to explain the lessons

[1] See W. M. Ramsay, *The Cities of St. Paul* (New York, 1908). pp. 180–86.

of the day at the Sabbath services, and Paul found in this his opportunity to present his Christian point of view. The uniformity with which it was rejected is proof of the inner coherence of the scattered Judaism of the time. In Palestine itself intolerance of foreign rule was steadily growing. In the year 66 this led to open revolt, which in the year 70 resulted in the destruction of Jerusalem and the final annihilation of the temple.

97. Jamnia.—Before the destruction of Jerusalem the city of Jabneh in the Philistine plain, called by the Greeks Jamnia, had become an important center of Jewish learning. It is the same as the Jabneel of Josh. 15:11. Upon the destruction of Jerusalem the Sanhedrin moved to Jamnia, where its sessions were held most of the time until the rebellion of Bar Chocheba, 132–35 A.D. The famous Rabbi Akiba, who was born about 50 and died 132 A.D., lived here. In the discussions of the rabbis at Jamnia the oral law was further developed, and it was decided that Ecclesiastes and the Song of Songs are canonical Scripture. This decision finally closed the Old Testament Canon.

98. The Talmudic period.—The Talmud consists of two main strata, the Mishnah and Gemara. Each of these consists of several strata of traditions. The Mishnah rests upon the collection of the traditions made by Rabbi Judah, the Prince, in the early part of the third century A.D. These traditions were of gradual growth. They had been given shape by the pupils of Hillel and Shammai in the first century. In time the wording of the traditions was found to differ in different schools, and the Sanhedrin of Jabneh at the end of the first century examined them, assorted them, and

determined their exact wording. Later they were
revised by Rabbi Akiba, who excluded many traditional
interpretations and abbreviated others. By the end
of the second century many variations had again crept
into the traditions, and Rabbi Judah, the Prince, in
order to secure uniformity, re-examined the interpretations and committed them to writing. Up to this
time there had been a strong prejudice against allowing
the traditions to be written. The edition of Rabbi
Judah was so convenient and his reputation was so great
that his revision soon supplanted all traditional forms of
the text in the schools both of Palestine and of Babylonia. Thus the Mishnah was completed. The name
means "repetition," and then "law learned by repetition." It is derived from the method of study in the
rabbinical schools, where the pupil repeated the words
of the teacher until he knew them by heart. The
rabbis who formulated the traditions of the Mishnah
are called Tanaim or "Repeaters." They lived before
200 A.D.

After the formation of the Mishnah the development
of the traditional law went on for three hundred years
in the schools of Palestine and of Babylonia. As the
advancing life of the community called for the application of the law to new situations, the law was developed by interpretation. In the sixth century the
traditions later than the Mishnah were written down in
the Gemara. The rabbis who contributed to the traditions of the Gemara are called Amoraim or "Sayers."
They did not lay claim to as high an authority as the
Tanaim and their words are even less fresh and vital
than those of their predecessors. The Gemara is in

reality in the nature of a commentary on the Mishnah. The two together constitute the Talmud.

Although the Talmud is not inspiring reading, it reveals to us a people of great religious devotion and earnestness—a people groping after God, anxious in every detail of life to do his will, and ready to make any and every sacrifice to obey him. If they lived on tradition, because they thought the voice of God now silent, they did not in this respect differ from the Christians of the time. The Talmud shaped the main course of orthodox Judaism and is, after the Bible, its chief religious book. Philo and Alexandrian Jewish thought left no permanent impress on Judaism, partly because of the Jewish aversion to Christianity, which had appropriated the Alexandrian conceptions, and partly because of the decline of philosophical thinking.

99. The Geonim.—The head of a rabbinical school in Babylonia was given the title Gaon, "Majesty"—in the plural, Geonim. After the completion of the Talmud until the eleventh century the schools of Babylonia had such a reputation that the decisions of these Geonim were widely accepted. After the Mohammedan conquest in the seventh century the Geonim were accepted as the arbiters of practice in the countries under Mohammedan rule—the East and Spain—but later their decisions were eagerly sought and widely accepted all over Europe. Their authority waned in the eleventh century.

100. The Karaites are a Jewish sect which split off from the main body in the eighth century. The sect had its origin in Babylonia; its founder was Anan ben David, an Exilarch, or leader of the Captivity, as the

Jewish colony in Babylonia was still called. The movement was a revolt against tradition and rabbinism and
an attempt to follow the Bible only. The name of the
sect comes from *kārā*, "to read," and expresses the desire
of its members to guide their lives by what could be
read in the Bible rather than by what had been handed
down by tradition. Anan recognized, however, that
the biblical laws could not apply literally to all the
details of the life of his day, and through the influence
of the system of Abu Hanifa, a Mohammedan lawyer, he
recognized that biblical laws could be extended by
analogy and by allegorical interpretation. Allegorical
exegesis really opened the way to extend the law by
speculation, though the speculations were introduced
under cover of biblical interpretations.

While the Karaites rejected the traditions, they did
not succeed in entirely emancipating themselves from
them. They are accused by orthodox Jews of reverting
to principles of the Sadducees and the Essenes as well
as of being profoundly influenced by Mohammedanism.
During the first two or three centuries of their existence
the Karaites made many converts in Babylonia, Persia,
Syria, Palestine, and Egypt. In the twelfth century
they began to make converts in Europe, gaining
many in the Byzantine Empire, where they flourished
until its fall in the fifteenth century. Later many
were found in Lithuania and in Russia. In Russia
they exist in considerable numbers at the present
time.

101. Jews in the Middle Ages.—By the beginning
of the eleventh century the influence of the Babylonian
schools upon Judaism had begun to decline. Babylon

had given to Jewry the written Law, and, in the Babylonian Talmud, the traditional law in its most widely accepted form. The decisions of her Geonim had been widely accepted; but now the glory departed from the Jewish communities of Babylonia. Babylonian scholars are said to have migrated and founded rabbinical schools in Alexandria, Kairwan, near the site of Carthage, Cordova, and perhaps at Narbonne. Until the sixteenth century the life of the Jews was comparatively free in the countries around the Mediterranean. Jewish scholars distinguished themselves among the scholars of the world, and a number of Jewish poets flourished.

Among the gifted poets was Moses Ibn Ezra (1070–1138); among the distinguished philosophers of the time was Ibn Gabirol (Avicibron) (1021–58). In this period four scholars flourished who profoundly influenced the Judaism of the West. They were Solomon Bar Isaac, called Rashi (1040–1105), who lived in France and whose commentaries on the Bible and the Talmud were very influential; Abraham Ibn Ezra (1093–1138), a native of Toledo in Spain, whose commentaries on the Pentateuch and many other books of the Bible were of great importance; Moses Ben Maimon, or Maimonides (1135–1204), who was a philosopher as well as an exegete, who endeavored to reconcile Aristotle with the Bible, and whose principles of interpreting the Talmud, though they really set some parts of the traditional law aside, were generally accepted; and David Kimchi (1160–1235), who learned from the Arabian scholars the grammatical science which they in turn had learned from the Greeks, and who applied it to the interpretation of the Hebrew Bible. Kimchi was influential, not only among

Jews, but among the Christian reformers who studied his grammatical works, and through them he profoundly influenced the Protestant scholarship of a later age. Maimonides surpassed all these in influence. He is often called by the Jews the second Moses. In this period Jewish scholars and religious thinkers were more able and were better equipped than those of Christendom.

102. **Period of the Ghetto.**—In 1492 the Jews were expelled from Spain, and in the next century in most European countries they were compelled to live in separate quarters of the towns where they resided. If these quarters were sufficiently large at first, they soon ceased to be on account of the natural increase of the population. Herded in these narrow ghettos and prohibited generally from acquiring an education in the languages of the countries in which they resided, they made the synagogue the center of Jewish life. Through centuries of ostracism they kept their faith, though they produced no such thinkers as in the preceding period.

103. **Jewish emancipation.**—Moses Ben Menahem-Mendel, or Moses Mendelssohn (1729–1786), is counted by the Jews as Moses the Third, or Moses the Emancipator. He was born at Dessau and educated in Berlin. Having himself by indomitable energy gained an education, he formed friendships with a number of distinguished Germans, the most important of whom was Lessing. He translated the Pentateuch into German. His coreligionists, studying this, became acquainted with the language of the country and thus had access to modern learning. One of his most famous works was entitled *Jerusalem*. In it he made a plea for the emancipation of Judaism and argued for the separation

of church and state. This work had a wide influence. The emancipation of the Jews in France, begun in 1784, was completed by the French Revolution. Between 1782 and 1814 it followed in Austria and Germany. Other countries took similar action, so that in Western Europe the shackles were struck from the Jews, though in Russia the mediaeval conditions prevailed until the revolution of 1917.

104. Zionism.—During the centuries of the Christian era Judaism never entirely lost the messianic hope. In times of persecution it was revived, and at all times the prayers recited in the synagogue asked for the coming of Messiah and the restoration to Palestine. The long residence of the Jews in different lands, where, after the emancipation, they became the citizens of different countries, led in some sections to an abandoning of Israel's national hopes.

Nevertheless, since 1895 an extensive movement for the recovery of Palestine and the establishment of a Jewish state has arisen, and is backed by an extensive organization. This movement is due to the influence of Theodor Herzl's book *The Jewish State*, the German original of which was published in 1895. It is called Zionism. As a result of the Zionistic movement a Jewish homeland has been established in Palestine. Jewish institutions, including a university, are being built up, and Hebrew as a spoken language revived.

105. Reform Judaism.—Reform Judaism began in Germany about 1845, but has its center now in the United States. It is the result of the impact of modern science—evolution, biblical criticism, and philosophy— upon Jewish teachers. Reform Judaism rejects the

messianic hope and looks for no restoration to Palestine.
It regards Judaism simply as a religion. It distinguishes
between the moral and the ceremonial law, regarding
all ceremonial laws as natural evolutions, and holds
itself at liberty to reject them except in so far as time-
honored custom is psychologically necessary to religion.
The dietary laws are generally disregarded, and the
prayers of the synagogue are much modified. Organs
and mixed choirs furnish music in the reform synagogues.
Reform Jews substitute for the messianic hope the conception of Israel as a messianic people, chosen to teach
the world of the one true God. They believe that the
Aaronic priesthood has passed away; every Jew is a
priest. The world and humanity are, in their view,
under God's guidance; humanity is not innately sinful;
it is Israel's mission to acquaint every being with the fact
that he is a child of God and to call him to a righteous life.

106. **The spirit of Judaism,** whether orthodox or
reform, is still noble. Jews regard themselves as the
heirs of the prophets, as the preachers of monotheism,
and the champions of social righteousness. Among
themselves they exhibit a good degree of social solidar-
ity, helping one another now, as they have during
centuries of persecution, in many practical ways. They
have in modern times furnished, too, a good quota of the
world's notable philanthropists.

SUPPLEMENTARY READING

CLASS A

On secs. 87 and 89–93: cf. G. A. Barton, *The Religion of Israel*,
chaps. viii–xvi; or J. P. Peters, *The Religion of the Hebrews*,
chaps. xxiv–xxix, and "Synagogue" in the *Jewish Encyclopedia*.

On sec. 88: J. A. Montgomery, *The Samaritans, passim.*

On sec. 94: the article "Oral Law" in the *Jewish Encyclopedia.*

On sec. 95: "Philo" in the *Jewish Encyclopedia;* or James Drummond, *Philo Judaeus* (London, 1888).

On secs. 96–98: "Mishnah" and "Talmud" in the *Jewish Encyclopedia;* and Hershon, *Treasures of the Talmud* (London, 1882), *passim;* also Hereford, *Christianity in Talmud and Midrash* (London, 1903), *passim.*

On secs. 99, 100: "Geonim" and "Karaites" in the *Jewish Encyclopedia.*

On secs. 101, 102: "Ghetto" in the *Jewish Encyclopedia;* or I. Abrahams, *Jewish Life in the Middle Ages* (Philadelphia, 1906), *passim.*

On secs. 103–105: "Emancipation," "Zionism," "Reform Judaism," "Moses Mendelssohn," "Theodor Herzl" in the *Jewish Encyclopedia,* and David Philipson, *The Reform Movement in Judaism* (New York, 1907).

On sec. 106: "Judaism" in the *Jewish Encyclopedia;* M. Friedländer, *The Jewish Religion* (London, 1900); I. Abrahams, *Judaism* (London, 1910).

CLASS B

I. Abrahams, *Judaism,* 1910.

CHAPTER VI

MOHAMMEDANISM

Say: He is God alone, the everlasting God; he does not beget, and he is not begotten; and there is not one equal to him.—Koran, Sura cxii.

Fear God . . . . surely God is knowing and wise.—Koran, Sura xxxiii, 1.

God is forgiving and merciful.—Koran, Sura xxxiii, 5.

Those who misbelieve, for them are cut out garments of fire. There shall be poured over their heads boiling water, wherewith what is in their bellies shall be dissolved and their skins too, and for them are maces of iron. Whenever they desire to come forth therefrom through pain, they are sent back into it: "And taste ye the torment of the burning."—Koran, Sura xxii, 20.

Is the reward of goodness aught but goodness? Then which of your lord's bounties will ye twain deny? And beside these, are gardens twain, ... with dark green foliage. . . . . In each two gushing springs. . . . . In each fruits and palms and pomegranates. . . . . In them maidens best and fairest! . . . . Bright and large-eyed maidens kept in their tents . . . . whom no man or jinn has deflowered before them . . . . reclining on cushions and beautiful carpets. . . . . Blessed be the name of the Lord possessed of majesty and honor.—Koran, Sura lv, 60–75.

107. **Arabia,** the cradle of Islam, is one of the most sterile portions of the earth's surface. The greatest length of the peninsula is 1,000 miles, and its average breadth is 600 miles. This area consists of great stretches of upland gravel on which only hardy thorn bushes grow, of sandy deserts, and of extensive tracts

of igneous rock. A few scattered oases, produced by isolated springs, and a comparatively fertile strip along the southern end of the peninsula slightly relieve its sterility.

From this barren land from time immemorial Semites have been pouring into other lands, carrying with them the peculiar type of Semitic religion alluded to in chapter i. By the sixth century A.D. the old Semitic religion had been in some degree transformed and had lost something of its hold upon the people.[1] Jews and Christian ascetics had to some degree penetrated the peninsula. At Mecca, the seat of the powerful tribe of Koreish, a center to which people from all parts of the peninsula came each year to celebrate a festival and to trade, four men had broken away from heathenism and called themselves "Inquirers." They professed to be searching for the catholic faith of Abraham.

108. Mohammed.—It was under these conditions that Mohammed was born at Mecca about 570 A.D. Left an orphan at an early age, he was cared for first by his grandfather and then by an uncle. He appears to have been a quiet and an exemplary youth, and, with the exception of two visits to Syria with trading caravans, passed the first fifty years of his life at Mecca. At the age of twenty-five he married a widow, Khadijah, who bore him two sons and four daughters. The sons died in infancy, but the daughters grew up. When about forty years old Mohammed was agitated by grave

[1] For conditions in Arabia before Mohammed, see W. R. Smith, *Kinship and Marriage in Early Arabia*, 2d ed. (London, 1903); G. A. Barton, *A Sketch of Semitic Origins* (New York, 1902), chaps. ii and iii; and for the peninsula itself, S. M. Zwemer, *Arabia the Cradle of Islam* (New York, 1900).

doubts and, withdrawing from the city, spent two years in a cave in prayer and meditation. He came forth with the conviction that God had commissioned him to be a prophet to his people, as the Hebrew prophets and Jesus had been commissioned to the Jews. He at once began to preach and for ten years labored in Mecca against great odds. Converts were never numerous, and during the first part of this period they were very few. At one time Mohammed and his followers were confined by a ban to a narrow section of the city and endured great hardship. Under such circumstances a little group of believers were gathered about the prophet.

109. Doctrines.—The cardinal doctrine of Mohammed was the oneness and aloneness of God, whom he called Allah, "The God." The one God was conceived by him as a great human being or a transcendent man. He had hands, eyes, and human attributes. He was thought to be all-wise and all-powerful, and to be the absolute despot of the world. It was useless for man to hope to understand him, but God would be merciful if man submitted to him. Next in importance to the doctrine of God was the doctrine of the prophetic function of Mohammed. Through Mohammed, God made his final revelation; Mohammed was the seal of the prophets; no prophet was to come after him. Religion is supposed to make a man "whole," to give him "peace." The root by which this is expressed in Arabic is *salama*, the infinitive of the causative stem of which, *islām*, means "to submit." As Mohammed preached the doctrine of submission to God he called his religion Islām.

To these doctrines Mohammed added, from the time of his earliest ministry, a doctrine of material rewards and punishments. Believers were to be rewarded with a material paradise, and unbelievers were to be tortured in a very material hell. His ideas on this point are indicated in the quotations at the head of this chapter. The outward duties of believers were to pray five times a day, as well as to be just and kind to the poor. The doctrines of angels and of Satan were taken over from Judaism, though the figure of Satan was blurred by conceptions of the jinn inherited from Arabian heathenism.

110. The Prophet at Medina.—In the year 622 the Prophet fled from Mecca and took up his abode at Medina.[1] This was accomplished through a secret understanding with the men of Medina and in spite of the determination of the men of Mecca to prevent it at any cost. The flight marked such an epoch in the life of Islam that Mohammedans begin their era for reckoning time from its date. At Medina, Mohammed was accepted by the Arabs as ruler of the city. At Medina, Islam was transformed in many ways. Until Mohammed had resided in Medina for some time he had prayed with his face toward Jerusalem. He fondly hoped that the Jews, of whom there were numbers in Medina, would accept him as a successor of their prophets. When this hope was disappointed, the Prophet changed the *Kibla*, or the direction of the face in prayer, from Jerusalem to Mecca. Henceforth the ideals of Arabian heathenism

[1] The real name of the city was Yathrib. It was so called when Mohammed moved thither. Later it was called Medinat un-Nabi, "the city of the Prophet," afterward shortened to Medina.

were more influential in Islam than those of Jerusalem
and Israel. At Medina the Prophet, as the head of the
state, engaged in successful wars, in raids for robbery,
and not only descended to trickery and violence, but
had revelations justifying these practices. Islam was
no longer a religion of moral suasion; the alternative
became conversion or death.

Khadijah had died before Mohammed left Mecca,
and during his career at Medina he extended, sometimes
by revelation,[1] his marriages far beyond the number
four, which he allowed to other believers. Before the
end of the period Mecca was captured by him, and the
pilgrimage to Mecca, with the heathen ceremonies involved in it, became a part of Islam. The black stone
of the Kaaba thus became sacred to him who abhorred
idols; it became a sacred privilege to drink from the
waters of the well Zemzem in Mecca; and sacrifice
became a part of a religion that recognizes no place for
atonement. Before the Prophet died, in 632 A.D., all
Arabia had given him a nominal allegiance.

III. **The Medina caliphate and the Koran.**—Following the death of Mohammed a chief was chosen to
govern the community. He was called *al-khalifa*, "the
follower" or "successor" of the Prophet. He did not,
like the Prophet, receive revelations from heaven. He
was guided by the prophet's words and by what he
thought the Prophet would do if he were alive. The
caliphate of Medina lasted from 632 to 660. During
this time the conquests of Islam were extended over
Palestine, Egypt, and Persia. The early policy, that
those who would not accept Islam should be put to the

[1] See Sura xxxiii, 37 ff.

sword, was modified; they were permitted to pay a tax. This tax went to swell the fortunes of the ruling congregation of Medina. During this period the Koran was compiled and its text fixed. In the Prophet's lifetime many of the suras had been carried in the memory of his devout followers. Of some of them notes had been made on bits of bone, leather, or palm leaf. In the reign of Abu-Bekr, 632–34, these were brought together in a book. The longer were placed first, and the shorter after them. No attempt was made to place them in chronological order. As most of the longer ones were uttered at Medina, the arrangement brings the greater number of the later suras at the beginning of the book. In the reign of Othman, 644–56, the text of the Koran was fixed by the addition of vowel points. The book thus formed became, as the Prophet intended it should, the fundamental religious and civil law of the Mohammedans. It was believed to be eternal. Its heavenly counterpart had existed with God in the highest heaven from all eternity. God intrusted copies of it to the angel Gabriel and permitted him to take them to the lowest heaven, and to impart the contents to Mohammed bit by bit as the Prophet needed it. This revelation was thus held to be fundamental and final. That later parts sometimes contradicted earlier parts did not seriously trouble the early generations of Islam.

In 656 Ali, the Prophet's cousin and son-in-law, was chosen caliph. The Prophet had expressed the wish that Ali succeed him, and many thought that he should have been chosen when the Prophet died. At this juncture Muawia, a descendant of Omeyya, a cousin of

Mohammed's grandfather, revolted. Before his revolt Muawia had been governor of Damascus for several years, and pushed his revolt from that vantage-ground. The whole of Ali's caliphate was occupied with the civil war thus precipitated. Finally in 660 Ali was assassinated and Muawia triumphed.

112. **The Damascus caliphate.**—Muawia established the Omayyad caliphate of Damascus upon the ruins of the caliphate of Medina. His family, though kinsmen of Mohammed, had clung to their heathenism as long as they could. During the Prophet's ministry at Mecca and most of his residence at Medina they had been among his most bitter enemies. Muawia changed the character of the caliphate. At Medina it had been an elective office; at Damascus it became hereditary in the Omayyad Dynasty. Heathen at heart, possessing only a veneering of Islamism, these successors of the Prophet secularized the Mohammedan organization. During their ninety years of rule (660–750 A.D.) Moslems conquered the rest of North Africa and the southwestern half of Spain; they surged into France and were turned back by Charles Martel at the battle of Tours. The armies of this caliphate also carried the conquests eastward to the borders of India and into Turkestan and Samarcand beyond the Oxus and Jaxartes rivers.

During this caliphate Mohammedans came into contact with the literature and learning of the Greeks, which had been cherished in the monasteries of Syria.

113. **Abbasside and Spanish caliphates.**—In 750 A.D. the house of Omayya was overthrown by Abul-Abbas, a descendant of Abbas, an uncle of Mohammed, who established the Abbasside caliphate. The caliphs of

this line also formed a dynasty. The success of Abul-Abbas forever divided politically the Moslem world, for North Africa and Spain never accepted the sovereignty of the Abbassides. Abd-er-Rahman, a scion of the Omayyad house, escaped the slaughter visited upon his kinsmen and fled to Spain, where he became ruler. His descendants established the Spanish caliphate, which continued until 1027 A.D. The second of the Abbasside caliphs founded the city of Bagdad as a capital city. Under the caliphs of both Bagdad and Cordova literature and philosophy flourished and the brilliant period of Moslem intellectual life began. The Koran is everywhere anthropomorphic in its conception of God. It insists on the eternity of the unrevealed exemplar of itself. The study of philosophy led in many quarters to pronounced skepticism on these points. Even Mamun, caliph of Bagdad, 813–33 A.D., became a philosophical skeptic much to the horror of most of the Moslem world. These skeptics were often called Mutazilites, or Seceders.

Before the middle of the tenth century the Bagdad caliphs lost their political power. Their empire had gradually broken up, dissolving into a number of petty political states which have changed many times in the lapse of centuries. The Abbasside caliphs continued to be the religious heads of Mohammedanism, except that in Spain and North Africa their authority was not acknowledged until after the fall, in 1171, of the Fatimite caliphate. This caliphate had arisen at Kairwan in North Africa in 909 and conquered Egypt in 968. The Abbasside caliphs continued to reside at Bagdad until 1258 A.D., when they removed to Cairo. When

Egypt was conquered by the Ottoman Turks in 1517 A.D., the last of the Abbasside line sold the office of caliph to the Sultan of Turkey, who, since that time, has been regarded as the successor of the Prophet.

114. **Missionary efforts.**—Throughout its history Islam has aimed at making converts. In the course of the centuries it has penetrated India, China, Africa, and the isles of the Pacific, and has made many converts. As it had its birth in a crude civilization and is in its original form a peculiarly objective faith, it is well adapted to the intelligence of the half-savage tribes of Africa and other backward lands. It is estimated that at present there are about 240,000,000 Mohammedans in the world. If this is true, they constitute nearly one-sixth of the population of the globe.

115. **The development of Mohammedan law.**— Mohammed regarded the Koran as God's revealed law for both sacred and secular things. In his legal decisions at Medina he sometimes followed Arabian tribal custom and sometimes the precedents of Jewish law. Where these failed him, he usually received a special revelation which was believed to disclose the divine will with reference to the matter in hand. Upon his death the revelations ceased; nevertheless, novel situations were continually rising. His successors had little difficulty in cases to which the words of the Koran were applicable, or in cases analogous to those that the Prophet had decided. In other cases they had recourse to tradition. "The Companions of the Prophet," as those who had come in contact with him as faithful believers were afterward called, would, in such emergencies, recall that on such and such an occasion the

Prophet had said or done so and so. After the death of the Companions, the memories of those who had known the Companions were drawn upon. They would say that they had heard so and so say that on such and such an occasion the Prophet said or did thus and so. And so the process went on. It must be admitted that the Companions and their successors often drew upon their imaginations, so that in time the body of traditions grew to enormous proportions, containing many items that were fictitious. Al-Bokhari, who died in 870 A.D., collected and sifted the traditions in his *Sahih*. He rejected many, but his collection contained about seven thousand traditions. Other collections were made, but that of Al-Bokhari, who possessed great critical insight, is the best. Simple tradition did not, however, always suffice. In Syria and other territories conquered from Byzantium, Moslem courts had taken over precedents and principles from the Roman courts that they found established there. It accordingly became necessary to justify the actual practice of Mohammedan tribunals from the Moslem point of view. The conditions varied in different parts of Islam. In applying the traditions to these conditions four schools of law were developed:

(1) The earliest was that of Malik ibn Anas, a lawyer of Medina, who died in 796 A.D. Malik lived in the city of the Prophet, and sought to build up a body of jurisprudence on the basis of the precedents and traditions of the Prophet. He represents a reaction from Abu Hanifa, and is the exponent of law based on tradition only. He was not careful as to the correctness of a tradition, but only of its value in

legal practice. His system is still followed in North Africa.

(2) A second school was that of Abu Hanifa, a resident of Kufa, a man of Persian birth, who died in 767 A.D. He was a lecturer on law—a speculative lawyer, rather than a practical jurist. He depended very little on the traditions, preferring to go directly to the text of the Koran. As this was in most cases inapplicable, he introduced the rule of analogy, which was practically identical with legal fiction. Even analogy he modified by what he called "holding for the better." Admitting that analogy pointed to such and such a rule, he would say, "Under the circumstances I hold it better to rule thus and thus." He thus made Moslem law so flexible that regulations made for the desert need not ruin city life. The Ottoman Empire and Orthodox India still follow his legal principles.

(3) A third school of law was founded by Ash-Shafi'i, who resided at times in Arabia and at times in Egypt, and who died in 820 A.D. In addition to the Koran and tradition, both of which he regarded as inspired, he introduced the principle of agreement. If, for example, Moslem communities were found to follow customs for which there was no authority in the Koran or traditions, it was assumed that the Moslem communities had agreed that such practices were right. As the first caliphs had attached weight to the agreement of the Companions of the Prophet, so Ash-Shafi'i made the agreement of Mohammedan communities a source of authority. Ash-Shafi'i also held that in drawing an analogy between a rule of the Koran and any particular case the reason lying behind the Koranic rule should be

taken into account. On the principles of Ash-Shafi'i any law or custom could be adopted and naturalized in Mohammedan law. The jurists of the Dutch protectorates still follow the principles of Ash-Shafi'i.

(4) A fourth school was formed by the disciples of Ahmad ibn Hanbal of Bagdad, who died in 855 A.D. He was a resident of Bagdad, who revolted against the rationalism of the ninth-century caliphs there. He swerved to literal traditionalism, suffered severe persecution, and was regarded by his disciples as a saint. He developed Moslem law in no way, his influence being wholly reactionary. His followers in modern Islam are few and are found chiefly in Arabia.

116. Sects.—Mohammedan sects are almost as numerous and varied as the sects of the Christian church. Attention can be given here only to the most important. The Karejites (*Khawagri*), or "Come-outers," were a group that grew up in the early days of Islam. They were radical reformers, and sought to establish a theocracy, urging that a pious man of whatever tribe or nation might be called to the caliphate. They, too, afterward broke up into many minor sects. The greatest cleavage in Islam is, however, that between the Shiites and Sunnites.

(1) *The Shiites* had their origin at the end of the caliphate of Medina and were the outgrowth of a group that had been discontented ever since the Prophet's death. This group had held that the first three caliphs were interlopers; that the Prophet desired Ali, the husband of Fatima, to be his successor. When Ali became caliph after the assassination of O⁺hman, Muawia resisted him, professing to be an avenger of the murdered

Othman. Ali fought him for a time, but was finally persuaded to refer the dispute to arbitration. The decision went against Ali, and the Karejites were so disgusted with him that one of them assassinated him. His eldest son Hasan was regarded for a time by a small coterie as caliph, but was poisoned in 669. His other son, Hosein, eleven years later headed an insurrection against the Omayyad caliph Yezid and was killed in battle. The slaughter of Ali and his sons, descendants of the Prophet, at the hands of Moslems seemed to the Shiites the greatest outrage. The Shiites were at first largely of the Persian race, and the Persians are still Shiites. Of Aryan stock, they believe more easily than the Semites in incarnations. The tragic deaths of Ali and his sons led them to regard these heroes as almost divine. Their tombs are to this day sacred shrines to the Shiite sects, and passion-plays still keep alive the memory of their sufferings. Among all the Shiites, Ali is regarded as an incomparable warrior, concerning whose prowess the most extraordinary legends are told. They regard him also as a saint whose miracles equal those of the prophets. In contrast with the Shiites are the Sunnites, or traditionalists, or those who follow the ordinary traditions of Islam and who recognize the legitimacy of the first four caliphs. The Turks are Sunnites. The Shiites have broken up into many sects, among whom the Nusari and the Ali-ilahi believe Ali to be an incarnation of God. The Nusari believe him to be the first of the three persons of the Trinity. The Shiites have a tendency to adopt Aryan types of mysticism, which sometimes strain their monotheism almost to the breaking point. According to the more general Shiite view Ali and his two sons were *imams*, or divinely appointed leaders, who were succeeded for a time by other *imams*. Some of the sects regard the *imams* as *Nuqat*, or "Points" of divine manifestation. Some Shiites hold that there were seven *imams*, others twelve. Both agree that the last *imam* did not die, but is concealed, awaiting the proper time for his full manifestation.

(2) *The Ismailites*, or "Seveners," were a Persian sect of Shiites, who believed that Ismail, who had been adopted by Abd-Allah ibn Maimun, the sixth *imam*, upon the death of the latter in 766 A.D. became the seventh and last *imam*. They believed in reality in a system of incarnations by sevens. In this system Ismail was the forty-ninth incarnation.

(3) *The Druses.*—In the eleventh century Darazi, an Ismailian, went to Egypt and persuaded the Fatimite caliph Hakim that the caliph as a descendant of Ali was an incarnation of God. After the disappearance of Hakim, who appears to have been insane, Darazi went to Syria and taught. He was opposed in some tenets by one Hamzah, whose opinions finally prevailed among the followers of Darazi. It thus happens that Darazi is counted a heretic by the sect which bears his name. This sect is now known as the Druses and is quite numerous in the neighborhood of the Lebanon Mountains and in the Hauran to the east of the Sea of Galilee.

(4) *The Assassins* is a name given by Europeans to another of the Ismailian sects. This sect made much of the doctrine of *imams*. It spread to Syria in the time of the Crusaders, and its leader, Rashid ed-Din Sinan, "the Old Man of the Mountain," who claimed to be

not only an *imam* but an incarnation of Deity, was for many years the terror of the Lebanon. The Assassins, with many other Ismailians, held to the "inner meaning" of the Koran rather than to its outward form, and could thus set aside its obvious precepts. A band of disciples was ever ready to assassinate those marked out by the head of the order for death.

(5) *Babism and Bahaism.*—On May 23, 1844, Mirza Ali Mohammed, a merchant of Shiraz in Persia, announced that he was the Bab, or gate through which men might hold communion with the concealed *imam*. Later he declared himself to be an incarnation of God. The claim was admitted by a number of enthusiastic followers, some of whom suffered martyrdom for the belief. The Bab was martyred at Tabriz, July 9, 1850. Bahaullah, one of the Bab's followers, proclaimed himself in 1866–67 "He whom God manifests." He claimed that the Bab had foretold his coming, being simply his forerunner. The followers of Bahaullah are called Bahis. After the Bab was put to death his followers fled to Bagdad, whence some years later the Turkish government removed them to Adrianople. It was here that Bahaullah proclaimed himself—an act which caused schism and bloodshed among the Babists. In consequence of this the Bahaites were removed to Akka in Palestine, and the Babists to Cyprus. The Babists soon dwindled in numbers and influence, while the Bahaites have increased in importance, and have carried on a somewhat successful propaganda in the United States.

117. Scholastic theologians.—As Moslems imbibed the principles of Greek philosophy, there were a number who began to apply these principles to the Koran and the articles of the Moslem faith. They were called Mutazilites, or Seceders, and were numerous and popular among the Shiites. The first of a long line of scholastic theologians who opposed the Mutazilites and endeavored to justify the tenets of Islam by the use of reason was Al-Ashari, who died in 933. He was of Arab stock, but, according to tradition, brought up by a Mutazilite stepfather. He was himself a Mutazilite until he was forty years of age, when he underwent a conversion to orthodox views. His conversion has given rise to several legends. He devoted the rest of his life to the defense of the Koran and the traditions—a task for which his previous education peculiarly fitted him. No one with sufficient intellectual equipment had before undertaken it. He handled the questions with great acuteness, and in one respect (the definition of what a thing is) he anticipated Kant.

The greatest of all the Mohammedan theologians was, however, Al-Ghazali, who was born in 1059 and died in 1109. He was the St. Augustine of Islam. He combined great philosophical ability with a profound type of mystical piety. During his earlier years he was a pupil of Mutazilite teachers, and at one time became a thorough skeptic. After this he experienced a conversion so remarkable that it is quoted by William James in his *Varieties of Religious Experience*. During his closing years he was a Sufi or mystic, as well as a defender of the faith. There was a tenderness and charity about all his judgments of others that is very winning.

In philosophy Al-Ghazali, like Hume, was a thorough skeptic. He held that we can know the cause of nothing

We only know that events succeed one another; whether one is caused by the other is a matter beyond our ken All our knowledge is due to revelation, whether in the religious or in the scientific sphere. According to him existence has three modes. The first is the world that is apparent to the senses; it exists by the power of God and is in constant change. Then there is the unseen, eternal universe that exists by God's eternal decree, without development and without change. Between these is an intermediate universe, which seems externally to belong to the first, but in respect of the power of God really belongs to the second. Al-Ghazali refused to allegorize the Koran, but, holding that angels, the Koran, Islam, and Friday are not corporeal realities, but actual existences in the unseen, eternal universe, he avoided the crass concreteness of much of Moslem thought. In dogmatic theology Al-Ghazali resembled Albrecht Ritschl. He rejected metaphysics and opposed the influence of any philosophical system on his theology. Theology must be based on religious phenomena, simply accepted and correlated. Like Ritschl, he laid stress on the *value for us* of a piece of knowledge. Al-Ghazali led Islam back to reality in religion. He would have been called in Christianity a biblical theologian. He combined with his genuine attachment to the Koran and traditions a genuine piety and religious experience.[1] He is probably the most influential figure in Islam after Mohammed.

118. Modern reactionary sects.—Arabia, always largely untouched by outside influences, produced in the

[1] This statement of Al-Ghazali's thought is based on D. B. Macdonald's "Life of Al-Ghazali," *Journal of the American Oriental Society*, XX, 71–132.

eighteenth century in the person of Abd-al-Wahab, a native of the Negd, who died in 1787, a reactionary reformer. It was his aim to restore Islam to its primitive purity, and to lop off all later accretions. He was the founder of the Wahabites, who take the Koran literally, and follow the legal maxims of Ibn Hanbal. The movement soon produced a dynasty that early in the nineteenth century ruled all of Arabia. The political power has vanished and Wahabism has become, as at the first, a religious sect. It doubtless had some influence upon Mohammed ibn Ali as-Sanusi, who in 1837 founded the Brotherhood of as-Sanusi for the purpose of reforming and spreading the Mohammedan faith.

119. The mystics.—The unseen world has always been very real to Mohammedans and has always seemed very near. From the earliest times there has been an element in Islam which was repelled by traditional teaching and intellectual reasoning. Such persons often became ascetics, and sought by mortifying the flesh to commune with God through direct vision. Such persons are called Sufis, from *sufi*, "wool," because in the early days they wore rough woolen garments. The tendency to asceticism has led to the organization of numerous religious orders and to a great variety of types of thought. The orders are often called "dervishes," from a Persian word meaning "seeking doors." The term is now not restricted to mendicant orders. Some of the mystics came under the influence of Greek mystical writings, and are scarcely to be distinguished from pantheists. Others, like the Christian Gnostics, exalt knowledge. Others simply accept God's immanence in the world and exalt the life in God. Ascetic and mystic sects have flourished among the Berbers of North Africa. One of these, the Al-Morabits (Almoravides), or "Monastics," established a dynasty which conquered Spain in 1087, and was overthrown by the Al-Mohads, a dynasty founded by another fanatical Berber sect. The Mohads were founded by Ibn Tumart, a pupil of Al-Ghazali, who emphasized the unity, *tawhid*, of God. *Tawhid*, however, as he employed it, stood for the spirituality of God.

While often leading to political consequences, asceticism and mysticism have opened the way in Islam to the religious life as a vocation for both men and women. While much that is bizarre and fanatical, and even demoralizing, has found expression in these orders, they have helped to keep the religious life of Islam in touch with reality, and have been one of the means of so diversifying Islam that it could meet a great variety of religious needs.

120. Estimate of Islam.—Mohammedanism began as the religion of a semibarbarous people. Though a great advance upon the Arabian heathenism which it displaced, it appeals, in its primitive form, essentially to backward peoples. Though Mohammed endeavored so to fetter it that progress would be impossible, the genius of the best Mohammedan thinkers has been able to find avenues of expansion and to make Islam a fairly exalted religion. The varieties of Islamic thought rival those of Christianity, and the number of its mystical sects surpasses that of Christianity. Much must be conceded to a religious system that commands the devotion of nearly one-sixth of the population of the globe, even if it must be recognized that it is not the natural instrument for the expression of the religious feeling of the most refined.

SUPPLEMENTARY READING

CLASS A

On sec. 107: cf. S. M. Zwemer, *Arabia the Cradle of Islam* (New York and Chicago, 1900), chaps. i and ii.

On secs. 108–10: cf. Sir William Muir, *Mahomet and Islam* (London, 1895); or A. Gilman, *The Saracens* (New York and London, 1887), chaps. iv–xxii.

On secs. 111–13: A. Gilman, *The Saracens* (New York and London, 1887), chaps. xxiii–xli; S. Lane-Poole, *The Moors in Spain* (New York and London, 1891); or Ameer Ali, *A Short History of the Saracens* (London, 1899).

On sec. 114: cf. D. B. Macdonald, *Aspects of Islam* (New York, 1911), chap. viii.

On sec. 115: cf. D. B. Macdonald, *Muslim Theology, Jurisprudence, and Constitutional Theory* (New York, 1903), pp. 65–118.

On secs. 116, 118: cf. D. S. Margoliouth, *Mohammedanism* (London), chap. v, and "Assassins," "Babis and Bahais," and "Druses," in Hastings' *Encyclopaedia of Religion and Ethics;* or I. Goldziber, *Mohammed and Islam* (New Haven, 1917), chap. v.

On sec. 117: cf. D. B. Macdonald, *Muslim Theology, Jurisprudence, and Constitutional Theory* (New York, 1903), pp. 186–242.

On sec. 119: cf. R. A. Nicholson, *The Mystics of Islam* (London, 1914); or D. B. Macdonald, *Religious Attitude and Life in Islam* (Chicago, 1909), Lectures VI, VII; or D. B. Macdonald, *Aspects of Islam* (New York, 1911), Lectures V, VI.

CLASS B

D. S. Margoliouth, *Mohammedanism* in the "Home University Library."

CHAPTER VII

ZOROASTRIANISM

O Ahura Mazdah, most beneficent Spirit, Maker of the material world, thou Holy One!—Vendidad ii, 1.

I conceived of thee, O Mazdah, in my thought that thou, the First, art also the Last—that thou art Father of Good Thought, for thus I apprehended thee with mine eye—that thou didst truly create Right, and art Lord to judge the actions of life—Yasna xxxi, 8.

I will speak of the Spirits twain at the first beginning of the world, of whom the holier thus spake to the enemy: Neither thought nor teachings nor wills nor beliefs nor words nor deeds nor selves nor souls of us twain agree.—Yasna xlv, 2.

All the pleasures of life which thou holdest, those that were, that are, and that shall be, O Mazdah, according to thy good will apportion them. Through Good Thought advance thou the body, through Dominion and Right at will.—Yasna xxxiii, 10.

It is they, the liars, who destroy life, who are mightily determined to deprive matron and master of the enjoyment of their heritage, in that they would pervert the righteous, O Mazdah, from the Best Thought.—Yasna xxxii, 11.

In immortality shall the soul of the righteous be joyful, in perpetuity shall the torments of the liars. All this doth Mazdah Ahura appoint by his Dominion.—Yasna xlv, 7.

121. **Persia** is geographically a great tableland or plateau. This was called Iran and extends beyond the borders of modern Persia into Afghanistan on the east. The area of this elevated region is nearly one-fifth of the United States of America. Mountains bound it on nearly every side, opening only through rocky passes.

Frequently they stretch far into the interior. While parts of this tableland are well watered, it has no rivers worthy of the name. Most streams are absorbed by the soil before they reach an outlet. In many portions of the land irrigation is a necessity, if crops are to be wrung from the arid wastes. Nevertheless the soil responds readily to tillage. It is natural that in such a country irrigation should become synonymous with righteousness, as it was in the Zoroastrian religion, and that agriculture should be regarded as a religious duty.[1]

122. The people of Iran, as we know them in history, belonged to the Aryan branch of the Indo-European stock. At some remote period their ancestors had lived on the great plain to the north of the Hindu Kush Mountains side by side with the ancestors of the Aryans of India. At what date they migrated into Parthia, Media, Persia, etc., we cannot now determine. Aryan names are found among the Mitanni of the upper Euphrates Valley and among the Hittites of Boghaz Kui about 1400–1300 B.C. Among the Mitanni the names of Mitra, Indra, and Varuna, Aryan gods, are found during the same period.[2] It seems probable that the Mitannians and Hittites were a mixture of races, but the presence of these gods, which appear also in India, prove that there were Aryans among them. Whether the migration of Aryans into India and Persia occurred before or after 1400 B.C. it is impossible at present to determine.

[1] Compare A. V. W. Jackson, *Persia, Past and Present* (New York, 1906), pp. 23 f.

[2] See Winckler, *Mitteilungen der deutschen Orient-Gesellschaft*, No. 35 (1907), p. 51.

The most that we can say is that the Medes were in the region of Media in the ninth century B.C., for in the year 836 B.C. Shalmaneser III of Assyria invaded their land.[1] It seems probable that by this time the Aryan stock had penetrated those parts of Iran in which we find them in later times.

The struggle with nature in this elevated tableland produced an efficient, practical people, not unlike the ancient Romans in their general characteristics. Their kinsmen of India became in the milder Indian climate contemplative, speculative, mystical. The Persians remained to the end active and alert, more deeply interested in objective realities than in metaphysical speculations. On this account the religion of Zoroaster was very different from the religions of India.

123. **The sources** of our knowledge of the religion of Zoroaster are extant portions of the Avesta,[2] collected probably in the last period of the Achaemenian Dynasty after 400 B.C., and the Pahlavi-texts, the most important of which is the Bundahishn. These were collected during the Sasanian Dynasty (220–641 A.D.) and the centuries immediately following, having been edited not later than 881 A.D. The Pahlavi writings bear about the same relation to the Avesta that the Talmud does to the Old Testament, or the patristic writings to the New Testament, though the analogy is not quite complete, since it is probable that in parts of the Bundahishn lost portions of the Avesta are reproduced in a late form. The Avesta consists of three parts, the Vendidad, the Yashts,

[1] See Schrader, *Keilinschriftliche Bibliothek*, I, 143.

[2] The etymology of the name *Avesta*, despite proposed explanations such as "knowledge," or again "text," or the like, remains uncertain.

and the Yasna. These are not all of the same age. The oldest portion is Yasna xxviii–liii, hymns that are called Gathas, written in a very old dialect. It is generally agreed that these are as old as Zoroaster himself, and contain, besides his own words, as sage, seer, and religious teacher, our most authentic information about the prophet.

These seventeen psalms form an especially sacred part of the Avesta. They are called "holy" in the later texts. Like the Hebrew Psalms, they are collected into five groups named the "Five Gathas." Throughout them runs the tone of a prophet proclaiming a faith not known before.

The other parts of the Avesta contain material that is undoubtedly old, though later in form of redaction. The Vispêrad and the liturgical Yasna, which contains litanies for the sacrifice, may be later than the Gathas, but in the Yashts there is much that dates back to antique times. It is in a measure pre-Zoroastrian.

The Yashts are poetic expressions of the mythology and historical legends of ancient Iran, and represent, it has been conjectured, the popular religious beliefs which the prophet opposed, but was unable to suppress, and which, after his death, found a place among the sacred writings.[1] The Vendidad is a compilation of ritual laws and of mythical tales possibly of non-Aryan origin.[2] It is the Book of Leviticus of Zoroastrianism. It has been conjectured that this ritual was introduced by the Magi at the end of the Achaemenian period, i.e., between 405 and 331 B.C. At any rate, it reproduces old Iranian

[1] See J. H. Moulton, *Early Zoroastrianism* (London, 1913), p. 182.
[2] So Moulton, *ibid.*, p. 183.

material, which probably represents the attitude of Zoroaster as little as the Levitical laws represent that of the prophet Amos.

The term "Bundahishn" means "creation of the beginnings" or "original creation." The work is a collection of fragments relating to cosmogony, mythology, and legendary history. It is compiled in the Pahlavi dialect, that stage in the development of the Persian language when the older inflectional endings had been dropped and before the modern Persian alphabet had been introduced. Its legendary history contains accounts of Zoroaster's life.

124. **The Iranian religion before Zoroaster** was clearly a type of polytheism kindred to that of the Vedas. Mithra, a sun-god kindred to the Vedic Mitra, was widely worshiped, as was Ahura, who corresponds to the Vedic Asura, and the Greek Ouranos,[1] and was apparently originally a sky-god. Varuna is sometimes called Asura (the Sanskrit form of Ahura), which means "lord." Ahura appears to have been called among the Persians, even before the time of Zoroaster, Ahura Mazdah, the Wise Lord, for his name appears in a list of gods compiled for the library of Ashurbanipal, king of Assyria (668–626 B.C.), where it occurs near that of an Elamite deity.[2] As this inscription was written before Zoroaster began to preach, it affords positive proof of the existence of Ahura Mazdah as a pre-Zoroastrian divinity. The prominence of fire even in the religion of Zoroaster

---

[1] See M. Bloomfield, *Religion of the Veda* (New York, 1908), pp. 136 ff.

[2] See H. Rawlinson, *Cuneiform Inscriptions of Western Asia*, III (London, 1870), p. 66, col. IX, 24; cf. also F. Hommel in the *Proceedings of the Society of Biblical Archaeology*, XXI (1899), 127, 132.

indicates that the Iranians reverenced a fire-spirit kindred to the Indian Agni. That these gods were related to those of India is further shown by the prominence of Haoma, the Vedic Soma (an intoxicating drink), in their cults—a feature that later found its way back into Zoroastrianism.[1] In later tradition Haoma was thought to be an angel with whom Zoroaster once conversed. Together with these deities many *daēvas* were feared. In later times these were regarded as demons, but before Zoroaster they may have been reverenced as gods, since the corresponding word *dēva* in Sanskrit means god. This is, however, uncertain.

The conditions of existence on the elevated plains of Iran colored the religious thought of the people. It was not easy for the agricultural communities to wrest the means of subsistence from an arid soil that must be continually irrigated. From the sterile steppes, especially from Turan (Turkestan) to the north, unsettled nomads were ever ready to swoop down and plunder the crops and cattle of Iran. The world naturally seemed to them, because of this, a struggle between good and evil—between light and darkness. All that promoted agriculture and the raising of cattle was good; whatever destroyed these was evil. As time passed, this view of the universe was intensified.

125. Life of Zoroaster.—The Gathas, our only contemporary source, are religious hymns. They contain no biography of Zarathushtra or Zoroaster, and the traditions in later documents are conflicting. It seems

---

[1] See, for example, Yasht xxiii of the Avesta in F. Max Müller, *Sacred Books of the East*, Vol. XXIII, and Yasna ix, 1-16, *ibid.*, Vol. XXXI.

certain that Zoroaster was born in Iran, but whether in Bactria or Media it is difficult to say. Professor Jackson favors the view that he was born in Atropatene in the neighborhood of Lake Urumia.[1] Little is known of his early life. According to tradition he retired from the world when about twenty years of age, giving himself for a number of years to religious meditation. During these years he fought out the fight of his own faith and doubtless began the formulation of the general truths of his religious system. When about thirty the revelation came to him. In a vision that was repeated thrice in one day he was admitted to the presence of Ahura Mazdah[2] in heaven, and the Supreme Being himself instructed Zoroaster, by the Omniscient Wisdom, in the doctrines of the faith. Upon returning to earth Zoroaster began to preach to the ruling priests the new religion—the worshiping of Mazdah, the anathematizing of demons, the glorification of the archangels, and the marriage of the next of kin.

During the next seven or eight years he was granted six more visions, in which each of the archangels appeared to him: Vohu Manah, or "Good Thought"; Asha Vahishta, or "Perfect Righteousness"; Khsha-thra Vairya, or "Wished-for Kingdom"; Spenta Armaiti, a feminine personification of harmony and the earth; Haurvatat, "Health" or "Salvation"; and

[1] Cf. A. V. W. Jackson, *Zoroaster the Prophet of Ancient Iran*, pp. 16–22. No certain account of the prophet's life or the early development of the religion is possible. The account given in the text is confessedly conjectural, though based on legends which may have had facts behind them, since Zoroaster was a historical personage.

[2] Spelled also in Pahlavi as Aūharmazd and in later Persian as Ormuzd.

Ameretat, or "Immortality." In Zoroaster's thought these six personified qualities, or institutions, became the chief attendants and agencies of Ahura Mazdah. Possibly he substituted them for spirits which the earlier heathenism had associated with Ahura, for in the list of Ashurbanipal, Ahura Mazdah is referred to in connection with the seven Igigi, or spirits of heaven. For ten years Zoroaster presented his doctrine in vain at court after court of the petty rulers of Iran and Turan. But one disciple had been won, Maidyōi-maonha, Zoroaster's cousin. At the end of this period of preaching and communion with the powers of heaven Zoroaster underwent a severe temptation.

In the eleventh year of his mission Zoroaster sought out the court of a certain Vishtaspa (Hystaspes), where he spent two years trying to convert the monarch. Of course he met with much opposition, but finally he was successful, and Vishtaspa became a disciple and a champion of the faith. His court followed the example of the ruler, and the subjects of the realm came into outward conformity. The conversion of Vishtaspa changed the whole outlook of Zoroastrianism. The prophet was no longer a lonely preacher; he had now a powerful royal patron who could back the appeal of the new religion with force of arms.

If we follow the traditional chronology of the life of Zoroaster, as Professor Jackson is inclined to do, the prophet was born about 660 B.C. His preaching began about 630 B.C., and, when Vishtaspa was converted in 618 B.C., Zoroaster was forty-two years old. The same tradition says that he lived to be seventy-seven years old. If this be true, his ministry continued thirty-five years after the conversion of Vishtaspa. During these years various sages are reputed to have come to the court of Vishtaspa in order ·to refute Zoroaster, and to have been converted by him. The chief of these was the Brahman Cangranghācah. Perhaps the story of this Brahman is historical, though those relating to Greek conversions are doubtless apocryphal.

According to traditions Vishtaspa was compelled to fight two wars in consequence of the new religion. These wars were fought with Arejat-aspa (Arjasp), a Turanian, who invaded Vishtaspa's kingdom from the north. The first invasion of Arejat-aspa resulted in the complete defeat of the unbelievers. This was accomplished through the heroism of a gallant crusader of the faith, Isfendiar, who was rewarded for his valor with the hand of Vishtaspa's daughter. Between the first holy war and the second a considerable period elapsed. Jamasp is said to have written down the teachings of Zoroaster and the scriptures were circulated even to distant lands. Isfendiar, who had expected to succeed the monarch, was thrown into prison through the jealousy of another prince. While Vishtaspa was absent in Seistan, Arejat-aspa again invaded the kingdom. There was only his aged father Lohrasp to defend it. He was unequal to the task. The kingdom was overrun and Zoroaster slain. This was, on the traditional chronology, in the year 583-582 B.C. The Iranians were beleaguered on a lonely height and all seemed to be lost, when Isfendiar was released from prison and saved the day. Jamasp is said to have been the prophet's first successor.

126. **Teachings.**—Zoroaster was a practical monotheist. In his thought Ahura Mazdah was the One

Supreme Deity. He appears to have taken this god from among those revered by his Aryan ancestors and to have done for him what Amos and the prophets of the eighth century did for Yahweh. To him Ahura Mazdah was the all-wise Creator, who knows all inexplicable things.[1] He knows men's secret sins;[2] he is absolute Lord.[3] The absolute sovereignty of Ahura Mazdah was in the present state of the world potential only. Though Zoroaster in the Gathas does not have much to say of Angra Mainyu, it is nevertheless assumed that the spirit of evil is as eternal as Ahura Mazdah himself, and exists independently of him.[4] Nevertheless Ahura Mazdah will in the end achieve dominion over him.[5] The agencies employed by Ahura for the accomplishment of his will were the heavenly helpers, Good Thought, Perfect Righteousness, Wished-for Kingdom, etc., though in the thought of Zoroaster Good Thought and Perfect Righteousness are far more important than the others. Popular Iranian belief held the animistic idea that each person had a guardian spirit or double called a Fravashi, which seems to have been analogous to the Egyptian Ka. Zoroaster appears to have rejected this idea, but he retained an analogous one that there is a heavenly ox-soul which bore a similar relation to cattle as the Fravashis to men.[6]

Zoroaster proclaimed that Ahura Mazdah demands righteousness of men, and that his help is promised to those who desire it.[7] It is assumed that man is the

[1] See Yasna li.

[2] Yasna xxxi, 13.

[3] Yasna xxxi, 21.

[4] Yasna xlv, 2.

[5] Yasna xlv, 10, 11.

[6] Yasna xxix, 1.

[7] Yasna xxxiv, 15; xliii, 1.

arbiter of his own destiny; that he can do right if he will. Right is truthfulness, the practice of justice, and the fostering of agriculture; wrong is lying, robbery, and the destruction of irrigation and cattle. On the last day the characters of men will be tried by the ordeal of passing through molten metal.[1] The righteous, who come out unharmed, will be accorded eternal bliss; the evil will be assigned to the house of liars forever.[2] The gospel of Zoroaster was characterized by its power of abstract thought, as well as by its ethical and practical insight. It was distinctly an effort of religious reform. The prophet rejected the popular gods as *daēvas* or demons,[3] and apparently most of the popular religious practices.

127. Under the Achaemenians.—The details of the early progress of Zoroastrianism are shrouded in obscurity. How far the wars of Vishtaspa, the patron of the prophet, carried it we have no means of knowing. It seems probable, though not certain, that the kings of the powerful Achaemenian Dynasty, founded by Cyrus the Great in 553 B.C., were from the first Zoroastrians. It is true that Cyrus in the one inscription of his that has come down to us—an inscription written in Babylonian and found at Babylon[4]—speaks of himself as a worshiper of the Babylonian god Marduk. This he probably did for reasons of state, and he may well have thought that all gods were but other names for Ahura.

[1] Yasna xxxiv, 4; cf. I Cor. 3:13: "The fire shall try every man's work."

[2] Yasna xliii, 5; xlv, 7; xlviii, 7; xlix, 11, 1, 2, etc.

[3] Yasna xlviii, 1.

[4] See G. A. Barton, *Archaeology and the Bible* (5th ed.), p. 445, for a translation.

That he named his daughter Atossa, the same as Huta-osa, the queen of Vishtaspa, has been held to indicate that he probably reverenced everything connected with the prophet.[1] Darius I and Xerxes in their inscriptions constantly refer to Ahura Mazdah as their god. It is true that there is no real certainty that they thought of Ahura as Zoroaster thought of him, but they say nothing to indicate that they thought of Ahura as only one among many deities.[2] Apparently Darius was a mono-theist. The father of Darius, too, bore the name Hystaspes, or Vishtaspa—a fact that creates a probability that also in this branch of the Achaemenians Zoroaster and his patron were honored.[3]

It seems probable that Zoroastrianism was the religion of Persia at this time, for Herodotus, who visited the country in the reign of Artaxerxes I, describes the religion as substantially that represented in the Yashts of the Avesta. He says that they worship the whole circle of heaven under the name of Zeus. This was the Greek way of indicating the equivalent of Zeus. It is testimony that Ahura Mazdah, who, as already shown, was originally the sky-god, was the chief deity. Along with him he says they worshiped the sun (Mithra),[4] the moon,[5] the earth,[6] fire,[7] water,[8] and the winds,[9] as

---

[1] Cf. J. H. Moulton, *Early Zoroastrianism*, pp. 88 f.

[2] See the inscriptions of Darius translated in *Assyrian and Babylonian Literature*, edited by R. F. Harper (New York, 1901), pp. 174–93.

[3] See Moulton, *ibid.*

[4] See the Mihir Yasht, *Sacred Books of the East*, XXIII, 119–58, and A. J. Carnoy, *Iranian Mythology* (Boston, 1917), pp. 287–88.

[5] *Ibid.*, pp. 8, 16, 19.

[6] *Ibid.*, pp. 286 ff.

[8] *Ibid.*, pp. 16, 356 f.

[7] *Ibid.*, pp. 358 f.

[9] *Ibid.*, p. 18.

well as a mother-goddess whom they had borrowed from the Semites.[1] She was the Avestan Anâhita.[2] In the Yashts and Sirozas of the Avesta the worship of these elements appears in conjunction with Ahura Mazdah and the six good spirits: Good Thought, Perfect Righteousness, etc.; hence it seems probable that by this time the pure ethical teaching of Zoroaster, which was probably in advance of the thought of the majority, had been fused with much of the earlier heathen practices. Among these practices was, apparently, that of maintaining the sacred fires. Tradition attributed the kindling of some of these to Zoroaster. Except for the compromise with older customs Zoroastrianism could probably not have survived. In this respect the experience of Zoroastrianism was parallel to the religion of Israel, to Mohammedanism, and even to Christianity. A place was found for these additional objects of worship by supposing that they were reverenced as creations of Ahura.

Under the Achaemenians the Magi, originally a Median tribe,[3] gradually attained power through royal patronage and became the priests of Zoroastrianism.[4] It was probably due to their influence that during the

[1] The passage is Herodotus i. 131. Herodotus confused Mithra with Anâhita.

[2] *Ibid.*, pp. 52–84, and Moulton, *op. cit.*, pp. 66, and 238 f. Artaxerxes Mnemon, 405–359 B.C., is the first to mention these new deities in inscriptions.

[3] Herodotus i. 101.

[4] They came into favor through Cambyses, who appointed one of them as his steward (Herodotus iii. 61). They were in disfavor after the accession of Darius I, but later Artaxerxes Mnemon became their patron, and their triumph was complete. See Berossos as quoted by Clement of Alexandria, *Exhortation to the Greeks*, V, 65.

closing decades of the Achaemenian Dynasty the Avesta was completed by the addition of the Yashts and the Vendidad. By these additions the ethical system of Zoroaster was grafted into a mass of nature-myths and ritual with which it originally had little in common. The ritual is as arid as that connected with any Semitic religion.

One other theological addition can be traced—the raising of Angra Mainyu to the position of an archfiend. Zoroaster, as already pointed out, had recognized that at the beginning there were two spirits.[1] These two spirits he described as twins and defined them as the Better and the Bad (Angra) in thought, word, and action;[2] it was the Bad Spirit who taught the daēvas and liars to ruin mankind.[3] Beyond this Zoroaster did not go, but in the Vendidad, Angra Mainyu, or the Bad Spirit, is portrayed as the evil counterpart of Ahura Mazdah, who at the time of creation met each beneficent creation of Ahura Mazdah by a counter-creation of evil.[4] Whereas in the thought of Zoroaster, Angra Mainyu was apparently thought of as a spirit who could be largely ignored, and whose influence could be overcome by right-doing, in the Vendidad he had become an active and malignant devil, whose presence it was necessary to banish, along with that of other demons, by powerful incantations.[5]

128. **Under Greeks and Parthians.**—The conquest of Persia by Alexander the Great gave the development of Zoroastrianism a great check. Greek cities were

[1] Yasna xlv, 2.

[2] Yasna xxx, 3. [4] See *Sacred Books of the East*, IV, 4 ff.

[3] Yasna xxxii, 5. [5] *Ibid.*, pp. 142 f.

founded in many parts of Persia. Zoroastrians were no
longer the ruling caste, and there was a popular movement in favor of polytheism. Later the Zoroastrian
countries passed under the sway of Parthia, but this did
not permanently improve the status of the religion. At
first the Magi were held in high esteem and had much
influence,[1] but later they fell into disfavor and were
deprived of power.[2] The Parthians were tolerant of all
religions, and, even if in theory Zoroastrianism was maintained, that which most impressed a foreign observer was
the worship of Mithra, or the sun,[3] and the adoration of
rivers[4]—both features of the cult of the later Avesta.
While this may have been the official cult, the people
worshiped with special ceremonies household gods represented by images.[5] Josephus calls these "ancestral,"
and it was doubtless an old cult that Zoroastrianism had
never suppressed. In spite of these disintegrating influences the religion maintained itself and the sacred fires
were kept burning during the five hundred and fifty
years from the conquest of Alexander to the establishment of the second Persian empire under the Sasanian
Dynasty in 220 A.D.

129. The Sasanians, who were intensely patriotic
Persians, regarded Zoroastrianism as their ancestral faith
and inaugurated an enthusiastic revival of it. The
sacred Avesta was not only copied and studied, but,
since in the lapse of centuries the inflections of spoken

[1] Strabo, XI, ix, 3.
[2] Agathias ii. 26.
[3] Herodian iv. 30.
[4] Justin xli. 3.
[5] Josephus, *Antiquities of the Jews*, XVIII, ix, 5.

Persian had so worn away that the language of the Avesta was no longer understood, paraphrases in the vernacular were circulated. Such paraphrases were also necessary because in the Sasanian period an alphabet was in use different from that employed in the Avesta. The paraphrases of the Sasanian time, like the Jewish targums to some of the biblical books, were often free reproductions into which much new material was woven. Such texts are known as Pahlavi-texts—Pahlavi being the name of the writing of this period. It is generally accepted that "Pahlavi" is a corruption of "Parthian." While the Pahlavi-texts were based on the Avesta, and are believed in parts to preserve the substance of Avestan books that are now lost, they represent the final doctrinal development of Zoroastrianism. To the doctrine of this period we shall presently return. Under some of the Sasanians Zoroastrianism became again a militant religion. At times it was propagated by the sword. One king actually imposed it for a time on the Armenian Christians.[1] The four hundred years of Sasanian supremacy witnessed the last triumph of this faith.

130. **Since the Mohammedan conquest** Zoroastrianism has declined. Under the early caliphs Zoroastrians were, with Jews and Christians, accorded the privilege of retaining their religion and paying a head tax, since they, too, were "people of a book" (i.e., possessed scriptures). Later they were denied this exemption. Until the ninth century they appear to have flourished, since Pahlavi-texts were written in considerable numbers until then, but after this they began to decline. The cause is obscure. It may have been due to the influence

[1] Cf. George Rawlinson. *The Seventh Oriental Monarchy*, chap. xv

of fanatical Shiites and to the oppression by Seljuk Turks. Two hundred years ago Zoroastrians were estimated at one hundred thousand in Persia; today they number only about ten thousand souls.[1]

In the early centuries of Islam, Zoroastrians established themselves in India. Their descendants now number about a hundred thousand. They reside chiefly in the Bombay presidency and are very prosperous. They had become very ignorant of their sacred books, which they could read only in imperfect translations, though in the last fifty years, through a revival of learning, they have revived their religion through a clearer knowledge of its sources. Through all the centuries they have adhered with considerable fidelity to their ritual.

131. **Final form of the doctrines.**—The historical development of Zoroastrianism from the Gathas to the Bundahishn resulted in a theory of the world based on a well-defined dualism. The forces of good were led by Ahura Mazdah and the six archangels, who were followed by many angels and lesser divine beings. The archangels were, as in the time of Zoroaster, Vohu Manah, Asha Vahishta, Khshathra Vairya, Spenta Armaiti, Haurvatat, and Ameretat. In the Bundahishn these six are called Amesha Spentas ("Immortal Holy Ones"). The angels and lesser divine beings are called Yazatas ("Worshipful Ones"). Mithra and Anâhita had in this period become angels. Opposed to Ahura Mazdah is Angra Mainyu (also called Ahriman) and his hosts. The hosts of evil were not so well organized as the hosts of good. After Ahriman the demon Aehsma (Daeva)[2]

---

[1] Cf. G. F. Moore, *History of Religions* (New York, 1913), pp. 378 f.

[2] See Tobit iii. 17, where he is called Asmodaeus.

seems to have been the most prominent. To him were given seven powers.[1] The other archdemons, mentioned incidentally in the Avesta, in the Pahlavi-books were named Akoman, or Ako Manu ("Bad Thought"), Andar (who is no other than the Vedic god Indra),[2] Sôvar, Nâkahêd, Tâîrêv, and Zâîrîk. These six, in some passages, form with Angra Mainyu a group antithetic to Ahura Mazdah and the Amesha Spentas.[3] To many other demons proper names and special functions were assigned;[4] and in addition many other demons were supposed to exist. Nevertheless Ahriman was not believed to be either eternal or omniscient.[5]

Ahura Mazdah created the world, making first the sky, then water, then the earth, plants, animals, and mankind, in the order named.[6] The creation occupied a year of 365 days, and was divided into six periods of two months each.[7] When Ahriman rose from the abyss[8] and beheld the work of Ahura Mazdah, he desired to destroy it. Ahura Mazdah met him and offered him an opportunity to co-operate with the good, but Ahriman refused. Ahriman was then granted by Ahura Mazdah a period of nine thousand years in which to contest the mastery of the world,[9] and proceeded to bring evil thoughts into men's minds and to mingle disagreeable elements with the good works of the Creator. For example, Ahriman mingled smoke and darkness with fire.[10]

---

[1] Bundahishn (in *Sacred Books of the East*, V) xxviii, 15.
[2] See chap. viii.
[3] Bundahishn i, 27.
[4] *Ibid.* xxviii, 7 f.
[5] *Ibid.* iii, 9, 13.
[6] *Ibid.* i, 28.
[7] *Ibid.* xxv, 1.
[8] *Ibid.* i, 9.
[9] *Ibid.* i, 20.
[10] *Ibid.* iii, 24.

The nine thousand years just mentioned bring to our notice the Zoroastrian theory of the world. According to this theory the world-cycle consisted of 12,000 years. Of these, 3,000 passed while all creatures were unthinking and unmoving. This was the spiritual state,[1] when only the Fravashis existed. This was followed by 3,000 years of confusion. The confusion was caused by Ahriman, but during it Ahura Mazdah created his material creatures.[2] During the third period of 3,000 years Ahriman descended to the earth and brought evils upon men.[3] This was the period of greatest distress. The wills of Ahura Mazdah and Ahriman were mingled in the world. Toward the end of the ninth millennium Zoroaster was born. This last millennial age is presided over by Zoroaster, whom the Bundahishn regards as divine, and his three posthumous sons, the last of whom, Soshyans ("Savior" or "Benefactor"), will be a kind of Messiah. He will render the evil spirit impotent and cause the resurrection of the dead.[4] Ahriman will be disabled and overthrown.[5] This cycle of 12,000 years may have belonged to primitive Zoroastrianism. It is clearly based on the conception of a world-year—a thousand years for each of the twelve months. Zoroastrianism looked forward, however, to the ultimate triumph of Ahura Mazdah, just as the Jews looked forward to the ultimate triumph of Yahweh and his Messiah.

Zoroastrians believe in a resurrection of all men. At the resurrection a wicked man will be as conspicuous as

---

[1] Bundahishn xxxiv, 1.

[2] *Ibid.* i, 23.

[3] Cf. *ibid.* xxxiv, 1 with iv, 1 ff.

[4] *Ibid.* xi, 6 and xxxii, 8.

[5] *Ibid.* i, 20.

a white sheep in a flock of black ones.[1] The righteous
are destined for heaven and the wicked for hell. All
will be tested by passing through molten metal. It will
seem to the righteous that they are walking in warm
milk, but to the wicked, that they are walking in molten
metal forever.[2] Relatives will then be reunited with
the greatest affection,[3] and the righteous will be conveyed to paradise and the heaven of Ahura Mazdah.[4]
Hell was thought to be in the midst of the earth, where
Ahriman pierced it and rushed into it when he first
attacked it.[5] Into hell all the demons will be cast at
the end of the period of 12,000 years. Then Ahura
Mazdah, the good Creator, will be completely triumphant and a new and perfect world established for all
time.

132. Estimate of Zoroastrianism.—Next to Judaism
Zoroastrianism is the oldest ethical monotheism in the
world. Zoroaster was a great religious genius who
caught something of eternal truth and successfully interpreted it to men. He and his followers were keenly
alive to the struggle between good and evil. To them
the world was a great battlefield on which this struggle
was being fought out. They laid great stress on conduct and demanded a noble ethical life. They had firm
faith in God as they saw him, faith in man, and faith in
the ultimate triumph of right and of God. The thought
and development of Zoroastrianism are in many ways
parallel to those of Judaism. Some scholars have
endeavored to show that Zoroastrianism borrowed from

---

[1] Bundahishn xxx, 10.

[2] Ibid. iii, 27.

[3] Ibid. xxx, 20.

[4] Ibid. xxx, 21.

[5] Ibid. xxx, 27.

Judaism; others that Judaism borrowed from Zoroastrianism, but no considerable borrowing in either direction can be proved. Each religion appears to have grasped some truth, and to have developed in its own environment independently of the other. Such likenesses as there are came from similarity of conditions and the psychological unity of man.

SUPPLEMENTARY READING

CLASS A

On secs. 122, 124: cf. J. H. Moulton, *Early Zoroastrianism* (London, 1913), Lectures I, II.

On sec. 125: cf. A. V. W. Jackson, *Zoroaster, the Prophet of Ancient Iran* (New York and London, 1901), *passim*.

On sec. 126: cf. J. H. Moulton, *Early Zoroastrianism*, pp. 343–90.

On sec. 127: cf. Jackson and Gray, "The Religion of the Achaemenian Kings," *Journal of the American Oriental Society*, XXI (1900), 160–84; L. H. Gray, "Achaemenians" in Hastings' *Encyclopaedia of Religion and Ethics*, I, 69–73; and J. H. Moulton, *Early Zoroastrianism*, Lectures VI, VII.

On sec. 128: cf. George Rawlinson, *Sixth Oriental Monarchy*, chap. xxiii.

On sec. 129: George Rawlinson, *Seventh Oriental Monarchy*, chap. xxviii.

On sec. 130: A. V. W. Jackson, "Zoroastrianism," in the *Jewish Encyclopedia*, XII, 695–97; G. F. Moore, "Zoroastrianism," *Harvard Theological Review*, V, 180–226; or J. H. Moulton, *Early Zoroastrianism*, Lectures IV, V.

CLASS B

G. F. Moore, *History of Religions* (New York, 1913), chaps. xv, xvi.

CHAPTER VIII

THE RELIGION OF THE VEDAS

Thou Indra who createst light where there was no light, and form, O men! where there was no form, hast been born together with the dawns.—Rig-Veda, I, 6, 3.

Indra speaks: Almighty strength be mine alone, whatever I may do daring in my heart; for I indeed, O Maruts,[1] am known as terrible: of all that I threw down, I, Indra, am lord.—Rig-Veda, I, 165, 10.

Protect the dear footsteps of the cattle. O Agni, thou who hast a full life, thou hast gone from covert to covert.—Rig-Veda, I, 67, 6.

May Varuna, Mitra, Aryaman, triumphant with riches (?), sit down on our sacrificial grass as they did on Manu's.—Rig-Veda, I, 26, 4.

May we unharmed stand under the protection of Agni, Indra, Soma, of the gods; may we overcome our foes.—Rig-Veda, II, 8, 6.

Your greatness, O Maruts, is to be honored, it is to be yearned for like the light of the sun. Place us also in immortality; when they went in triumph, the chariots followed.—Rig-Veda, V, 55, 4.

Slay thou, O Kama, those that are my enemies, hurl them down into blind darkness. Devoid of vigor, without sap let them all be; they shall not live a single day!—Atharva-Veda, IX, 2, 10.

There is one eternal thinker, thinking non-eternal thoughts, who, though one, fulfils the desires of many. The wise who perceive him within their Self, to them belongs eternal peace, not to others.—Katha-Upanishad, V, 13.

[1] The storm-gods.

138

One hundred times that bliss of Pragâpati is one measure of the bliss of Brahman, and likewise of the great sage who is free from desires.—Taittiriyaka-Upanishad, II, 8, 4.

He who forms desires in his mind, is born again through his desires here and there. But to him whose desires are fulfilled and who is conscious of the true Self (within himself) all desires vanish, even here on earth—Mundaka-Upanishad, III, 2, 2.

133. The Land and People.—India, extending from 8 to 36 degrees of north latitude from the Himalaya Mountains far into the Indian Ocean, presents a great variety of temperature and climate. It is a great three-cornered country, about 1,000 miles from north to south and the same distance from east to west. The student of the Vedic religion is, however, chiefly interested in the two great river-valleys of the Indus and the Ganges. The upper part of the valley of the Indus, where the rivers are fed by the melting of the everlasting snows on the Himalayas and the climate is that of the temperate zone, is one of the favored portions of the earth's surface. The valley of the Ganges lies farther to the south; it is dependent for its fertility to a greater degree upon the rains brought by the monsoons; the climate is not favorable to human life, and the struggle for existence is intensely severe. As compared with Persia, Palestine, or Arabia, Northern India is a land of fertility.

From time immemorial India has been populated by a variety of tribes. It has become customary in recent years to call many of these Dravidian.[1] Not all the

[1] See the article "Dravidian" in Hastings' *Encyclopaedia of Religion and Ethics*, V, 1 ff. The term was first applied by Mann to a tribe of Southern India. It has been supposed that he meant to include all of them.

aboriginal tribes of India were of one stock, but, so far as we can trace them, they appear to have been backward races. At an unknown date, probably considerably more than a thousand years before the beginning of our era, there came into the upper Indus Valley through the passes of the Hindu Kush Mountains some tribes of Aryan stock. They were members of the great Indo-European race, and before their migration into India had lived with their kinsmen, the ancestors of the Persians, somewhere to the north of the Hindu Kush Mountains. They spread over the upper part of the valley of the Indus. The majority of them lived on the eastern side of that river in the region called Punjab, or the five-river region. They extended as far east as the Sutlej River. In this valley they lived for some centuries; here the Vedas were composed. Later, portions of this Aryan race pressed on into the valley of the Ganges, and it is held by some that the change in their religious thought, which we shall trace in this sketch, was due in part to the depressing effect of the climate of that valley.

134. **The sources** of information concerning the religion of the early Aryans of India are the Vedas, Brahmanas, and Upanishads, all of which are counted as Vedic by the people of India. More than a hundred books are called Vedas, some of which are little known to scholars.[1] The Vedas, properly so called, are the Rig-Veda, Yajur-Veda, Samá-Veda, and Atharva-Veda. The word "Veda" springs from the same root as the English "wit" and the German *wissen*, and means "knowledge," especially "sacred knowledge." The

---

[1] Bloomfield, *Religion of the Veda*, p. 17.

oldest of the Vedas is the Rig-Veda—"Rig" being from a stem which means "stanzas of praise." It consists of a little more than a thousand hymns, containing about 10,000 stanzas, and equals in bulk the *Iliad* and *Odyssey*. Not all these poems are "stanzas of praise." Some of the later ones are blessings and curses. Six of these books (II-VII) are called "family books." They are supposed to have been composed by different poets or seers, or families of such, each of whom claimed to trace his descent from a single seer. They are the earliest part of the Veda.

The Yajur-Veda takes its name from a word meaning "formulae in prose." It is later than the Rig-Veda, contains many of the same hymns, though with many new verses, and adds the formulae mentioned. These are sometimes mere dedications, sometimes short prayers, and at times long solemn litanies.

The Sama-Veda takes its name from a word which means "melodies" and is the Veda of music. It contains no connected hymns, but rather disconnected verses borrowed mainly from the Rig-Veda. Some practices not found in the other Vedas appear in it. With these a number of legends are connected. Even the sense of its verses is subordinated to the music. It is devoted largely to the worship of Indra.

The Atharva-Veda is named from one of two ancient families of priests who were supposed to understand potent charms. It is a collection of 730 hymns, containing about 6,000 stanzas, a part of which are blessings while others are "witchcraft charms" or curses. It is a most valuable collection of popular practices, superstitions, and folklore.

The Brahmanas are theological treatises attached sometimes to the Vedas. They are written in prose and deal with the sacrificial ceremonial. They were designed to explain the significance of the ceremonial to those who were familiar with its details. Sometimes they reveal a reflective spirit, unsatisfied with the mere offering of animal sacrifices, seeking for union with a spiritual being. The theological attitude of the Brahmanas is varied, veering from a very practical interest in the ritual to theological speculation far beyond the range of ritual.

Closely connected with the last-mentioned side of the Brahmanas are the Upanishads, which are sometimes counted with the Brahmanas, but really present a new religion. Next to the Rig-Veda the Upanishads are the most important literary productions of Vedic India.

135. Chronology.—It is generally agreed that the oldest Upanishads were written before the time of Gautama, called the Buddha, who died about 487 B.C. This seems certain, since the whole Buddhistic system of thought presupposes the philosophic conceptions of the Upanishads. Beyond this single fact we have no chronological datum from the Vedic period. No building, or monument, or coin, or jewel, or utensil has come down to us from the Vedic time. No ancient Indian historian has left us a chronicle or an outline of the chronology. It is not strange, therefore, that the estimates of scholars have varied widely. Some would put the Rig-Veda at 3,000 or 4,000 B.C.; others would bring it down to 1,000; advocates of 2,500, 2,000, 1,500, and 1,200 have not been wanting. Macdonell supposes that the Brahmanas and Upanishads developed in the period 800–500 B.C.[1] If this is so, one need not suppose that the beginnings of the Rig-Veda antedate 1,500 B.C., though they may go back to 2,000. From what we know of the appearance of the Hittites[2] in history, and of the beginnings of the Aryan occupation of Iran,[3] it does not seem probable that the Aryans entered India earlier than 2000 B.C., and it may well have been later than that. It must, however, be frankly recognized that we have no direct evidence on this point.

136. The social organization represented by the Rig-Veda was a simple patriarchal society, ruled by chieftains called *rajas* (*raja* is philologically equivalent to the Latin *rex*), who were often hereditary. In the Rig-Veda occupations were not differentiated; every man was a soldier as well as a civilian. The family was the foundation of society. The father was lord of the house; he was also a priest who offered the sacrifice. The wife, though subject to him, occupied a position of greater honor than in the age of the Brahmanas, for she participated in the offering of the sacrifice. She was mistress of the house and shared the control of the children, slaves, and unmarried brothers and sisters of the husband. Suitors asked the father for a daughter's hand, making the request through the mediation of a friend. Sons and daughters married usually in the order of age, but sometimes girls remained unmarried and grew old in their father's house. The standard of morality was comparatively high. The community was agricultural.

[1] A. H. Macdonell, *A History of Sanskrit Literature* (New York, 1900), chap. viii.

[2] See Barton, *Archaeology and the Bible*, chap. iii.

[3] See chap. vii, *passim*.

The standard of value was a cow. Horses, sheep, goats, asses, and dogs were also domesticated Gold is frequently referred to, and also bronze. The Indus (ancient *Sindhu*) is frequently mentioned, as are the five rivers of the Punjab under ancient names, viz., the Jhelum, Chenab, Ravi, Beas, and Sutlej. The sea is seldom mentioned, for the community was confined to the upper Indus.

Later, conquests were made of the aborigines in other regions, especially in the valley of the Ganges. In the course of the struggles thus entailed, a differentiation of occupations occurred, a priesthood, a warrior class, as well as an agricultural class, were developed, and the caste system came into being. This system was apparently due in part to the gulf which separated the Aryan from the colored race which they conquered, and in part to the effort of the priesthood, which had now emerged, to maintain its sanctity.

137. Vedic deities.—The Rig-Veda states that the number of gods is thirty-three, or thrice eleven. This number is not exhaustive, for it does not include the storm-gods. It is nevertheless in excess of the number of important deities, for there are scarcely twenty that have as many as three hymns addressed to them. Several of these gods were brought by the Indian Aryans from their home beyond the Hindu Kush. The most important of these was Indra, the national god of the Indians, who among the Persians was relegated to the place of a demon. The importance of Indra is shown by the fact that nearly one-fourth of the hymns of the Rig-Veda celebrate his praises. Like other early tribal gods, Indra was supposed to fight the national battles. This fighting character he never threw off. Like other fighters, Indra is full of brag and bluster. The first two quotations from the Rig-Veda at the head of this chapter sufficiently indicate his character and the attitude of his worshipers toward him. Indra paid the penalty of his early origin. Owing to the conservatism of religious thought, he never rose to the height of refinement of his later worshipers. He does not represent the best religion even of the Vedas. He is of the earth, earthy. He slays dragons and monsters; he is a glutton, a drunkard, and a boaster. One hymn[1] is generally interpreted as attempting to utter the vaunting of Indra when intoxicated with soma. It is the earliest attempt in literature to portray the maudlin exhilaration arising from the use of alcohol.

Another prehistoric god of India was Agni, the god of fire. The sacredness of fire among the Persians attests his antiquity. Next to Indra he is the most popular of the Vedic gods. More than two hundred hymns are addressed to him. While Agni is personified as a god, the consciousness of his origin was never lost. To the end all his qualities were qualities of fire.

Mitra and Varuna are also gods brought from the primitive Aryan home, for, as pointed out in chap. vii, they were prominent among the Persians also. Mitra was a sun-god; Varuna probably a sky-god.[2] Mitra is in the Veda almost submerged as a companion of Varuna. Only one hymn is addressed to Mitra alone. Varuna, though addressed in far fewer hymns than Indra, Agni, or Soma, is next to Indra the greatest of the Vedic gods.

[1] Rig-Veda, X, 119.

[2] See, e.g., Rig-Veda, VII, 86-89.

He was thought to be the upholder of the physical and moral universe. The hymns addressed to him are more devout and ethical than any others in the Veda and approach more nearly the strains of the Hebrew Psalter. His omniscience is a favorite theme. He witnesses the truth or falsehood of men. No creature can wink without him.[1]

Another sky-god, Dyaush pitar, "father Sky," appears to go back to pre-Indian days. Both his name and epithet are philologically identical with the Greek *Zeus pater*, the Latin *Diespiter*, or Jupiter. The personification of the sky as a god is shown by these correspondences to go back to primitive Indo-European times. In the Vedas, Dyaush is employed both as the name of the god and as the word for sky. The origin of the god is thus quite transparent.

Quite as old as Dyaush is his daughter Ushas, the Dawn, identical with the Greek *Eōs* (or *Heōs*), and the Latin Aurora. Like that of her father, the origin of the deity was always clear, and the beauty of the dawn inspired the Vedic poets to produce some of their most charming creations.[2]

The Açvins, or heavenly twins, who correspond to the Dioskouroi of Greek mythology, were also probably prehistoric. They, like Ushas, were the children of Dyaush pitar. It is not certain whether they were personifications of the morning and evening star, or of the sun and moon, or of the twilight, half-light, half-dark. In the Vedas they are the succorers who aid those in trouble.

[1] See, for example, Rig-Veda, VII, 89.
[2] *Ibid.*, I, 113.

Prithivī[1] matar, or "Mother Earth," who is represented as the wife of Dyaush pitar, is perhaps also as primitive as he. Only one separate hymn is addressed to her in the Rig-Veda, and even in that reference is made to her heavenly spouse.

Another god that would seem to have originated before the separation of the ancestors of the Indian Aryans from the Persians was Soma, the Persian Haoma. In the Yasna,[2] Haoma was an angel with whom Zoroaster once conversed. Soma was at once a plant and an intoxicating drink; it also became a god. In both Veda and Avesta it is described as dwelling or growing on a mountain. Its true abode was thought to be in heaven, whence it was brought down to earth. Its exhilarating power led to the belief that it was a drink that bestows everlasting life. From it the gods themselves were thought to gain their immortality. Naturally large quantities of soma were employed in the ritual; gods set men the example of drunkenness. It is a somewhat sad comment on Vedic morals, but others, as, for example, the Babylonians, believed that their gods were not above drunkenness,[3] even if they did not deify drink. In the latest hymns of the Rig-Veda, Soma is somewhat obscurely identified with the moon.

The ancient people of India manifested a strong bent toward the multiplication of gods through the personification of the powers of nature, and the multiplication of deities through the personification of different epithets of the same god. By these means several deities were

[1] Rig-Veda, V, 84. *Prithivī* is literally "the Broad One."

[2] Yasna ix, 1–16.

[3] See G. A. Barton, *Archaeology and the Bible* (5th ed.), p. 258.

added to the pantheon after the migration into India. Thus in the Vedas there are in addition to Mitra four sun-gods: Surya, Savitar, Pushan, and Vishnu. In the Vedas, Vishnu is not one of the most important gods, though he became such in later Hinduism. Similar personifications produced Vāta or Vāyu, the wind-god, Parjanya, the rain-god, and Rudra, the storm-god. In the Vedas, Rudra is a simple storm-god of no very great prominence. In Hinduism he assumed a different rôle. A group of storm-gods, indefinite in number, to whom many hymns in the Rig-Veda are addressed, is the Maruts. The terrific force of storms in India led to the belief that there were many such spirits, and magnified their terrifying powers.

The important Vedic gods have been classified as:

Celestial gods: Dyaush pitar, Varuna, Mitra, Surya, Savitar, Pushan, Vishnu, Ushas, the Açvins, and the Adityas, frequently associated with Varuna and Mitra.

Atmospheric gods: Vāta or Vāyu, Indra (who is frequently represented as a kind of storm-god), Parjanya, Rudra, and the Maruts.

Terrestrial gods: Prithivī, Agni, and Soma.

138. Cosmogony.—In the earlier hymns of the Rig-Veda creation is referred to as an act of natural generation.[1] In the later strata of the Rig-Veda we find the idea of a creator, or the material of creation, distinct from all the gods and superior to them. This creator is given various names, Prajāpati being one of the most important. He was in reality a huge man, whom the gods cut up as though he were a sacrifice, and from the parts made the various portions of the universe. His

[1] Rig-Veda, IV, 2, 2, and III, 4, 10.

head became the sky, his feet the earth, his navel the air, while from his eye sprang the sun, from his mind the moon, and from his breath the wind.[1]

139. The ritual and its purpose.—The hymns and prayers of the Veda were composed to accompany the sacrifices which were offered to the gods. These consisted of such viands as the worshipers regarded as delicious or necessary. Ghee, or melted butter, and soma were prominent elements in them. The purpose of the offerings was to propitiate the gods and bring them near. Thus one hymn prays:[2]

> May Varuna, Mitra, and Aryaman, triumphant with riches (?), sit on our sacrificial grass as they did on Manu's!

In the earliest time the sacrifices were offered by the heads of families, and chieftains offered their own sacrifices. There were no temples and no permanently holy places. A spot was chosen for a sacrifice and consecrated for the occasion. When the sacrifice was completed, the place became again as other places. Before the end of the Vedic period, through a natural differentiation of duties, certain men had assumed the function of the priesthood, and others had acquiesced in the arrangement. It thus happened that kings often employed others to officiate at sacrifices offered by them. Nearly all the hymns of the Rig-Veda appear to have been written by such priests, who had a pecuniary interest in the sacrifice, and who employed their poetry, not only to praise the god or gods, but to impress the king with the desirability of liberally rewarding the priest. It thus happens that most frank appeals for

---

[1] Rig-Veda, X, 90.　　　　[2] Ibid., I, 26, 4.

baksheesh, or a gift, are mingled by the singers with beautiful descriptions of the gods, and with genuine religious appeals. *Dakshina* is the Sanskrit term for "sacrificial fee." In the following translations by Bloomfield[1] it is rendered "baksheesh."

> Up the shining strands of Dawn have risen,
> Like unto glittering waves of water!
> All paths prepareth she that they may be easily traversed;
> Liberal goddess, kind, she hath become baksheesh.

And again:[2]

> Baksheesh's roomy chariot hath been harnessed,
> And the immortal gods have mounted on it,
> The friendly dawn, wide-spread, from out of darkness
> Has risen up to care for the abode of mortals.

> The mighty goddess rose before all creatures,
> She wins the booty and always conquers riches;
> The dawn looks forth, young and reviving ever,
> She came the first here to our morning offering.

For a time so early the poetry is beautiful. As Bloomfield remarks: "Never has sacrifice had such genuine poetry to serve it. But the reverse of the coin is that never has poetic endowment strayed so far from wholesome theme as to fritter itself away upon the ancient hocus-pocus of the fire priest and the medicine-man."

140. Vedic salvation.—Notwithstanding that the priests made the ritual and the poetry fill their own pockets, the Veda voices many an appeal for salvation as the people of that time understood salvation. They desired to be healthy and prosperous; to have good crops; that storms might not devastate, and to have

[1] *Religion of the Veda,* p. 69.

[2] Bloomfield, *op. cit.,* p. 71.

long life. One hymn appeals to Varuna, the god of justice, thus:[1]

> May I not yet, King Varuna,
> Go down into the house of clay:
> Have mercy, spare me, mighty Lord.
>
> Thirst has come on thy worshiper,
> Though standing in waters' midst:[2]
> Have mercy, spare me, mighty Lord.
>
> O Varuna, whatever the offence may be
> That we as men commit against the heavenly folk
> When through our want of thought we violate thy laws,
> Chastise us not, O God, for that iniquity.

Such an appeal presupposes a god that, though just, is merciful. There is no hint that he needed an atoning sacrifice to change his attitude toward the worshiper, though another hymn implies that he may exact from the sinner atoning suffering. It runs:[3]

> We ascribe to thee honor from of old,
> Now and in future, Varuna, thou mighty one;
> Upon thee we rest as upon a firm rock,
> Infallible one, the eternal laws.
>
> Take my peculiar misdeed from me,
> Let me not, O King, expiate a sin unknown;
> Should yet many brilliant mornings dawn,
> On them, O Varuna, thou wouldst lead us alive.

141. Heaven and hell.—In the Vedas, Yama[4] was the god of death. He was king of the regions of the

---

[1] Translated by Macdonell, *History of Sanskrit Literature*, p. 77.

[2] A reference to dropsy, with which Varuna was thought to afflict sinners, according to Macdonell.

[3] Translated from the German of Grassman's *Rig-Veda* (Leipzig, 1876), II, 28, 9, 10.

[4] Yama was probably a part of primitive Aryan mythology, since he appears in the Avesta as Yima.

departed, whether they had been good or bad. The poets of the Rig-Veda have, however, little to say about the after-life, and that little is vague. In Rig-Veda, V, 55, 4, the worshipers yearn for immortality, but whether it is immortality on the earth or in some other abode is not told. In Rig-Veda, X, 14, 1, a hymn devoted to funeral obsequies, Yama is celebrated as the god who first spied out a path to another world. That other world was, Sanskrit scholars think, in heaven. The dead are addressed thus:[1]

> Run on thy path straight forward past the two dogs,
> The sons of Sarama, four-eyed and brindled,
> Draw near thereafter to the bounteous fathers,
> Who revel on in company with Yama.

In the Atharva-Veda there is a definite belief in a pit of black darkness in the earth beneath, into which the wicked are to be hurled,[2] though the conditions which prevail there are only vaguely described. Evidence is also afforded that the good were taken to a place of happiness. In a charm against dropsy is the prayer:[3]

> Lift from us, O Varuna, the uppermost fetter, take down the nethermost, loosen the middlemost! Then shall we, O Aditya, in thy law, exempt from guilt, live in freedom! Loosen from us, O Varuna, all fetters, the uppermost, the nethermost, and those imposed by Varuna! Evil dreams and misfortune drive away from us: then may we go to the world of the pious!

In later literature, the Upanishads and the epic of the Mahābhārata, there are clear traces of an Indian belief

---

[1] Rig-Veda, X, 14, 10, translated by Macdonell, *op. cit.*, p. 118.

[2] See *Sacred Books of the East*, XLII, p. 191, vs. 49; p. 211, vs. 32; p. 222, vs. 10.

[3] *Ibid.*, p. 12 (VII, 3, 4).

in a hell and a heaven.[1]   Because the rewards of heaven
were of a material nature, the thinkers of the Upanishads
frown upon the hope of heaven as unworthy of a
philosopher.[2]

142. Magic and demonology.—In its main contents
the Atharva-Veda is more superstitious than the Rig-
Veda. It represents the popular beliefs rather than
those of the more intelligent. It betrays a belief in the
existence of many demons, and contains many charms
by which it was supposed their attacks could be warded
off. It was compiled later than the Rig-Veda, and
where it reflects the conceptions entertained of the
higher gods they are often more advanced than those of
the Rig-Veda. Some of its charms against the demons
of sickness originated perhaps before the Indo-Europeans
separated, for they agree to some extent in content as
well as in purpose with certain old German, Lettic, and
Russian charms.[3] While parts of the Atharva-Veda
clearly developed in India, it reveals to us the fact that a
belief in numerous demons, and a magic art believed to
be potent against them, existed through the entire period
of Vedic development.

143. The Brahmanas, which probably began to be
composed as early as 800 B.C. in prose, represent a theological transition. The Aryan people had now been long
exposed to the Indian climate, had occupied, in addition
to their original territory, the valley of the Ganges in
which the climate was more depressing, and had, independently of climate, reached a more mature period of

[1] See Hopkins, *The Great Epic of India* (New York, 1901), pp. 184–86.
[2] See *Sacred Books of the East,* XV, p. 30, vs. 10.
[3] See Macdonell, *op. cit.,* pp. 185 ff.

thought. In the Brahmanas, too, we have evidence that the fluid society of the time of the Rig-Veda had crystallized into the four castes: the Brahman, or priestly class, who now became the real rulers; the Rajanya or Kshatriya, the warrior class; the Vaisya, the agricultural class, and the Sudra or serf caste. While most of the Brahmanas are occupied with practical sacrificial directions, others undertake to explain the meaning of the ritual. A few passages indicate that the more thoughtful had passed beyond the stage of culture in which gods are believed to be material beings and animal sacrifices are thought to be potent. Religion was becoming a thing of the spirit; they were questioning the utility of the ritual. The priests, or Brahmans, as they were called, had a pecuniary interest in the ritual, which to many was still a sacred necessity. This pecuniary interest they sometimes manifested in repulsive ways.[1] It became the duty of the Brahmans, however, to explain to the worshipers the spiritual significance of the time-honored material ceremonies. For example, certain sacrifices by their burning took the sacrificer up to the god-world; others by their noise made him master of the father-world; still others of the man-world. Fire, which consumed the sacrifice, was interpreted as speech.[2] In such ways the ritual was given a more intellectual and spiritual interpretation. In the Brahmanas one beholds the minds of the thinkers traveling away from old beliefs toward another kind of religion.

144. **The Upanishads,** into which the Brahmanas merge, contain the essence of this new religion, if religion

[1] See, for example, *Sacred Books of the East,* XV, 121 ff.

[2] See Bloomfield, *op. cit.,* pp. 190 ff.

it can be called.   It is rather a philosophy and a pessimistic one at that.

(1) The heart of the philosophy of the Upanishads is that there is but one real existence in the universe, the supreme *Brahman, Atman,* or Self.   All creatures are but evanescent manifestations of this Self.   This doctrine is reached even in the Brahmanas, where it is taught that no material thing may be loved for itself, but for the Self that is manifest in it:

Verily, a husband is not dear, that you may love the husband; but that you may love the Self, therefore a husband is dear.

Verily, a wife is not dear, that you may love a wife; but that you may love the Self, therefore a wife is dear.

Verily, sons are not dear, that you may love the sons; but that you may love the Self, therefore the sons are dear.

Verily, wealth is not dear, that you may love wealth; but that you may love the Self, therefore wealth is dear.

The list continues and enumerates even the Vedas and the gods as things that are to be loved only because of the Self.   A monistic doctrine could not well be more pronounced.

(2) The Upanishads are saturated with a profound pessimism.   In the Vedas there is manifest a genuine youthful joy in life; in the Upanishads, on the other hand, life is considered an evil.   The essential element of life is desire; desire leads to pain; he only reaches the happiness of Brahman or the Self who is free from desire.

(3) *Transmigration.*—The pessimism of the Upanishads is intensified by the belief in the transmigration of souls.   This belief is not peculiar to India; we hear of it in Egypt, among the Celts, and among the Greeks. Hindu pessimism made it, however, especially terrible.

How it arose in India is not known. There is no trace of it in the earlier Vedic literature. It was possible for any man in the animistic stage of culture to reach it, if he reflected on three facts in which all men believed: (*a*) man has a soul separate from the body; (*b*) animals have souls; (*c*) all souls can change their habitation.

In the Vedic literature the souls of the departed went to the realm of Yama; in later times to heaven. In the Upanishads belief in transmigration is grafted on to this earlier belief. The ascetic, who retires to the forest, goes at death on the path of the gods not to return. Those who practice the ordinary callings of life go at death by the path of the fathers to the moon, where they remain until the influence of their good deeds is exhausted, when they return by the same path and are reborn. They may be reborn as a person, an animal, or an herb. If their conduct has been good, they will attain to some good birth, such as a Brahman; if it has been evil, they will quickly attain some evil birth, such as a dog, or a hog.[1] The influence of deeds on rebirth was called the doctrine of *Karma*, or the deed.

(4) *The abolition of desire* became, under these circumstances, the great aim of the believers in this philosophy. Desire led to rebirth; rebirth led to suffering; and so the wheel of pain rolled on forever. Salvation lay in the abolition of desire.[2]

It has been frequently held that this pessimistic philosophy is the natural outcome of the conditions of

[1] The fullest description of transmigration is in the Upanishad translated in *Sacred Books of the East*, I, 80 ff.

[2] *Sacred Books of the East*, XV, p. 40, vs 2

life in India, which, it is declared, are harder than those of any other civilized country.[1]

145. The evolution of religious thought in the Vedic literature is most striking. The Indians reckon the Upanishads a part of the Vedas. The religion of the earliest hymns of the Rig-Veda is that of buoyant, joyous youth; that of the Upanishads is the religion of a world-weary people for whom life held no treasure great enough to offset its agony. This was, however, only the religion of philosophers. As will appear in chap. x, the older Vedic religion long survived among the common people.

SUPPLEMENTARY READING

CLASS A

On sec. 133: cf. Hunter's "India" in Lodge's *History of the Nations*, chap. 1, or A. A. Macdonell, *History of Sanskrit Literature* (New York, 1900), pp. 139–44.

On sec. 134: cf. Macdonell, *op. cit.*, chaps. iii, vii, and viii; or Bloomfield, *The Religion of the Veda* (New York, 1908), pp. 17–59.

On·sec. 135: cf. Bloomfield, *op. cit.*, pp. 18 ff.

On sec. 136: cf. Macdonell, *op. cit.*, chap. vi; or Hoernle and Stark, *History of India* (Cuttack, 1904), chaps. ii and iii.

On sec. 137: cf. Bloomfield, *op. cit.*, Lectures III and IV; or Macdonell, *op. cit.*, pp. 67–107.

On sec. 138: cf. Macdonell, *op. cit.*, pp. 131 ff.

On sec. 139: cf. Bloomfield, *op. cit.*, Lecture II.

On sec. 140: cf. Macdonell, *op. cit.*, pp. 116 ff.; and E. W. Hopkins, *The Great Epic of India* (New York, 1901), pp. 184 ff.

On sec. 142: cf. Macdonell, *op. cit.*, pp. 185–201.

On secs. 143, 144: Bloomfield, *op. cit.*, Lectures V and VI.

CLASS B

G. F. Moore, *History of Religions*, chap. xi.

CHAPTER IX

BUDDHISM AND JAINISM

There are two extremes, O Bhikkus, which the man who has given up the world ought not to follow—the habitual practice, on the one hand, of those things whose attraction depends upon the passions, and especially of sensuality—a low and pagan way (of seeking satisfaction), unworthy, unprofitable, and fit only for the worldly-minded—and the habitual practice, on the other hand, of asceticism (or self-mortification), which is painful, unworthy, and unprofitable.

There is a middle path, O Bhikkus, avoiding these two extremes, discovered by the Tathâgata[1]—a path which opens the eyes, and bestows understanding, which leads to peace of mind, to the higher wisdom, to full enlightenment, to Nirvana!

What is the middle path, O Bhikkus, avoiding these two extremes, discovered by the Tathâgata—that path which opens the eyes, and bestows understanding, which leads to peace of mind, to the higher wisdom, to full enlightenment, to Nirvana? Verily! it is the noble eightfold path; that is to say:

Right views;
Right aspirations;
Right speech;
Right conduct;
Right livelihood;
Right effort;
Right mindfulness; and
Right contemplation.

—Dhamma-Kakka-Ppavattana-sutta,[2] 2, 3, 4 (Buddhist).

He who knows wrath, knows pride; he who knows pride, knows deceit; he who knows deceit, knows greed; he who knows greed, knows love; he who knows love, knows hate; he who

[1] An epithet of Buddha.

[2] That is, "The Foundation of the Kingdom of Righteousness."

knows hate, knows delusion; he who knows delusion, knows conception; he who knows conception, knows birth; he who knows birth, knows death; he who knows death, knows hell; he who knows hell, knows animal existence; he who knows animal existence, knows pain.

Therefore, a wise man should avoid wrath, pride, deceit, greed, love, hate, delusion, conception, birth, death, hell, animal existence, and pain.   —Akârânga Sutra, I, iv, 4 (Jain).

146. The sources of Buddhism.—Buddhism has died in India, the land of its birth, but flourishes in many other countries. As Gautama, its founder, committed nothing to writing, his teachings were intrusted to tradition, and were not written down until later. In the course of the centuries much has been added to the tradition. From Ceylon and neighboring lands have come sacred books of Buddhism (the Pitakas[1]) in the Pali language, estimated by Rhys Davids to be in bulk about four times that of the Old and New Testaments. These consist of discourses (*Suttas*) attributed to Gautama, commentaries upon them, wonderful stories of the birth of the Buddha (Jatakas), and traditions of his life.[2]

From Nepal, in the north of India, Buddhistic scriptures have also come. Among these are Ashvaghosha's poem on the life of Buddha,[3] descriptions of the land of bliss,[3] and a work of a miscellaneous character, entitled *The Lotus of the True Law.* In China and

[1] The Sanskrit for "basket." Used as the name of a "collection" of books.

[2] Pali works are translated in the *Sacred Books of the East*, XI, XVII, XX; M. P. Grimblot, *Sept suttas pâlis* (Paris, 1876); and in K. E. Neumann, *Die Reden Gotamo Buddho's* (Leipzig, 1896–1905).

[3] Nepalese Buddhistic scriptures are translated in the *Sacred Books of the East*, XXI and XLIX.

Tibet[1] also Ashvaghosha's poem on the life of Buddha has been found, and from China[2] many other Buddhist scriptures have come. As the religion spread into these countries either before the Christian era, or at the very beginning of it, the existence of the same work in Pali, in the Sanskrit texts of Nepal, in Tibetan, and in Chinese is proof of a high antiquity. There is reason to believe that some of these works were composed less than a century after the death of Gautama.

147. Life of Gautama to his enlightenment.—In the sixth century before Christ an Aryan tribe named Sākyas was living at Kapilavastu on the little river Rohini in the valley of the Ganges about 130 miles north of Benares. Forty miles to the north rose the great peaks of the Himalayas. There were but two tribes of Aryans farther east than the Sākyas. They were the Lichavis and the Magadha. Suddhodana, the raja of the Sākyas, married the two daughters of the raja of the Koliyans, a neighboring tribe. The elder of these sisters became the mother of Gautama, afterward called the Buddha, about 567 B.C.[3] At the time of his birth the

[1] Translations from Tibetan sources are found in W. W. Rockhill, *Life of the Buddha* (London, 1884).

[2] Chinese Buddhistic sources are made accessible in English in Samuel Beal, *Catena of Buddhist Scriptures from Chinese* (London, 1871), his *Abstract of Four Lectures on Buddhistic Literature in China* (London, 1882), and his translations in the *Sacred Books of the East*, XIX.

[3] This date is obtained in the following way: Asoka, king of Western India, who says in his inscriptions that he was converted in his ninth year, says that he sent missionaries to Antiochus of Syria, Ptolemy of Egypt, Antigonus of Macedonia, Alexander of Epirus, and Magas of Cyrene (see V. A. Smith, *Asoka* [Oxford, 1901], pp. 129–32). These rulers were all ruling at the same time only between 262 and 258 B.C. (see A. J. Edmunds, *Buddhist and Christian Gospels*, 4th ed. [Philadelphia

mother was on her way to her father's house, but her son was born under some tall trees in a pleasant grove called Lumbini. The mother died a week later, and the child was brought up by her childless sister, his father's other wife. When of suitable age Gautama was married to his cousin, the daughter of the raja of Koli. A later tradition seems to show that Gautama was never interested in the ordinary occupations of a prince, but it is certain that in his twenty-ninth year, shortly after the birth of his only child, he abandoned home and family to devote himself to the study of religion. This was in accord with an ascetic custom then already old in India. Coeval with the rise of the Upanishad philosophy, there had grown up a body of ascetics who abandoned the world, lived in poverty in the forests or mountains, and begged their bread. Gautama is said to have been led to this step by four visions: that of a man decrepit through age, a sick man, a decaying corpse, and a dignified hermit. Before leaving home he stole into the chamber of his sleeping wife, to take a last look at her and his child. This parting the Buddhists call the "Great Renunciation."

Gautama traveled eastward beyond the Koliyan territory with his horse and then sent back his horseman to tell his wife and father what had become of him. He

1908], I, 58). If we take the average of 260 for the conversion of Asoka, his reign began in 269 B.C. A Ceylonese tradition states that Asoka began to reign 218 years after Buddha died. This tradition is followed by leading Buddhist scholars; it fixes Buddha's death in 487 B.C. Tradition also has it that Gautama was eighty years old at his death. If so, his birth occurred in 567 B.C. On this reckoning there is an uncertainty of four years as to the accession of Asoka, and consequently as to the birth and death of the Buddha. It should be added that some scholars discredit the Ceylonese tradition.

then changed his princely clothing for that of a poor man, cut off his long hair, and became a wandering mendicant. He first went southeastward to the kingdom of Magadha, on the south of the Ganges, where he spent some time studying the philosophy of the Brahmans under two distinguished teachers. The Brahmans insisted that the practice of penance was an efficient aid in gaining super-human power and insight. Gautama, unsatisfied by his study with the philosophers, withdrew with five faithful disciples into the jungle, and for six years gave himself to the severest asceticism, until he had wasted to a shadow. Since asceticism was in India a sufficient title to sanctity, his fame had by this time spread far. Gaining no peace, he intensified his fasting until one day he fell in a swoon and was regarded by his disciples as dead. When he came to himself he was convinced that fasting was not the way to his goal; he therefore abandoned it. Upon this his disciples left him and went away to Benares.

The depression that Gautama now suffered surpassed all that had preceded. Philosophy and asceticism, the outward helps on which his countrymen leaned, had both failed him. Wandering toward the river Nairan-jara, he sat down one morning under the shade of a ban-yan tree, reviewed the years of his life, and fought with temptation through the long hours of the day. As the day ended he beheld in mental vision a new path. He became Buddha, the enlightened one. This tree was accordingly called the Bo-tree, or tree of enlightenment. He gained peace *in the power over the human heart of inward culture, and of love to others.* At last he had found certitude. He then made another renunciation, greater than his first; he renounced asceticism and

penance.   Because of Gautama's experience the Bo-tree
has become to Buddhists almost what the Cross is to
Christians.   Gautama's first thought was to announce
his religious discovery to his · previous philosophic
teachers.   They, however, rejected him, but, nothing
daunted, he went on to Benares and began to preach
there.[1]

148. Gautama's doctrine was really not a religion,
but a method of ethical culture.   He recognized no
supreme God.   The *dēvas*, or the gods of the old religion,
were real beings, but they were, like men, caught in the
meshes of the material universe.   Gautama proposed no
reformed worship of these.   He accepted the pessimistic
point of view which is reflected in the Upanishads, and
the doctrines of transmigration and of *Karma*.   Salvation as he conceived it was escape from the pain and the
necessity of continuous reincarnation.   His formulation of this thesis he called the four "Noble Truths":
(1) The experiences of life—birth, growth, decay, illness,
death, separation from objects we love, hating what cannot be avoided—are all sorrowful.   That is, such states
of mind as are inseparable from conscious personality
are states of suffering and sorrow.   (2) The causes of
suffering and sorrow are the action of the outside world
on the senses.   These objects excite a craving, or a
delight, which leads to action, which leads in turn to
rebirth, continued existence, and misery.   (3) The
complete subjugation and destruction of this eager thirst
or lust is that which causes sorrow to cease.   (4) The
path which leads to the cessation of sorrow is the Noble

[1] This statement is abridged from that of T. W. Rhys Davids,
Buddhism (London, 1903), pp. 25-45.

Eightfold Path: right views or beliefs; right aspirations or aims; right speech; right conduct or action; right livelihood (or means of living); right effort or endeavor; right mindfulness; right contemplation or meditation. Gautama taught that one who followed this path would become an *Arahat*—a man set free by insight from the desire for material or immaterial existence; from pride and self-righteousness and ignorance. As one traveled the Noble Eightfold Path on the way to *Arahat*ship, one would conquer ten errors or evil states of mind: self-delusion; doubt; dependence on works; sensuality or bodily passions; ill-feeling or hatred; love of life on earth; desire for life in heaven; pride; self-righteousness; ignorance.

One who became an *Arahat* had attained *Nirvana*, a state to which Buddhist writers devote many pages of awe-struck praise. An *Arahat* was not, however, a saved soul, for Gautama denied the reality of the soul's existence. The soul, he held, was only an ensemble of sensations, desires, and fears. Apart from these it has no reality any more than a chariot has reality apart from its wheels, axle, pole, and body. Denying the reality of the soul, he should in consistency have denied transmigration also, but the fascination of this doctrine he could not shake off. Though there was no soul to migrate, he held that there was a *Karma*—a kind of character attained through what one had done, and according to this character one's next incarnation would be shaped. Here Gautama agreed with the philosophers of the Upanishads. He also held that one might be so good as to attain temporary *Arahat*ship in some heaven without attaining Nirvana. Such a person would dwell in heaven until the virtues of his *Karma* were exhausted, and would then be compelled to begin again the round of incarnations.

As an *Arahat* was not a soul, so Nirvana was not heaven. It is rather[1] the extinction of that sinful, grasping condition of mind and heart which would otherwise, according to the great mystery of *Karma*, be the cause of renewed individual existence. It is the same thing as a sinless, calm, unconscious state of mind. It is Buddhistic holiness—a holiness of perfect peace, goodness, and wisdom. The doctrines of Buddha, though they centered one's thought on himself, gave a great impulse to ethical living. The world's tragedies and injustices spring from the selfish desires of men for things. As Buddhism aimed to destroy this desire, it produced an unselfish morality that at times has rivaled that of Christianity.

149. The years of Gautama's ministry.—When Gautama arrived at Benares he went to the Deer Park or Migadaya Wood, about three miles north of the city. Here he continued to teach for some time. Three months later, and five months after the crisis under the Bo-tree, he called together his disciples, who are said already to have been about sixty in number, and sent them forth to preach. During the rest of his life Gautama was accustomed to travel about and preach during the eight pleasant months of the year. During the four rainy months he remained in one place and taught. He soon returned to Rajagriha, the capital of the kingdom of Magadha, where Bimbisara, the king,

---

[1] This definition is taken from T. W. Rhys Davids, *op. cit.*, p. 111, a book to which the writer is greatly indebted.

became his patron, assigning him a bamboo grove, in which Gautama spent many rainy seasons. The traditions tell us in what localities he traveled for about twenty years of his ministry, but we have not space to follow the details.[1] He died at the age of eighty at Kusinagara, the modern Kasia, from a fit of indigestion induced by eating mushrooms.

The first disciples of Buddha gathered about him, leaving all and becoming an order of mendicants. He himself was the leader of this order. The order was established, not because Gautama attached any value to ascetic practices as such, but because he held that men occupied with the things of life could less easily so eradicate desire as to attain Nirvana. He recognized also the desirability of encouraging those who were not ready to join the order to make an endeavor to enter upon the Noble Eightfold Path. From an early period in his ministry, therefore, a lay membership was organized. Indeed, as in other ascetic orders of India, many entered this order temporarily. The two types of members have ever since characterized Buddhism, though the wandering mendicants have become a settled, celibate clergy. At a comparatively early period in his ministry the Buddha returned to Kapilavastu, his birthplace, when his wife Yasodhara and his son Rāhula were converted to his teaching. His son joined the order at once. Later, when Gautama organized an order of female mendicants, Yasodhara became one of its first members.

150. Buddhist orders and laity.—When one joins the Sangha, or Buddhist order, he is required to subscribe

[1] For details see T. W. Rhys Davids, *op. cit.*, pp. 69 ff.

to no creed. In one part of the ceremony of initiation he says:

> I go for refuge to the Buddha.
> I go for refuge to the Law.
> I go for refuge to the Order.

He vows not to destroy life, not to steal, to abstain from social impurity, not to lie, to abstain from intoxicating drinks, not to eat at forbidden times, to abstain from dancing, singing, music, and stage plays, not to use garlands, scents, unguents, or ornaments, not to use a high or broad bed, and not to receive gold or silver.[1]

The rules of the order are very elaborate.[2] They define four faults which are regarded as fatal to the status of a regular disciple of the Buddha. They are: any act of sexual intercourse, theft, taking human life or even encouraging anyone to self-destruction, and pretending to knowledge that one does not possess. Next to the four great offenses are thirteen that deal with "formalities." Several of these have to do with cleanness and uncleanness; others with so building huts that no animal may be inconvenienced or killed. Other rules deal with the uses of robes, rags, bowls, etc., and restrict monks to the use of certain medicines. The Pacittiya rules, which are ninety-two in number, are of a most miscellaneous nature. Five are directed against taking life. A monk is forbidden to dig, lest worms should be accidentally killed. Twenty rules guard against immorality; about ten are directed against lying, slander, etc.

---

[1] See T. W. Rhys Davids, *op. cit.*, p. 160.

[2] Compare for a more elaborate statement T. W. Rhys Davids, *op. cit.*, pp. 162–73; and R. S. Copleston, *Buddhism* (London, 1892), chaps. xiii, xiv, xviii, and xix.

One is directed against the use of intoxicating drinks. As it is followed by several against indecorous conduct, it is probable that drink was forbidden because it led to levity and a lack of decorum. Much space could be devoted to the rules of the order, which are very elaborate, but enough has been said to indicate their character.

The rules for the nuns contain little of importance. They were required to follow the rules for monks as far as they were applicable, and in other matters to follow their own judgment. They were altogether dependent upon the community of men. They had to go to the monks for instruction, and their acts were not valid unless confirmed by the monks.

The laity, so far as the Buddhistic community was concerned, were really outsiders. Buddha's teaching was applicable to all living creatures in three worlds—for gods, men, and animals. The discipline was, however, for human beings. In order to adapt the rules to the laity, some of the requirements were modified. A layman is not called to celibacy, but is required to be faithful to his wife. He may kill animals for the table, though he will have to suffer for it in future births. He need not abstain from alcohol, except after a special vow.

151. Early history of Buddhism.—The sources, both Pali and Sanskrit, agree that immediately after Gautama's death the older members agreed to hold a council to settle the rules and doctrines of the order. It would seem that these had not been fully determined by the Buddha himself. The first council was accordingly held in the rainy season, or the season *was*, following his death. Five hundred members attended the council.

It was held in a cave near Rajagriha, which had been prepared by Ajatasatru, king of Magadha. It is regarded as probable by Rhys Davids that the kernel of the later sacred books of Buddhism dates from this time. The next information about the history of Buddhism concerns the Council of Vaisali, which was held about one hundred years after the first one. Some of the monks desired this council to adopt what are known as the ten indulgences, among which was the permission to drink intoxicants, if they looked like water, and to receive gold and silver. The indulgences were condemned by the council, and a schism resulted. Although this was the first open schism, others occurred later, for the Ceylon chronicles enumerate eighteen sects. They were probably not sects in the modern sense of the term, though they formed different governments and lived apart from one another.

By the time of the Council of Vaisali the kingdom of Magadha had become supreme in Eastern India. In 325 B.C. Alexander the Great reached the most easterly point of his Indian invasion, and at the request of his soldiery abandoned the invasion of the valley of the Ganges. Before he turned back, his camp was visited by Chandragupta, a low-caste rebel from Magadha, whom Alexander spurned. Later, when Nanda, king of Magadha, was murdered, Chandragupta seized his throne, and after Alexander's death he drove the Greeks from India and established an empire that controlled all of Central India. He ruled from 322 to 298 B.C. His capital was at Pataliputra at the junction of the Ganges and Gandak rivers. Being of low caste, Chandragupta apparently favored Buddhism. His son Bindusara succeeded him.

Bindusara was followed some time between 271 and 267 B.C. by his son Piyadasi, or Asoka, who was in his ninth year converted to Buddhism, and became the Constantine of that faith. He enjoined its precepts upon his subjects, inscribing them upon rocks in many parts of the country, and sent missionaries to foreign lands to preach it. Some of these missionaries visited Syria, Egypt, Macedonia, Epirus, and Cyrene. In his eighteenth year Asoka held a council at Patna and appointed a chief minister of religion, whose duty it was to preserve the purity of religion and see that subject races were properly treated. Asoka's edicts show that, along with many other good works, he established hospitals even in foreign lands for the care of men and animals. The most important of Asoka's missionary enterprises was the mission sent to Ceylon, for it resulted in the introduction of Buddhism into that country, where it has flourished with especial vigor. Here in the fifth century A.D. Buddhaghosa, the famous monk who compiled an encyclopedia of Buddhist doctrine, lived. Asoka's efforts seem also to have introduced Buddhism into Kashmere—at least it reached that part of India in his century.

Space forbids us to follow in detail the later history of Buddhism. About the beginning of the Christian era it found its way into China. Probably even earlier it had become naturalized in Tibet. From China it spread to Korea and Japan. In the fifth century A.D. Buddhism was adopted in Burmah, and in the seventh century in Siam. In India proper it was already decadent in the sixth century A.D., when the Chinese pilgrim Yuan Chwang visited the country. It lingered on, however, till the twelfth or thirteenth century, when it was expelled by Hinduism and Mohammedanism. Although it has practically vanished from the land of its birth, it is estimated that there are today perhaps 500,000,000 Buddhists in the world. In other words, it is a religion of about one-third of the human race!

152. The transformation of Buddhism.—Buddhism, which remained comparatively pure until the time of Asoka, has in the centuries since been greatly transformed. Gautama himself recognized no God, but quite early in its development Buddhism had made him a god. He is regarded as omniscient and as perfectly sinless. Soon the doctrine arose that he had no earthly father; that he descended of his own accord from his throne in heaven into the womb of his mother, who was the purest of the daughters of men. After his birth the very trees bent of their own accord over him, and in many miraculous ways he gave evidence of his heavenly character. Around this conception of him all the marvels of the Jatakas, or Birth Stories, grew up. These were in part the outgrowth of a certain doctrine which, it is alleged, Gautama taught. According to this doctrine twenty-four Buddhas had appeared before him. After the death of each one the world grew gradually worse until a new one appeared. After five thousand years the religion revealed to Gautama under the Bo-tree will become so corrupt that a new Buddha, Buddha Maitreya, the Buddha of kindness, will appear and again open to men the door to Nirvana. Thus the pre-existent Buddha, who had appeared many times, newly reincarnated in Gautama, took the place of a God in the religion.

Along with this development many beautiful stories and parables were incorporated in the Buddhist scriptures and attributed to Gautama. Some of these, like the story of the penitent and impenitent robber,[1] and the parable of the prodigal son,[2] somewhat resemble passages in the Gospels. It has been maintained that Christianity borrowed these from Buddhism, and that Buddhism borrowed them from Christianity. Albert J. Edmunds and Garbe earnestly advocate the indebtedness of Christianity to Buddhism.[3] Such borrowing has not yet been fully proved, though shown to have been possible. One form of the legend of the Buddha became, however, so popular that it was given a Christian form, and, as St. Josaphat, the Buddha is revered as a Christian saint on the twenty-seventh of November!

The development which made Buddha a god is known as *Mahayana* Buddhism, or Buddhism of the Great Vehicle. The Little Vehicle, or *Hinayana*, accepted in Ceylon, Siam, and Burma, represented Gautama as a simple teacher who uttered elementary truths easily comprehended by all.[4] This, as already noted, did not long satisfy. In the Great Vehicle Gautama's activity was divided into five periods. In the first his doctrine proved too advanced for the multitude, hence there followed a period of twelve years called the Deer Park. In this period Gautama set forth the doctrines of the

[1] Albert J. Edmunds, *Buddhist and Christian Gospels*, II, 14 ff.

[2] *Sacred Books of the East*, XXI, 99–106; Vol. X of American edition.

[3] See Edmunds' *Buddhist and Christian Gospels*, II, 14 ff.

[4] See *Sacred Books of the East*, XIX, 168–79.

Little Vehicle as an accommodation to human infirmity. The third was a period of expansion, when he preached to *Boddhisattwas* in ten regions a doctrine of greater profundity. This was only preliminary to a fourth period in which Gautama taught the doctrine of the Absolute, "which is the negation of all that is finite, and can be neither described nor comprehended by the ordinary processes of the intellect." In the fifth period he set forth more fully the nature of the Absolute, which constitutes and pervades all things, but which becomes incarnate in successive Buddhas. This last period is called Nirvana.[1] Thus in the Greater Vehicle Gautama was exalted to an incarnation of the Absolute. Along with the transformation of the conception there developed a transformation of the means of grace. In early Buddhism the efforts of each individual constituted his means of grace; in the Mahayana system great stress is laid upon prayer. The Absolute is merciful and may be appealed to.

In Tibet and Nepal the development of this system has taken a peculiar form. According to this view there were three Buddhas before Gautama. The Buddha Maitreya, who will finally bring in the Golden Age, will be the fifth. Each of these mortal Buddhas has his counterpart in the mystic world free from the corrupting influences of material life. These are called Dhyāni Buddhas. Each one of the five has a *Boddhisattwa*—a being, either man, angel, or animal, whose *Karma* is capable of producing other beings in a continually ascending scale of goodness until it becomes a Buddha.

[1] Compare the statement in G. W. Knox, *The Development of Religion in Japan* (New York, 1907), pp. 95 f.

According to this scheme the fifteen Buddhas are as follows:

Dhyāni Buddhas	Boddhisattwas	Human Buddhas
Vairochana	Samanta-bhadra	Kraku-chanda
Akshobya	Vajrapāni	Kanaka-muni
Ratna-sambhava	Ratnapāni	Kāsyapa
Amitabha	Padmapāni (or Avalokitesvara)	Gautama
Amogasiddha	Visvapāni	Maitreya

Some of these, like Avalokitesvara, "the lord that looks down from on high," are metaphysical inventions, but Vajrapāni, "the thunderbolt handed," or "hurler of the thunderbolt," is no other than the Vedic god Indra, under one of his epithets. Thus the old religion has crept back into Gautama's system of ethical culture! Another infusion from the old religion is the belief in heaven and hell. This belief is interwoven with the doctrine of transmigration. In heaven the good, who are not good enough for Nirvana, rest awhile before they are again incarnated. Hell is similarly a temporary abiding-place for the wicked.

In Tibet alone of Buddhist countries the Buddhist order has developed into a hierarchy. Avalokitesvara is conceived as the Spirit of the Buddha who is present with his church. He is supposed to be incarnate in the Dalai Lama, the infallible Head of the Church. The temples in Buddhist countries are supposed to be places for meditation and reading of the sacred books of Buddhism. There are altars on which incense is burned to the statue of the Buddha. Prayers are also said or chanted in parts of the Buddhist world. In Tibet the mechanical saying of prayers is thought to be a virtue.

Even their presentation in written form is of value, hence prayer wheels have been invented, to which written prayers are attached. Every time the wheel, turned by wind or water, bears the prayer upward merit accrues to the devotee! In Nepal the early discipline of the order has so far relaxed that there are monasteries swarming with married monks.[1]

153. **The founder of Jainism,** Vardhamana or Mahavira, was born near Vaisali, the modern Besarh,[2] in the valley of the Ganges. His father appears to have been a petty chieftain. Mahavira lived in the same general period as Gautama, but probably a little before him, and founded a system of ethical culture which so much resembles Buddhism in some points that it has at times been regarded as a Buddhist sect. In many respects, however, it differs strikingly from Buddhism. Mahavira, until he was thirty years old, lived a normal life. He became an ascetic and practiced asceticism for twelve years, when he received enlightenment and became the Jain, or the Victorius One. He then founded the Jainist order of monks, over which he presided until his death, when he was seventy-two years old.[3]

154. **Jainism,** like Buddhism, was a revolt from the Brahmanic system. With reference to the gods Mahavira went farther than Gautama. Gautama admitted their existence, but denied them worship; Mahavira was thoroughly skeptical about them.[4] Like Gautama, he

[1] V. A. Smith, *Early History of India* (Oxford, 1914), p. 367.

[2] See Jacobi, *Sacred Books of the East,* XXII, x, xv; and A. Cunningham, *The Ancient Geography of India* (London, 1871), p. 443.

[3] *Sacred Books of the East,* XXII, 269.

[4] *Ibid.,* p. 152

retained the doctrine of transmigration and of *Karma*, but, unlike him, he held with many Brahmans to the value of asceticism. Notwithstanding his faith in transmigration, he still retained the Vedic doctrine of hell, to which the wicked went between births. Mahavira had practiced ascetic austerities twelve years before he became victorious, and he held that twelve years was the appointed time, if such practices were to be efficacious. The five vows taken by the Jainist monks are not to kill any living being, not to tell lies, not to steal, not to indulge in sexual pleasures, and to renounce all attachments.[1] These are in many respects similar to the vows of the Buddhist monks, but Jacobi has made it probable that both are influenced more by earlier Hindu asceticism than by each other. Although Mahavira had a very poor opinion of women,[2] he permitted them to become ascetics. His rules apply to nuns as well as to monks. There are at present two orders of Jain monks, one of which wears clothes and admits women, while the other does not admit women and goes nude.[3] Deliverance from rebirth is to be attained by right knowledge of the relation between spirit and non-spirit; by right intuition, or absolute faith in the Master and the declarations of the sacred texts; and by the right practice of the virtues, or observance of the five vows in all their details. The belief that it is wrong to kill anything leads the Jains to the most absurd tolerance of vermin. At times they fear to move or to breathe freely lest they kill some of the small insects with which the very air of India

[1] *Sacred Books of the East*, XXII, 202 ff.

[2] *Ibid.*, pp. 21, 48.

[3] E. W. Hopkins, *Religions of India* (Boston, 1895), p. 295.

frequently swarms. In almost every town where Jains live animal hospitals abound. One at Kutch is said to have contained five thousand rats!

The followers of Mahavira regard him as a pre-existent being, who of his own accord was born of his mother. In practice, therefore, they accord him divine honors. Hopkins declares that a religion that denies God, worships man, and nourishes vermin has no right to exist![1] Its one virtue, that of not killing, it holds in such exaggerated form that it becomes grotesque.

SUPPLEMENTARY READING

CLASS A

On secs. 146–49: cf. T. W. Rhys Davids, *Buddhism* (London, 1903), chaps. i–iv.

On sec. 150: See *ibid.*, chaps. v and vi; and R. S. Copleston, *Buddhism* (London, 1892), chaps. xiii, xiv, xviii, and xix.

On secs. 151, 152: cf. T. W. Rhys Davids, *op. cit.*, chaps. vii–ix.

On sec. 152; cf. James B. Pratt, *The Pilgrimage of Buddhism*, New York, 1928.

On secs. 153, 154: cf. Hopkins, *Religions of India*, chap. xii; S. Stevenson, *The Heart of Jainism* (Oxford University Press, 1915); and *Sacred Books of the East*, XXII (American ed., Vol. X, second half).

CLASS B

George F. Moore, *History of Religions*, I, chap. xii.

[1] *Ibid.*, p. 297.

CHAPTER X

HINDUISM

The Veda is the source of the sacred law.—GAUTAMA[1], *Institutes of the Sacred Law*, i, 1.

There are four castes—Brahmanas, Kshatriyas, Vaisyas, and Sudras. Amongst these, each preceding [caste] is superior by birth to the one following. . . . . To serve the other castes is ordained for the Sudra.—ĀPASTAMBA, *Aphorisms*, I, 1, 1:4, 5, 8.

There are four orders, viz., the order of house-holders, the order of students, the order of ascetics, and the order of hermits in the woods. If he lives in all these four according to the rules, without allowing himself to be disturbed, he will obtain salvation.
—ĀPASTAMBA, *Aphorisms*, II, 9, 21:1, 2.

Heaven is their reward, if they speak the truth; in the contrary case hell.—GAUTAMA, *Institutes*, xiii, 7.

He who receives a (gift) from an avaricious king who acts in opposition to the treatises goes in succession to these twenty-one hells.—*Ordinances of Manu*, iv, 87.

Leaving his good deeds to his loved ones and his evil deeds to his enemies, by force of meditation he goes to the eternal Brahma.—*Ordinances of Manu*, vi, 79.

All this depends on meditation, whatsoever has been declared; for no one who knows not the supreme self obtains the fruit of his deeds.—*Ordinances of Manu*, vi, 82.

And consecrated altar built and raised of bricks of gold,
Shone in splendor like the altar Dasha raised in days of old,
Eighteen cubits square the structure, four deep layers of brick in
     height,
With a spacious winged triangle like an eagle in its flight!

---

[1] Not to be confused with the founder of Buddhism.

Beasts whose flesh is pure and wholesome, dwellers of the lake
    and sky,
Priests assigned each varied offering to each heavenly power on
    high.
Bulls of various breed and color, steeds of mettle true and tried,
Other creatures, full three hundred, to the many stakes were tied.

. . . .

Birds and beasts thus immolated, dressed and cooked, provide
    the food,
Then before the sacred charger priests in rank and order stood,
And by rules of Veda guided slew the horse of noble breed,
Placed Draupadi, *Queen of yajna,* by the slain and lifeless steed.
    —*Mahābhārata,* Book xii (Dutt's translation, pp. 167 f.).
Krishna (said):

I am the creature seated deep in every creature's heart;

. . . .

Of poets Usana, of saints Vyâsa, sage divine;
The policy of conquerors, the potency of kings,
The great unbroken silence in learning's secret things;
The lore of all the learned, the seed of all which springs.
Living or lifeless, still or stirred, whatever beings be,
None of them in all the worlds, but it exists by me!
    —*Bhagavad-Gita,* Book X (Sir Edwin Arnold's translation).

155. History.—Neither the Vedic religion nor the
philosophies of the Upanishads was supplanted by the
Buddhistic and the Jainistic heresies. Each lived on and
has undergone multiform developments in the course
of the centuries. The history of India has witnessed
many upheavals. The chief events down to the reign
of Asoka have already been noted. The descendants of
Asoka lingered as petty rajas of Magadha and of parts
of Western India for several centuries. In 206 B.C.
Antiochus III of Syria is said to have made an incursion
into India, and in the following century parts of India
were at several times subject to kings of Bactria.

After Bactria had been overthrown by Parthia, Parthian princes at various times ruled portions of India to about 60 A.D. Legend has it that the apostle Thomas visited and preached in India at this time. These conquerors from the West left no permanent influence upon the country.

In 185 B.C. the descendant of Asoka at Pataliputra was overthrown and a Sunga dynasty was established there. Pushyamitra, its founder, inaugurated a reaction against Buddhism and revived the horse sacrifice. The Sunga dynasty was succeeded by the Kanva dynasty in 73 B.C. The Kanvas were in turn overthrown in 28 B.C. by the Andhra dynasty, a Dravidian people who lived in the region of the Godavari and Kistna rivers, where the Telugus are now found. The Andhra dynasty had been founded in that region after the death of Asoka, where it had gradually increased its power until it finally overthrew the Kanva dynasty and controlled the valley of the Ganges. The Andhra kings flourished until about 225 A.D.

While these events were in progress a Scythian dynasty called Kushan, that had established itself in Bactria about 10 B.C., invaded Northwestern India about 20 A.D. and established itself in the region of Kabul and the upper Indus. This dynasty was not expelled from India until about 225 A.D. During a part of its career in India it controlled much of the valley of the Ganges. One of its kings, Kanishka, is said to have been converted to Buddhism.

For about a hundred years we have no knowledge of the events occurring in Central India, but about 320 A.D. a man bearing the historic name of Chandragupta established a dynasty at or near Pataliputra, which lasted till 606 A.D. and withstood an invasion of the Huns. It was followed by the powerful reign of Harsha of Thānēsar, who flourished until 647 A.D. After Harsha's death the country broke up into petty states which were often at war with one another, and the history of which we have not space to follow. From the end of the tenth century (986) to the thirteenth century the Mohammedans made many conquests in Northwestern, Central, and Southern India, compelling many of the people to accept Islam. The Mohammedans established monarchies in various parts of the land—Bengal, the Deccan, Delhi, etc.—and became the most important political force in the country until 1803. Since that time India has gradually passed under the control of Great Britain.

156. Systems of philosophy.—Before entering on the development of religion in the narrower meaning of the term, it is convenient to trace the various systems of philosophy that were evolved out of the thought of the Upanishads or in reaction against it. These systems were regarded by their adherents as religions, or substitutes for religion. Some of them profoundly influenced the law books and the epics.

The oldest of these philosophies was the Sankhya system, which is said to have originated with Kapila, a pre-Buddhistic thinker. Kapila revolted from the monism of the Upanishads, and maintained that there are two eternal things: matter and an infinite number of individual souls. An account of the nature and the mutual relation of these two forms the main content of the system. The philosophy is atheistic, as it recognizes no God. What are called gods were no more than individual souls. Salvation, according to this system, is deliverance from the misery of transmigration, and is accomplished by the recognition of the absolute distinction between matter and the soul.

The Yoga system was founded by the grammarian Patanjali two or three centuries later. The system takes its name from a word meaning "union," etymologically related to the Latin *jugum*, "a yoke," and had for its aim, some think, union with God. Others say that it means "exertion" and refers to ascetic labors. Like Sankhya, it held to the distinction between spirit and matter, but unlike it, it held to faith in a personal God. The Yoga theory of salvation was practical rather than theoretical. It laid emphasis on asceticism and experience rather than upon knowledge. Fasting and other penances had long prevailed in India. The Yoga system took them up and enforced them with a philosophical explanation. The object of these practices was to isolate the soul from matter, that it might be united to God. To stand with mud caked in one's hair till birds nested in it, immovable because the soul was in ecstatic abstraction, was an extreme manifestation of the practice of Yoga principles.

Still another philosophy, a development of that of the Upanishads, passes under the name of Vedanta. It is chiefly influential in the form given to it by Cankara, a commentator on the Veda who lived about 800 A.D. It is built on the conception of Brahman, which is explained at times as Absolute Being, at times as the ground of being or soul of the universe, and at times as a personal God. According to this philosophy the

phenomenal world has no real existence, though a
kind of existence, like that of a dream, is accorded to it.
Dreams are for a time real, though there is no outward
reality to correspond to them. The bad dream of death
and rebirth will go on until each recognizes that there
is no real existence in the world except Brahman-Atman.
This knowledge is salvation. Passages in the Upanishads which speak of Brahman as a personal supreme
God were, Çankara taught, accommodations to the limi-
tations of human understanding. On account of such
limitation Brahman might be adored as Lord. This
was, however, a lower view than the other. There
was thus a distinction between a higher and a lower
Brahman. (The Sanskrit term *Brahman* and its deriva-
tives are employed in Indian religious literature in a
variety of ways. The term meant originally "to think
holy thoughts," "worship," "adore," etc. Then a
Brahman was a member of the priestly caste. The religion conducted by this priestly caste came in time to be
called *Brahmanism*—a term which in modern times is
sometimes used as a synonym of Hinduism. *Brahman*
was at times also employed to designate the object of
worship. In this sense it is another name for *Atman*, the
Soul of the universe.)

Opposed to this school is that of Ramanuja, who
lived about 1100 A.D. According to this system Brahman is not a metaphysical Absolute, but his essence is
intelligence. He is all-enveloping, all-knowing, all-
merciful. He is goodness and is unalterably opposed to
evil. Souls, far from being troubled dreams, constitute
the very body of Brahman. Ramanuja, like the others,
accepted the doctrine of death and rebirth. On his view

one could gain salvation from this by loving God, seeking him, adoring him. God would then mercifully grant the seeking soul release and permit it to share his own bliss.

There are three minor orthodox systems of philosophy, the Mimansa, which explains the value to be derived from Vedic ceremonies; the Nyaya, a system of logic and argumentation; and the Çarvakas, a materialistic philosophy which regards the soul as a kind of ferment produced by the elements of the body.

The influence of these philosophic sects upon Hinduism has been profound. One consequence of this is the widespread belief that salvation may be attained by contemplation of Brahman and intellectual absorption rather than by ethical endeavor and attainment of character. Religion thus becomes a matter of thought, and the life remains untouched.

157. Religion of the earlier law books.—Perhaps the earliest sources of information concerning the religion of the period just outlined are the law books of India, the sutras of Gautama, Āpastamba, and Manu. These are, if not the earliest, the most conservative sources. It is thought that the Institutes of Gautama may be as early as the rise of Buddhism. This work makes the Veda the source of sacred law; a king and a Brahman are to be deeply versed in the Veda. The work is a set of rules defining the duties of each of the four castes. Incidentally it ordains certain sacrifices to Agni, the Maruts, and to Prajāpati, the Vedic Creator.[1] Adoration of Rudra, Mitra, Indra, Agni, Soma, and all the gods is also prescribed.[2] Heaven is the reward of witnesses who speak the truth; hell, of those who lie.[3]

[1] Gautama, v, 10.   [2] *Ibid.*, xxvi.   [3] *Ibid.*, xiii, 7.

In the *Aphorisms* of Āpastamba there is more variation from Vedic worship. Offerings and hymns were to
be presented to "Earth, Air, Heaven, Sun, Moon, the
Constellations, Indra, Brihaspati, Prajāpati, and Brahman."[1] Brihaspati, "Lord of Prayer," is a deity of the
Rig-Veda, but Brahman, the universal substance of the
monistic philosophy of the Upanishads, has been taken
from later strata of thought. His presence is evidence
that even these law books were not untouched by the
speculations of the philosophers. In this work, as in
that of Gautama, the distinctions of caste are everywhere
presupposed, and are rigidly enforced. It is assumed
that the doctrine of transmigration and of *Karma* may
to some extent relieve men from the prison-house of
caste. Those who do well may in successive births enter
higher castes; those who do ill, if members of a noble
caste, will be born in the future in lower castes.[2] In the
Ordinances of Manu (about 200 B.C. ?) the influence
of philosophic speculation is still more pronounced.
While formally making the Veda the basis of legal practice, and enforcing the obligations of caste, many variations are introduced. The Lord, Creator of all things,
is Brahman. He is self-existent; he created all things,
even the gods; lightnings, thunderbolts, and Indra's
unbent bow are his work.[3] This one some declare to be
Agni, others Manu Prajāpati, some Indra, others breath,
others again the eternal Brahman.[4] The wicked man goes
not to one hell, but to twenty-one hells,[5] though in other
passages it is taught that sin may be punished by rebirths

[1] Apâstamba, II, 2, 4:4.
[2] *Ibid.*, II, 5, 11:10, 11.
[3] Manu, i.
[4] *Ibid.*, xii, 123.
[5] *Ibid.*, iv, 87 ff.

rather than in hells. Thus the crime of killing a beast will be punished by as many rebirths as there were hairs on the animal.[1] Salvation is, according to Manu, union with Brahman, but the thought as to how this union might be accomplished was evidently in a state of transition. At times it is said to be effected by study of the Veda, by vows, offerings, offspring, and sacrifice.[2] At other times it is said to be secured by meditation.[3] At times the rules of sacrifice are enforced with almost trivial literalness; at other times sacrifice is declared to be spiritual.[4] In such ways the old religion appears in the Laws of Manu to be in process of transformation.

In the estimation of the compilers of all these laws it was necessary to regard the Veda as the Hindu Bible, but the Veda to which they adhered was not always the same. Gautama built upon the Sama-Veda, Āpastamba and Manu upon the Yajur-Veda. The methods of treating Vedic texts and institutions differed, as the methods of interpretation applied to the Bible by modern Christian sects have sometimes differed. It was thus that one school could justify speculations which almost did away with Vedic gods.

158. The Mahābhārata, the great epic of India, is a work of much religious significance. It has profoundly affected large sections of Hindu religious life. Like the Gilgamesh Epic of the Babylonians and like the *Iliad*, it is not all from one hand or one age. It is a long conglomerate work, containing about eight times as much material as the *Iliad* and the *Odyssey* put together.[5]

[1] Manu, v, 38.
[2] *Ibid.*, ii, 28.
[3] *Ibid.*, iv, 87; vi, 79.
[4] *Ibid.*, iv, 22–28.
[5] Macdonell, *History of Sanskrit Literature*, p. 282.

This mass of material was a gradual growth, beginning as an epic not earlier than 400 B.C., and (with the exception of minor amplifications) completed about 400 A.D.[1] By 500 A.D. its contents were the same as at present.[2] The beginnings of the epic are based on stories that reach much farther back into Indian antiquity.

Even a brief outline of the epic story would occupy too much of our space. The scene is laid at Hastinā-pura, fifty-seven miles northeast of the modern Delhi. The region was called, from the ruling race, the land of the Kurus. Here two brothers ruled, Dhritarashtra and Pandu. Dhritarashtra being blind, Pandu reigned gloriously. Pandu had five sons, the chief of whom were called Yudhishthira, Bhima, and Arjuna; Dhritarashtra had a hundred sons. After Pandu's death Dhritarashtra took over the government, but made Yudhishthira the heir apparent. Soon the sons of Pandu were compelled by the hatred of their hundred cousins to flee the kingdom. They made their way to the king of Panchala, whose daughter, Draupadi, Arjuna won by a feat of arms. They soon formed an alliance with Krishna, the hero of the Yadavas, who from this time became the friend, adviser, and champion of the brothers, especially of the most warlike of them, Arjuna. Because of their powerful alliances their uncle now divided his kingdom with the five brothers in order to placate them. Through the machinations of one of their cousins a conflict was precipitated. With the account of this conflict the epic action begins. There were battles, victories, defeats, the loss of a kingdom by gambling, banishment,

[1] Hopkins, *The Great Epic of India* (New York, 1901), p. 398.
[2] Macdonell, *op. cit.*, p. 287.

and wars again. To the original story of war other stories have been added in the lapse of time. The different strata represent many varying religious conceptions. In parts of it the Vedic custom of animal sacrifice is described with approval, as in the case of the horse sacrifice in Book xii, quoted at the head of this chapter. In other parts philosophic speculations and anti-priestly utterances are enthusiastically set forth. The most significant religious feature of the epic is the way in which Krishna developed from an earthly hero to an incarnation of Vishnu. We learn from the Greek writer Megasthenes, who was in India about 300 B.C., that at that time the two gods Vishnu and Çiva were already very prominent, and that people were divided into Vishnuites and Çivaites. Çiva was originally the Vedic god Rudra, a god of storm and vengeance. Çiva means "auspicious" and was a euphemistic epithet given to Rudra. The new name seems gradually to have changed to some extent the character of the god, who became the auspicious deity to many, and vied with Vishnu, one of the Vedic sun-gods, for the devotion of the Indian peoples. The division into Vishnuites and Çivaites, noted by Megasthenes, became one of the most far-reaching distinctions in Hinduism. The *Mahābhārata* is one of the great products of a part of the Vishnuites.

Krishna was, it is thought, a real man, a nephew of Kamsa, king of the Yadavas. He was born at Mathura, between Delhi and Agra. An oracle warned Kamsa that a son of his brother would kill him; he therefore put his nephews to death as fast as they were born. Krishna's parents secretly conveyed their son to the other side of the river, where, with an older brother who had also escaped, he was brought up by a herdsman and his wife. The brothers became famous for their fights with demons and dragons. Their fame reached the uncle, who summoned them to his court, when the uncle was put out of the way, and Krishna became king. After many other victories he became the charioteer of the prince Arjuna, and took part in the wars which form the central theme of the *Mahābhārata.* Many years later internecine strife broke out among the Yadavas, when they killed one another to the last man, Krishna perishing with the others.

Why this hero became Vishnu incarnate we can now only conjecture. One plausible theory is that he was a religious reformer, who taught people to worship God under the name of Bhagavata, "the Adorable," and that he was afterward regarded as an incarnation of God, the Brahmans interpreting God as Vishnu.

159. The Bhagavad-Gita, or "Song of the Blessed," lends probability to the theory just mentioned. It is inserted as an episode in the sixth book of the *Mahābhārata.* It is placed at a point in the epic where Arjuna was compelled to lead the forces of the sons of Pandu against his cousins, the sons of Dhritarashtra, in fratricidal strife. Arjuna hesitated and Krishna proceeded to instruct him in the true doctrine of sacrifice—the sacrifice of the lower self to the higher self. The outward war of the brothers was thus made to interpret the inward war of the two natures in every man. The teaching is given in the form of a dialogue. Arjuna asked many questions, to which Krishna gave illuminating replies. In these replies the spiritual religion of the Krishna-Vishnuites is clearly set forth and at the same time is given practical application to the affairs of real life. Krishna, in the passage quoted at the beginning of this chapter, as the embodiment of Vishnu, is the all-embracing immanent deity.

In him pantheism is made personal. The great struggle of life is the struggle between one's lower and higher natures. In carrying on this struggle one should not flee arduous manly duty (not even the war which confronted Arjuna could be shirked), but one should stand up manfully to that which the immanent God laid upon him. The transmigration of the soul is assumed as an underlying philosophy all through the poem, and the philosophies of different schools find expression in different parts of the work.[1] The poem was in some form present in the epic, it is thought, as early as 250 B.C.,[2] though in parts it has been expanded since. Although an eclectic work, the *Bhagavad-Gita* is the finest ethical and religious product of non-Buddhistic Indian religious thought. Certain strains remind us of words of Jesus, as the following from Krishna:

> Who doeth all for Me; who findeth Me
> In all; adoreth always; loveth all
> Which I have made, and Me, for love's sole end,
> That man, Arjuna! unto me doth wend.[3]

Some modern Hindu sects and their admirers have had the *Bhagavad-Gita* printed in many translations, and circulate it as Bible societies circulate the New Testament

---

[1] These philosophies are outlined in sec. 156.

[2] So Garbe in the article "Bhagavad-Gita" in Hastings' *Encyclopaedia of Religion and Ethics*, II, 535 ff.

[3] *Bhagavad-Gita*, Sir Edwin Arnold's *The Song Celestial*, end of Book XI, pp. 128 ff

Such incarnations or descents (*avatāras*) of Vishnu and other deities are supposed in India to have occurred many times. These *avatāras* were sometimes in animal as well as in human form. Vishnu was believed to have manifested himself in this way nine times. Thus old cults were reinterpreted as ancient forms of later ones. In time it was supposed that whenever religion was in danger or iniquity was triumphant the god was incarnated to set things right. This view is expressed in the *Bhagavad-Gita*.

160. **The Ramayana** is another epic poem that has had great religious significance in India. In its present form it consists of seven books, and is said to have been composed by a poet named Valmiki. Jacobi has shown that the original kernel of the poem consisted of Books ii–vi, and there are reasons for supposing that these five books were composed before 400 B.C. and some think they antedate the beginning of Buddhism.[1] The scene of the *Ramayana* was the vicinity of Ayodhya, the modern Oudh, about 170 miles northwest of Benares. Daçaratha, king of Ayodhya, had three sons by three wives: Rama, son of Kauçalya; Bharata, son of Kaikeyi; and Lakshmana, son of Sumitra. Rama was declared the heir apparent, but Kaikeyi, anxious that her son Bharata should be the next king, persuaded Daçaratha to grant her any boon she might ask. Having obtained her request she asked that Bharata might be made heir apparent and Rama be banished for fourteen years. Rama was accompanied into exile by his wife Sita and his half-brother Lakshmana. All three lived happily in the forest of Dandaka. Upon the death of Daçaratha,

---

[1] Macdonell, *History of Sanskrit Literature*, p. 309.

Bharata refused to reign, but sought out Rama and implored him to return. When Rama refused, Bharata went back, placed a pair of Rama's shoes on the throne, and himself dispensed justice by their side. Rama continued to dwell in the forest, having various adventures, engaging in various wars, and making alliances with the monkeys. Once he was compelled to rescue his wife Sita from captors somewhat as King David did his.[1]

The original poem had to do with these adventures, but by the addition of Books i and vii Rama has been made an embodiment of Vishnu, so that the poem, like the *Mahābhārata*, is a glorification of Vishnu. In consequence of this, some Hindu sects regard the *Ramayana* as their Old Testament and use it for religious edification. Rama, the incarnate deity, is the type of the filial son; Sita, of the faithful wife; Lakshmana, of the devoted brother. The story of Rama and Sita is thought by some to have been heightened by an infusion of Vedic myth; others regard them as simply humanized mythical characters. The sects that reverence Rama are not as numerous as those that reverence Krishna.

161. The Institutes of Vishnu, not earlier than 200 A.D., is a law book that affords interesting evidence that such pantheistic theology as that of the *Bhagavad-Gita* was unable to expel the old ceremonies from any considerable section of even that part of Hindu life affected by the Vishnuite sects. In the *Institutes* it is still made obligatory to offer burnt offerings to Agni, Soma, Mitra, Varuna, Indra, and others;[2] such was the influence of Vedic scripture. Nevertheless in another

[1] Cf. I Sam. 30: 1–6.

[2] See *Sacred Books of the East*, VII, chap. lxvii, p. 3.

chapter the pantheistic doctrine of the all-embracing Vishnu is set forth.[1] While such sacrifices are inculcated in one chapter, another declares that a "Brahmana may beyond doubt obtain final emancipation by solely repeating (prayers), whether he perform any other religious observance or no; one who is benevolent towards all creatures (and does not slay them for sacrifice) is justly called a Brahmana (or one united to Brahman)."[2] Each of the twenty-one hells of Manu is declared to be the residence for a specified time of sinners who have not performed the proper penance,[3] but such sinners will be reborn, each as a different animal. One who steals vegetables containing leaves will become a peacock; one who steals a horse, a tiger; one who steals a woman, a bear,[4] etc. Nothing could better illustrate the confusion that arose from perpetuating the old, developing it at some points, and at the same time attempting to combine with it a philosophy which denied the validity of the old.

Many influences have in the course of centuries made themselves felt in Vishnuite thought and many sects have developed. This has been due in part to the philosophies described in section 156. Some of the sects stand for lofty ethics and real theism; some of them have degenerated to immorality. Those of the last-mentioned type are found most often among the sects that have substituted love of Krishna for intellectual contemplation of him. They frequently manifest this love by imitating his relations with his various wives. A good example of these is the sect of Vallabhācāris, named for its founder Vallabhācārya, who was born

[1] *Ibid.*, chap. xcviii.
[2] *Ibid.*, chap. IV, 21.
[3] *Ibid.*, chap. xliii.
[4] *Ibid.*, chap. xliv.

about 1478 A.D. The members of the sect work themselves up into great emotional manifestations, in which they frequently roll unconscious on the ground. They hold that love for Krishna should be manifested by imitating his devotion to his favorite concubine Rādhā, and, as they have abolished the rules of caste, many loose characters are found among them. Emotionalism thus naturally degenerates into license. The priests of the sect are regarded as representatives of Krishna on earth and claim and receive honors due to him. Women are taught that the highest bliss is secured to them and their families by receiving the caresses of Krishna's representatives. The priests also claim and receive the *jus primae noctis*.

162. **The Çivaites.**—Side by side with the evolution of the worship of Vishnu the worship of Çiva developed. As already noted, Çiva was Rudra under another name. Unlike Vishnu, Çiva is not believed to have become incarnate. Another divergence is found in the fact that with Çiva many goddesses appear to be associated. There is not only his wife Devi, but Gauri, the bright one; Sati, the faithful wife; Parvati, the daughter of the mountains; Kali, the black one; Bhairavi, the terrible; Karala, the horrible. Perhaps these were originally but various names of Devi. The conception of Çiva and his goddesses is not purely Aryan. Many elements from the aboriginal races of India have been gathered into it. To these goddesses the terrifying powers of the Vedic Rudra are now largely attributed, so that Çiva himself is more nearly the auspicious one. The most common emblem of Çiva is the phallus (*lingam*) and its female counterpart, the *yoni*. The philosophical affinities of Çivaism are with the dualistic philosophies

of Sankhya and Yoga rather than with the monistic systems. Though the Çivaite sects are not so numerous as the Vishnuite, there are several. To some of these Çiva is the "Great Yogin," who, besmeared with ashes and with matted hair, sits under the Pipa-tree, and who through meditation has become a god. Such worshipers imitate him. Megasthenes, when in India, saw another side to Çiva, whom he identified with the Greek Dionysos

In Çiva as worshiped by the Çakta sect the baser side of Vedic religion—that element that worshiped Soma—has survived and been reinforced by other elements drawn from aboriginal Indian cults. Man is recognized as a creature of passions, and it is held that it is by means of these passions that he is to cross the region of darkness to union with Civa. Passion is poison, but poison can be killed only by poison. Hence the five things that have caused man's ruin—wine, flesh, fish, mystic gesticulations, and sexual indulgence—are employed by them in religious orgies. In this sect the *çakti*, or female principle, assumes the leading place.

163. The triad.—Although there is much rivalry between the worshipers of Vishnu and of Çiva, this rivalry is not universal. In the south of India the two are often coupled together under the name Hari-Hara and worshiped as one god. In other places their temples are often in the same sacred inclosure. In certain circles Brahman was added, and the three adored as a triad. Thus Kalidasa, the Shakespeare of India, sang:

> In those three persons the one God was shown—
> Each first in place, each last—not one alone;
> Of Çiva, Vishnu, Brahma,[1] each may be
> First, second, third, among the Blessed Three.

[1] Another spelling of Brahman.

It was by the formation of a triad that certain thinkers reconciled the rival claims of various sects.

164. Temples.—While the Vedic religion had no permanent holy places, Hinduism has long erected temples all over India. Benares, the Jerusalem of India, has the largest number. There are at least two thousand temples there, not counting smaller shrines. The temples vary greatly in size and splendor.[1] Each contains one or more idols, except temples of Çiva, whose emblem is the *lingam*. The larger temples support extensive priesthoods as well as bands of musicians and dancing girls. In temples where there are idols it is the duty of the priests to awaken them each morning, make their toilets, burn incense before them, and offer them food. The number of temples and shrines is continually increasing. The scene of some unusual event, or the abode of some person accounted sacred, is sufficient to mark out a spot for a shrine. There is not an object in heaven or on earth that the Indian is not prepared to worship. He holds all life sacred, plant as well as animal. All living things are venerated, but the cow is regarded as most sacred. She typifies the all-yielding earth, and is the chief source of nourishment of every Hindu. The ox is the indispensable agent of agricultural labor. Images of the typical cow of plenty are sold in the bazaars and bought as objects of reverence, and sacred cows are found in many temples.

165. The Sikhs.—Early in the fifteenth century a reformer, Kabir by name, assailed idolatry and broke away from all authority, whether Hindu or Mohammedan. His followers were to conform to no rites. Several

[1] For pictures of some of these, see V. A. Smith, *Early History of India*, pp. 428, 465.

sects trace their spiritual ancestry to him. Of these the
Kabir Panthis regard Kabir as a god. The most important of them are, however, the Sikhs, founded toward
the end of the fifteenth century by Nanak, a professed
follower of Kabir. Under the influence of Islam he
endeavored to purge Vishnuism of superstition. He
taught a monotheistic faith. God is Supreme Lord by
whatever name he is called. Deliverance from the
round of rebirths and reabsorption into God was, he held,
an act of free grace, communicated by means of a formula
which could be taught only by one who stood in apostolic
succession to Kabir and himself. A successor, Arjun,
compiled the Granth, or Sikh Bible. It contains utterances of Kabir, Nanak, and of many of the older Hindu
saints, to which Arjun added some of his own. The
Sikhs became a wealthy and militant community, which
played an important part in Amritsar in the eighteenth
and nineteenth centuries. The fourth in succession
from Nanak built a temple at Amritsar.

166. Modern Hindu reforms.—The impact of Christianity and Western civilization upon India has led to
at least two noteworthy efforts to adjust Hinduism to
modern conditions. The earliest of these efforts is
the Brahma Samaj (Society of God), founded in 1828
by Ram Mohan Ray, a distinguished, broad-minded
Brahman. It has had since his death two other distinguished leaders, Debendra Nath Tagore and Keshab
Chandra Sen. As each of these leaders stood for a somewhat different religious position, and as there were some
members of the society who, at each new departure, preferred the older view, the Brahma Samaj is now composed
of three wings. All branches of it agree that God is

a personal being, that he never became incarnate, that he hears and answers prayer, that he is to be worshiped only in spiritual ways, that men of all castes may worship him acceptably, that repentance and cessation from sin are the only way to forgiveness and salvation, and that nature and intuition are the sources of the knowledge of God, no book being authoritative. The branch of it led by Keshab Chandra Sen is known as the "New Dispensation Samaj." It adds to the articles already mentioned belief that the soul is immortal; that God is a Trinity, Father, Son, and Spirit; that God is Mother as well as Father; that God speaks through inspired men as well as through nature and intuition; that Brahmanism is a universal religion; and that the Brahma Samaj is God's latest dispensation and its missionaries his apostles. In 1901 there were but 4,050 members in all three branches of the society.

The Arya Samaj (Society of the Noble) was founded in 1875 by Mul Sankar, better known as Swami Dayā-nand Sarasvati, who was born as a member of the Çiva cult, broke away from it for the Vedanta philosophy, and finally became a religious reformer on the basis of the Sankhya-Yoga philosophies. Dayānand Sarasvati had come in contact with modern civilization through many channels, and endeavored to reform Hinduism to meet the conditions of modern life. He taught belief in a personal God, who is all-truth, all-knowledge, incor-poreal, almighty, just, merciful, unbegotten, unchange-able, all-pervading, and the cause of the universe. The Vedas are the books of true knowledge; one should always be ready to accept truth; all ought to be treated with love, justice, and in disregard of their merits;

ignorance should be dispelled; and everyone should regard his prosperity as included in that of others. His great cry was "back to the Vedas." He professed to derive all his teaching from them, but the method of interpretation by which he extracted the true doctrine and put aside all that contradicted it was peculiarly his own. It conformed neither to Hindu canons of interpretation nor to those of scientific exegesis. According to him salvation was to be accomplished by effort. No distinctions of caste are regarded valid.

It is estimated that the adherents of the Arya Samaj now number about 100,000. The Samaj is now divided into a "cultured" and a conservative party. The former eats meat and fosters modern education, maintaining a creditable college at Lahore; the latter is vegetarian, and adheres to the ancient ideas of education.

167. Summary.—Hinduism, which is still the religion of some 200,000,000 people, presents almost endless variety of faith and practice. These diversities have been created by the various influences, internal and external, that have swept over India since the Vedic age. It has no rallying-point; it stands for no one great idea or ideal. Some of its ideas are beautiful; many of its ideals noble; but in general it lacks consistency and coherency. In most of its varied manifestations Hinduism suffers by the divorce of religion from life. Salvation is to be attained by intellectual absorption or by some ritual acts. That it should affect conduct most of the systems deny or ignore.[1] The ideals of the

---

[1] The separation between religion and morals is implied in chap. vi of the *Advanced Textbook of Hindu Religion and Ethics* used in the Central Hindu College at Benares, where emphasis is also laid upon religion as a contemplation of God. See pp. 221-37.

Bhagavad-Gita are noble, but Krishna as he is worshiped in Bengal fosters prostitution in his temples, while the cult of Çiva often degenerates to immoral orgies. For the most part Hinduism is ethically impotent and many of her holy men are gross.

SUPPLEMENTARY READING

CLASS A

On sec. 155: cf. V. A. Smith, *Early History of India, Including the Campaigns of Alexander* (Oxford, 1914), and A. A. Macdonell, *India's Past* (Oxford, 1927).

On secs. 156, 160: Hopkins, *Religions of India*, chap. xiv; F. Max Muller, *The Six Systems of Indian Philosophy* (New York, 1899).

On secs. 157, 159: Hopkins, *The Great Epic of India* (New York, 1901); or J. C. Oman, *Indian Epics, the Ramayana and Mahābhārata* (London, 1906); and the translations in Dutt, *Mahābhārata, The Epic of Ancient India* (London, 1899).

On sec. 158: Sir Edwin Arnold, *The Song Celestial* (Boston, 1909), and Franklin Edgerton, *The Bhagavad Gita* (Chicago, 1925).

On sec. 161: Hopkins, *The Great Epic of India*, chap. iii; or G. F. Moore, *History of Religions*, I, chap. xiii; J. E. Carpenter, *Theism in Mediaeval India* (London, 1921).

On secs. 162–65: cf. Jacobi, "Brahmanism" in Hastings' *Encyclopaedia of Religion and Ethics*, II; or Nicoll Macnicol, *Indian Theism* (Oxford University Press, 1915), chaps. vii–xi; or M. Monier-Williams, *Hinduism* (14th ed., London, 1901), chaps. vii–xii; J. E. Carpenter, *Theism in Mediaeval India* (London, 1921).

On sec. 166: cf. "Brahma Samaj" and "Arya Samaj" in Hastings' *Encyclopaedia of Religion and Ethics*, II.

CLASS B

G. F. Moore, *History of Religions*, I, chaps. xiii–xv.

CHAPTER XI

THE RELIGIONS OF CHINA

Always and in everything let there be reverence; with the deportment grave as when one is thinking (deeply) and with speech composed and definite.—*Lî Kî*, I, i, 1¹.

If a man observe the rules of propriety, he is in a condition of security; if he do not, he is in one of danger.—*Lî Kî*, I, i, 6²⁴.

That which I do not wish others to put upon me, I also wish not to put upon others.—CONFUCIUS, *Analects*, Book V.

The Way (Tao) that can be trodden is not the enduring and unchanging Way (Tao). The name that can be named is not the enduring and unchanging name.—*Tao Teh Ching*, I, 1, 1.

> Always without desire we must be found,
> If its deep mystery we would sound;
> But if desire always within us be,
> Its outer fringe is all that we shall see.
> > —*Tao Teh Ching*, I, 1, 3.

The highest excellence is like that of water. The excellence of water appears in its benefiting all things, and in its occupying, without striving (to the contrary), the low place which all men dislike. Hence (its way) is near to (that of) the Tao.—*Tao Teh Ching*, I, 8, 1.

168. The land, people, and history.—The cradle of Chinese civilization appears to have been the provinces of Shan-si and Shen-si in Northwest China—provinces watered by the Hwang-ho or Yellow River. The greater portion of these provinces lies between 35° and 40° north latitude; they possess a dry and bracing climate.   Millet grows here, as do apples, pears, grapes, melons, and walnuts.   Sheep and cattle are raised, and the two-humped camel furnishes transportation.   The date at which this civilization developed is uncertain. Chinese chronographers have transmitted a list of dynasties that, added end to end, take us back to 2850 B.C.[1] and tell us of long-lived mythological beings who ruled before this time and who invented the chief features of civilization.   Some scholars count all this material mythological down to about the tenth century B.C.,[2] though the lengths of the various reigns as given in the lists are not impossibly long.   The material is nevertheless most uncertain before 2258 B.C., when the Hia dynasty ascended the throne.   It is said to have ruled until 1766 B.C., when it was displaced by the Shang or Yin dynasty, which is said to have held the scepter until 1122 B.C.   As both Babylonian and Egyptian sources exaggerate the lengths of the reigns of the early rulers of those countries, it is quite possible that the Chinese sources do the same.   It may well be, therefore, that the beginnings of its civilization do not extend farther back than 2500 B.C.

The Chinese have no traditions concerning the entrance of their ancestors into the country.   Efforts have been made by some scholars to connect them with the Sumerians of Babylonia,[3] or the Elamites,[4] but the efforts are far from convincing.   It is probable that the

[1] See F. Hirth, *Ancient History of China* (New York, 1911), pp. 7 and 329.

[2] So H. A. Giles, *History of Chinese Literature* (New York, 1901).

[3] C. J. Ball, *Sumerian and Chinese* (Oxford, 1914).

[4] So Lacouperie; cf. Hirth, *op. cit.*, pp. 14 ff.

Chinese developed out of the Mongolian stock in the region where they still live.

The Shang dynasty was followed by the imperial Chow dynasty, 1122–249 B.C. During this period China, which had been extended considerably beyond its original borders, became a feudal state, whose nominal suzerains were, after about 700 B.C., often unable to control the nobles of its component parts. Nevertheless, by the sixth century B.C., society was tolerably stable and secure, people lived in well-built houses, dressed in silk and homespun, wore leather shoes, carried umbrellas, sat on chairs, used tables, rode in carts and chariots, ate their food from plates and dishes of pottery, and measured time by a sundial.[1]

The Chow dynasty was overthrown by the Prince of Tsin, the most northwesterly province of China, who took the name of Shi Hwang-ti, or "first emperor." He built the Great Wall to protect the country from incursions of Tartars on the north, and so impressed his influence upon the country that, though his dynasty fell in 205 B.C., the name of his province Tsin has ever since been applied to the whole country. It is the original of our English name China. Since its fall twenty-one dynasties have ruled in China, the last of which, the Tsing dynasty, fell in 1912.

The dominant race first pushed its way eastward along the Yellow River to the sea, through the provinces of Shan-si, Ho-nan, and Shan-tung, then southward to the Yang-tsze-kiang, then on to the borders of India. In the course of the centuries political ascendency has

[1] Cf. Giles, *op. cit.*, p. 5.

also been extended over Manchuria, Mongolia, Eastern Turkestan, and Tibet.

169. The primitive popular religion.—There is abundant evidence that when the Chinese civilization developed, the people were in that stage of evolution known as animistic, and believed every object to be the abode of a spirit.   Indeed, this is the belief of the common people of China at the present time.   Chinese tradition accounts for the origin of the universe by generation from two souls or breaths called *Yang* and *Yin*, "the *Yang* representing light, warmth, productivity, and life, also the heavens from which all these good things emanate; and the *Yin* being associated with darkness, cold, death, and the earth.   The *Yang* is subdivided into an indefinite number of good souls or spirits called *shen*, the *Yin* into particles or evil spirits called *kwei*, or specters; it is these *shen* and *kwei* which animate every being and every thing.   It is they which constitute the soul of man.   His *shen*, also called *hwan*, immaterial, ethereal, like heaven itself, from which it emanates, constitutes his intellect and the finer parts of his character, his virtues, while his *kwei*, or *poh*, is thought to represent his less refined qualities, his passions, vices, they being borrowed from the material earth.   Birth consists in the infusion of these souls; death in their departure, the *shen* returning to *Yang* or heaven, the *kwei* to the *Yin* or earth."[1]   The world is crowded with *shen* and *kwei*. The air swarms with evil spirits innumerable.   They infest public roads, especially at night, play all sorts of pranks upon people, and often kill them.   Against these, men defend themselves with drums, gongs, kettles, bows,

[1] J. J. M. DeGroot, *Religion of the Chinese* (New York, 1910), p. 7.

spears, and flaming torches. "The gods are *shen* who animate heaven, sun, moon, the stars, wind, rain, clouds, thunder, fire, the earth, seas, mountains, rivers, rocks, stones, animals, and plants. To these there have been added from time immemorial the souls of deceased men, especially of one's ancestors. To this innumerable company sacrifices of food and animals have been and still are offered. As among other animistic peoples, fear of the *kwei* or demons appears to be quite as potent as fear of the gods and ancestors. However, the Chinese believe that on the whole the *Yang* is above the *Yin* as the heaven is above the earth.

As there was among men a chief ruler, so among the spirits there was a Shang-ti or supreme ruler. Some scholars translate this "God" and hold that the Chinese had attained monotheism at a very early time. As Shun, the second of China's historic kings (2258–2206 B.C.), is said by the *Shu King*[1] to have sacrificed to Shang-ti, the Chinese would have attained monotheism at an early date, were the monotheistic claim true. Shun, at the time he sacrificed to Shang-ti, sacrificed also to six honored spirits, as well as to hills and rivers. He was accordingly not a monotheist. The people generally never worship Shang-ti so far as we know, and where Shang-ti is mentioned in the *Shu King* it is usually associated with Heaven,[2] a spirit that seems equally powerful with Shang-ti. Although in one passage the impartation of moral ideas to men is attributed to Shang-ti,[3] he is after all but a shadowy ruler, whose

[1] *Sacred Books of the East*, III, 39.

[2] *Ibid.*, pp. 126, 161, 165.

[3] *Ibid.*, p. 88.

importance is soon overshadowed by Heaven.[1] In one
passage even the earthly monarch is associated with
him. No Chinese monotheism can be made out.

170. **The state religion** of China is based on the
five canonical books, or the books which Confucius
rescued from the past and transmitted to posterity.
These are the *Shu Ching*, or book of history, the *Shi
Ching*, or book of odes, *Ch'un Ch'iu*, or spring and autumn
annals, the *Yî Ching*, or book of changes, a book of fanci-
ful state philosophy deducted from a system of linear anagrams, and the *Lî Kî*, or book of rites. In its later
form the state religion was also influenced by the Confucian classics, which were collected by later disciples and
include the works of Mencius. The emperor was thought
to be the son of Heaven, and the state religion was a
worship of Heaven, Earth, and the spirits of the seasons,
winds, sun, moon, and rivers, on which the prosperity of
the empire depends. Heaven is apparently not regarded
as a personal being, but rather as an ethical pattern.
Although frequently spoken of in a monotheistic fashion, the worship of Heaven is not monotheism. Heaven
is itself believed to be composed of numerous spirits,
and numerous spirits are worshiped in connection with it.
The state religion is a kind of polydemonism. Frequently at the annual worship of Heaven sacrifices have
been offered to the founders of dynasties, and to the
spirit of the sovereign's predecessor, as well as to the
spirits of the earth, rivers, etc.

The emperor was, until the establishment of the
republic in 1912, the religious head of the nation. He
could enlarge the pantheon by increasing the number of

[1] *Sacred Books of the East*, III, 99.

spirits that were to be venerated, or reduce its size. Upon the proper performance of his religious duties the prosperity of the whole empire was supposed to depend. It was his exclusive right to worship Heaven. The performance of such worship on the part of local governors was regarded as a declaration of rebellion. The local governors each in like manner worshiped the spirits of their respective provinces. The imperial sacrifices to Heaven were offered in the southern suburb of the capital; those to Earth, in the northern. The ceremonies varied in different dynasties. The *Li Ki* states[1] that the offering to Heaven was made on the grand altar with a blazing fire of wood; that to Earth, by burying the victim in the great mound. In both cases the victim was red. By burying a sheep and a pig at the altar of Great Brightness they sacrificed to the seasons. With similar victims they sacrificed to the spirits of heat and cold, sun, moon, stars, winds, flood, rain, mountains, valleys, forests, streams, etc. The spirits worshiped were not all imaginary; many of them were ancestors of the sovereigns and princes. Thus according to the *Li Ki* kings and feudal princes erected temples to father, grandfather, great-grandfather, great-great-grandfather. and remote ancestors. Each temple had a raised altar surrounded by an open area. In all of these, sacrifices were offered every month. There were two other temples for more remote ancestors to which the tablets of the earlier princes of the line were gradually removed. At these only the seasonal sacrifices were offered.[2]

[1] *Ibid.*, XXVIII, 202 f

[2] *Ibid.*, XXVIII, 204 f

The Chinese appear to have had no way of securing divine oracles, but there were many forms of divination practiced by emperors and feudal princes. One very ancient method has come down to us in the *Yi King*, or book of changes. The anagrams appear to us about as meaningless as they could well be, but, if they were originally figures made by the falling of stalks or straws of different lengths, one can see why at the dawn of history they may have been thought to foreshadow coming events.

The state religion was perpetuated down to the fall of the Manchu dynasty, so that it was possible for men now living to witness a form of worship the beginnings of which reach back far into the Bronze Age. The altar to Heaven, constructed of three terraces of white marble in an inclosure containing appropriate buildings for the preservation of tablets and for the convenience of the emperor, is entirely open to the sky.[1] It is situated on the south of Peking about three miles from the royal palace in a park of some five hundred acres surrounded by a brick wall fifteen feet high. The altar itself, together with the buildings mentioned, is surrounded by an inner wall. Here on the morning of the winter solstice the emperor, having passed the night in the Hall of Abstinence near the altar, in the gray dawn ascended the altar, prostrated himself in the prescribed manner and presented prayers to Heaven, sun, moon, stars, and planets, and to his ancestors. Tablets to all these had been placed upon altars appropriately erected on the different terraces, while in a great furnace, near

[1] See Henry Blodget's full description in the *Journal of the American Oriental Society*, XX, 58–6c

by, a sacrificial holocaust was burned. The altar to
Earth is at the north of the city in a park of about three
hundred acres two miles from the imperial palace. It
is square and built in two terraces of dark-colored marble.
In the dawn of the day of the summer solstice the
emperor here in a similar way worshiped Earth, two
mountains, three hills, four seas, and four great rivers.
Both services were accompanied by music, and are said
to have been simple and invested with a high degree of
reverence and solemnity.

171. **Confucius and Confucianism.**—The most influential man in the whole history of China is K⁣ung-
futze, or "master K⁣ung," whose name is Latinized as
Confucius. He was born in 551 B.C. in the little state of
Lu in the territory of the modern province of Shan-tung.
Little is known of his early life. "At the age of fifteen
he bent his mind to learning." When he was nineteen
he married, but the marriage was not a happy one,
and he afterward divorced his wife. The necessity of
supporting his family (his wife bore him a son) led him
to accept the office of keeper of the stores of grain, but at
twenty-two he was released from the cares of office and
became a teacher—an occupation in which he passed
the rest of his life. In teaching he found time to study.
He made the past, its history, records, and institutions,
the object of his loving research. The state with its
order and glory filled him with admiration. To order
it, as well as the lives of its citizens, aright was the aim
of his teaching. He thus became a great moral and
political philosopher. By thirty he "stood firm," he
tells us; that is, he had formed opinions of his own.
About this time his fame so increased that many noble

youths enrolled themselves as his pupils. As years passed, his pupils increased; at one time their number is said to have been three thousand. The life of Confucius fell in the feudal period, at a time when the central power found it difficult to maintain its authority over strong nobles.

In 517 B.C. Confucius visited the city of Lu, the capital of the empire, where he was able to see the altars on which Heaven and Earth were worshiped, and where he could inquire more carefully into the history and precedents of the Chow dynasty. At Lu he is said to have had an interview with Lao-tze, China's other great sage, who was then an old man. In 516 Confucius followed his sovereign into exile in the neighboring state of Ts'i, but, finding that he could be of little service, he returned to Lu the next year. By the year 500 some degree of order was restored and Confucius was appointed ruler of the town of Chang-tu, where he soon effected great reforms. From this post he became superintendent of public works and later minister of crime. In the first office he effected great improvements in agriculture; in the second his admirers say that he abolished crime. Nevertheless, in 495 he abandoned office because his sovereign did not live up to his high ideals. The next thirteen years were spent by Confucius in wandering from state to state, accompanied by a group of pupils. He hoped to find a prince who would listen to his counsels, but hoped in vain. In 483 B.C. he returned to the state of Lu, but did not re-enter public life. He died in 478 B.C.

Confucius left behind him a group of devoted pupils and four of the five canonical books, which he had collected and edited. His pupils collected a book of memorabilia of their master known as the *Lun Yu* or *Analects*. It is arranged in twenty short books or chapters, and records in a disconnected way many sayings of the master. One book of the *Analects*, the tenth, is occupied with a description of the personal appearance, dress, and manners of Confucius. We learn from this that he was a strict formalist in all things, careful even as to the posture in which he lay in bed!

Confucius was in no sense a religious reformer. To the end his religion was the religion of his ancestors. The remote past was to him a golden age, and his purpose was to perpetuate some of its golden characteristics. He aimed to establish a high code of morals and a pure and efficient civil administration. His noblest ethical utterance is the negative form of the Golden Rule quoted at the head of this chapter. While on the whole his precepts inculcate a high order of morality, they apply, like those of the biblical Book of Proverbs, to the conduct of practical affairs and constitute neither a system of philosophy nor a system of theology. In matters of civil administration Confucius had little opportunity to gain practical experience; he was from force of circumstances a theorist, but his insight into administrative affairs was keen and his maxims sound.[1]

A hundred years after Confucius died Mencius (Meng Tze) was born. He was a disciple of Confucius, and did much to focus the influence of the earlier teacher. Mencius laid less stress than his master upon sacrifices and the worship of Heaven and more on morals. The great emperor, Shi-Hwang-ti, of the Tsin dynasty,

[1] See *Analects*, Book XIII.

endeavored toward the close of the third century B.C. to uproot Confucianism. He made a systematic effort to destroy all Confucian books, but was fortunately not completely successful. It was natural that with the accession of the Han dynasty, 205 B.C., there should be a reaction in favor of Confucius, and since that time he has grown steadily in favor of the state. His teaching has been expounded and developed by three great teachers, the last and greatest of whom was Chu Hsi, who lived from 1130 to 1200 A.D. In 1 A.D. Confucius was canonized as "Duke Ni, the all complete and illustrious." In 57 A.D. it was ordered that sacrifices should be offered to him. In 492 A.D. he was styled "the venerable Ni, the accomplished Sage." In 609 a temple was erected to him at every seat of learning. In 659 he was styled "K'ung, the ancient Teacher, the perfect Sage." In 1907 the late Empress Dowager raised him to the first grade of worship,[1] ranking him with Shang-ti. In 1915 Yuan Shi Kai made Confucianism once more the religion of the state.

The philosophy of the Confucian school, which has had much influence, not only in China, but in Japan, is that the ruling principle of heaven and earth is virtue. "Order is Heaven's only law." It is relationship to others in an orderly series which gives value to the individual. Order forms the kosmos; without it there is chaos and evil. A man exists only for society; position is more important than personality. In the state the emperor is the pivot; in the family, the father. But even the emperor rules by virtue; if this be want-

[1] Cf. W. E. Soothill, *The Three Religions of China* (London, 1913), p. 34.

ing, he is only a usurper, and rebellion against him is justified.

172. Lao-tze and Taoism.—Lao-tze or Laocius, the second of China's great sages in importance, was born in 604 B.C. He is said to have lived to the ripe old age of eighty years. He was for some years keeper of the archives of the imperial court. In his old age Lao-tze, on account of the signs of decay in the state, resigned his position and set out for the West to retire from the world. When he reached the frontier one of his disciples, it is said, asked him to write a book, whereupon he wrote the *Tao Teh Ching*. This story comprises all that we know of the life of Lao-tze, and, as this comes from a writer many centuries later, its truth is involved in considerable doubt. Nevertheless the *Tao Teh Ching* gives us the oldest known form of the teachings of Lao-tze.

In the system of Lao-tze the great and adorable thing is called Tao, a word that is practically untranslatable. Perhaps "Nature" is its nearest equivalent in English, though it has been rendered "Way," "Power," "Reason," and even "God." To Lao-tze the Tao seemed the inexpressible Infinite. Here are some of his sayings about it:

The Tao that can be trodden is not the enduring and unchanging Tao.[1]

He who knows the Tao does not care to speak about it; he who is ever ready to speak about it does not know it.[2]

How pure and still the Tao is, as if it would ever so continue! I do not know whose son it is. It might appear to have been before Shang-ti.[3]

[1] *Tao Teh Ching* (*Sacred Books of the East*, XXXIX), 1:1.
[2] *Ibid.*, 56:1.   [3] *Ibid.*, 4:3.

Those who know the Tao are not extensively learned; the extensively learned do not know it.[1]

> The grandest forms of active force
> From Tao come, their only source.
> Who can of Tao the nature tell?
> Our sight it flies, our touch as well.
> Eluding sight, eluding touch,
> The forms of things all in it crouch;
> Eluding touch, eluding sight,
> There are their semblances, all right.
> Profound it is, dark and obscure;
> Things' essences all there endure.
> Those essences the truth enfold
> Of what, when seen, shall then be told.[2]

The relation of the Tao to all the world is like that of the great rivers and seas to the streams from the valleys.[3]

All-pervading is the great Tao! It may be found on the left hand and on the right.[4]

Such was Lao-tze's conception of the great Absolute into harmony with which man should try to come. The method of attaining this harmony was in his view a self-humiliating quietism. Thus he says:

When its [the Tao's] work is accomplished, it does not claim the name of having done it. . . . . Hence the sage is able in the same way to accomplish his great achievements. It is through his not making himself great that he can accomplish them.[5]

He who is satisfied with his lot is rich.[6]

He [the sage] is free from display, and therefore he shines; from self-assertion, and therefore he is distinguished; from self-boasting, and therefore his merit is acknowledged; from self-complacency, and therefore he acquires superiority.[7]

[1] *Tao Teh Ching* (*Sacred Books of the East*, XXXIX), 81:1.
[2] *Ibid.*, 21.   [4] *Ibid.*, 34:1.   [6] *Ibid.*, 33:1.
[3] *Ibid.*, 32:5.   [5] *Ibid.*, 34:2, 3.   [7] *Ibid.*, 22:2.

Who knows how white attracts,
Yet always keeps himself within black's shade,
The pattern of humility displayed,
Displayed in view of all beneath the sky;
He in the unchanging excellence arrayed,
Endless return to man's first estate has made.

Who knows how glory shines,
Yet loves disgrace, nor e'er for it is pale;
Behold his presence in a spacious vale,
To which men come from all beneath the sky.
The unchanging excellence completes its tale;
The simple infant man in him we hail.[1]

These quotations, like the two from the *Tao Teh King* which stand at the head of this chapter, prove that in a quietistic self-effacement and lack of desire Lao-tze found the key to salvation. Like Confucius, he turned his face toward the past. The golden age of mankind's infancy was to him the goal. The last poetical quotation made above clearly expresses this. To one who attained this "comes a kingliness of character; and he who is king-like goes on to be heaven-like. In that likeness to heaven he possesses the Tao. Possessed of the Tao he endures long."[2] Here we have presented both the primitive Taoist idea of salvation and the method of its attainment. This attitude led Lao-tze in practical ethics to take higher ground than Confucius. His general principle was: "The soft overcomes the hard; and the weak, the strong."[3] He once said: "I have three precious things that I prize and hold fast. The first is gentleness; the second is economy; and the third is shrinking from taking precedence of others."[4]

[1] *Ibid.*, 28:1.

[2] *Ibid.*, 16:2.

[3] *Ibid.*, 36:2; cf. 43:1.

[4] *Ibid.*, 67:2.

Again: "It is the way of the Tao . . . . to consider what is small as great, and a few as many; and to recompense injury with kindness."[1] He thus rose almost to the gospel rule: "Do good to them that hate you,"[2] and far surpassed Confucius' negative form of the Golden Rule.

As Confucius had his Mencius, so Lao-tze had a faithful disciple and interpreter in Kwang-tze, who was a contemporary of Mencius. Kwang-tze possessed one of the acutest minds China has produced, and devoted all his energies to the exposition and enforcement of the teachings of Lao-tze. His works rank next in importance to the *Tao Teh King* in the literature of Taoism.[3] He "was unable to persuade the practical Chinese nation that by doing nothing all things would be done."

Kwang-tze's method was to unite opposites. Thus he says: "If the affirmation be according to reality of the fact, it is certainly different from the denial of it—there can be no dispute about that. If the assertion of an opinion be correct, it is certainly different from its rejection—neither can there be any dispute about that. Let us forget the lapse of time; let us forget the conflict of opinions. Let us make our appeal to the infinite, and take up our position there."[4] His idea seems to have been that by "ignoring the existence of contraries we are embraced in the obliterating unity of God."[5] His

---

[1] *Tao Teh Ching* (*Sacred Books of the East*, XXXIX), 63:1.

[2] Luke 6:27.

[3] They are translated by Legge in the *Sacred Books of the East*, XXXIX and XL.

[4] See *Sacred Books of the East*, XXXIX, 196.

[5] See H. A. Giles, *History of Chinese Literature* (New York, 1901), p. 62.

description of the Tao is in full accord with that of his great teacher, though with greater philosophical power he endeavored to reach a mystical union with it.

After Kwang-tze, Taoism degenerated into the bizarre. This degeneration is said to have been greatly accelerated by Chang Tao Ling, born in 34 A.D., whose descendants are still, so to speak, Taoist popes in China. Taoists climb ladders of swords, seek for the elixir of immortality, and are dabblers in the occult. It adds each year fresh saints or gods to the pantheon, and fosters the worship of those spirits and ancestors in which the Chinese have always believed. The many secret societies of China are for the most part Taoist. The Boxer organization was one of these. Its tragic madness is still of recent memory.[1]

173. **Buddhism** in its northern form, Mahayana Buddhism, was introduced into China in the reign of Ming Ti, otherwise called Yung P'ing, 58–76 A.D., though a knowledge of it had reached China through her trade with Nepal and India long before. For two and a half centuries after its introduction into the country no Chinese were permitted to become monks. After this condition was removed the religion rapidly spread. In the fifth, sixth, and seventh centuries Fa Hien, Hieun Tsang, and I Tsin made pilgrimages to India and wrote accounts of what they saw. Buddhistic works were translated into Chinese. In 525 A.D. it is said that Boddhidharma, the twenty-eighth in the list of Buddha's successors, left his native land and migrated to China, where he became a kind of patriarch of Chinese Buddhism.

[1] W. E. Soothill, *The Three Religions of China* (London, 1913), p. 82.

Confucianism was from the beginning opposed to Buddhism. The Buddhistic order of monks tended to loose the bonds of the family and the state, on which Confucianism had always laid great stress. Finally in the eighth century A.D. a state persecution of Buddhists compelled more than 12,000 monks to return to secular life. Another persecution in the ninth century destroyed 4,600 monasteries and relegated to secular life 260,000 monks and nuns. Still another in the tenth century closed 30,000 temples. Buddhism was not, however, exterminated. There were many who found in it that which met a spiritual need.

Chinese Buddhism is closely akin to that of Tibet. There is the same belief in Boddhisattwas and in the efficacy of prayer. Tibetan Buddhism has taken up the Hindu notion of hell and heaven as temporary abodes between states of incarnation. The idea of transmigration has never taken a deep root in China. It is somewhat foreign to the national genius. The Buddhistic doctrines of heaven and hell have, however, given the Chinese an eschatology which neither Confucianism nor Taoism supplied.

The order of monks has in China degenerated into a professional clergy, who drone long invocations, twirl their beads, and keep the lamp burning before the shrine of Buddha. Invocation and ceremonial have taken the place of meditation and ethical culture as a means of salvation, and the souls of the departed are believed to gain release from hell only through the prayers of the priest, for which he receives a good fee.[1]

[1] W. E. Soothill, *The Three Religions of China*, pp. 105 ff.

174. The resultant religion.—Confucianism, Taoism, and Buddhism are not mutually exclusive religions, and in China millions think it better to gain what benefits they may from being on good terms with all three. One does not cease to be a devotee of one religion by appropriating the benefits of another. The older religions, especially Taoism, have accordingly been modified to some extent by Buddhism. The popular conception of the divine is still the primitive polydemonism. In every household new spirits are continually worshiped as ancestors take their place among the departed. The moral ideals of the early Chinese canonical books are high, and these were advanced by the Confucian and Taoist schools. From the earliest times of which there is record moral wrong was thought to incur the punishment of Heaven. Punishment was, however, confined to this life. It naturally followed that misfortune was thought to be the result of some sin. The ordinary Chinese term for sin therefore does not necessarily mean more than that one is miserable or unfortunate. Neither Confucianism nor Taoism carried punishment into a life beyond. Confucianism held that Heaven would receive the good man, hence one could be saved by effort. No Confucianist could think of an ancestor in hell; all one's ancestors took their places as a matter of course in heaven. Taoism taught a salvation by quietism, but was equally silent as to the fate of an evil man beyond this life.

With the coming of Mahayana Buddhism a definite idea of a future life was introduced, and Taoism at least has now taken over the beliefs in heaven and hell. It has taken over the Buddhistic eschatology and theory of salvation, but has discarded the foreign terminology and instead substituted Chinese names.[1] According to the Buddhist theory salvation should come as the result of works crystallizing in character, but it is often sought through prayers and the intervention of priests. Even Buddhism has shared the tendency to believe in a multitude of spirits or gods. Chief among these is its savior, Amitabha, the coming Buddha, and a goddess of mercy, Kuan-yin, to whom both men and women appeal.

The Taoists hold three deities in especial honor: Lao-tze, P'an-ku (Chaos, or the maker of the world), and Yü Hwang Shang Ti, a Taoist who was apotheosized by the emperor in 1116 A.D., and who is often popularly confused with Shang-ti. In addition to these, Taoists pray to Hsi Wang Mu, the Royal Mother of the Western Paradise, and T'ien Fei, the Queen of heaven.[2]

Sacrifices are freely offered, the favorite victim being a pig, but such sacrifices are not looked upon as expiating sin. They are rather to propitiate a god or a spirit, or are thank-offerings for favors already received.[3] Neither in the state religion nor in Confucianism has a priesthood ever developed. Buddhist and Taoist monks have become a sort of priesthood, but, even so, they are not wholly analogous to the priesthood of other countries. Divination is a very old art in China, where it has always been held that the will of the divine could be disclosed. In such divination Taoist monks and Buddhistic monks and nuns profess to be adepts. The favorite instruments of divination are stalks of grass

[1] Soothill, *The Three Religions of China*, p. 261.

[2] *Ibid.*, pp. 82 and 269 ff.

[3] *Ibid.*, p. 156.

and tortoise shells. The tortoise is to them the emblem of longevity or immortality. The marks on its back are regarded as significant.[1] There was no consulting of entrails as in the West. There is almost no trace of phallic worship, and the Chinese appear never to have sanctioned such orgies as those of the Semitic mother-goddess, or of the Çiva Çakta sect in India. Both Confucius and Lao-tze have shared the fate of Zoroaster, Gautama, Krishna, and Mahavira; they have been exalted by their followers from the earth and given a place among the gods.

It has been said that "Confucianism ministers to the moral man. Taoism deals chiefly with the problems of the spirit forces which play upon the present life of men, and Buddhism makes vivid the future life and thus appeals to the religious sense, to the imagination, and to devotion. Confucianism deals with the visible present, Taoism with the invisible present, and Buddhism with the invisible future."[2] While this is true, none of these religions is adequate to the needs of Chinese life. Confucianism presents a moral ideal, but offers no sufficient aid to its attainment. Taoism, always vague, is, in its modern debased form, a mass of superstitions which hold the devotee in perpetual fear. Buddhism, although its doctrines reach into the unseen and its ideals are noble, has long ago become formal and traditional. Its elaborate Mahayana doctrines are received by the mind, but are too often impotent to mold the life. Even in the mind they are clouded by

[1] Soothill, *ibid.*, pp. 163–70; cf. DeGroot, *The Religion of the Chinese*, p. 74.

[2] Sherwood Eddy, *The Students of Asia* (New York, 1915), p. 91.

the superstitions that other forms of Chinese thought foster.

SUPPLEMENTARY READING

CLASS A

On sec. 168: Hirth, *The Ancient History of China* (New York, 1911); or S. Wells Williams, *A History of China* (New York, 1897), pp. 1–52.

On sec. 169: J. J. M. DeGroot, *The Religion of the Chinese* (New York, 1910), chaps. i–iii.

On sec. 170: Blodget, "The Worship of Heaven and Earth by the Emperor of China," *Journal of the American Oriental Society*, XX, 58–68; or W. E. Soothill, *The Three Religions of China* (London, 1913), Lecture XI.

On secs. 171, 172: J. Legge, *The Religions of China* (London, 1881); R. K. Douglas, *Confucianism and Taoism* (London, 1900); or J. J. M. DeGroot, *The Religion of the Chinese*, chaps. v and vi; or Soothill, *Three Religions of China*, Lectures II and III; or H. A. Giles, *Confucianism and Its Rivals*, Lectures III, IV, V, and VIII.

On sec. 173: W. E. Soothill, *The Three Religions of China*, Lecture V; or J. J. M. DeGroot, *The Religion of the Chinese*, chaps. vi and vii; or Giles, *Confucianism and Its Rivals*, Lectures VI and VII.

On sec. 174: W. E. Soothill, *The Three Religions of China*, Lectures, V–X, XII.

CLASS B

G. F. Moore, *History of Religions*, I, chaps. i–v.

CHAPTER XII

THE RELIGIONS OF JAPAN

Now of the various offences to be committed . . . . some are of heaven and others of earth. Heavenly offences are the breaking down of divisions between rice-fields, filling up of water-courses, removing water-pipes, flaying alive, flaying backwards. . . . . Earthly offences are the cutting of living bodies, the cutting of dead bodies, leprosy, incest, calamities from creeping things, from the high gods and from high birds, killing of cattle, bewitchments.

Whensoever these offences are committed, for committed they will be, let the great Nakatomi[1] clip heavenly twigs at the top and clip them at the bottom, making thereof a complete array of one thousand stands for offerings. Having trimmed rushes of heaven at the top and trimmed them at the bottom, let them split them into a manifold brush. Then let them recite this great liturgy.

When they do so, the gods of heaven, thrusting open the adamantine doors of heaven and cleaving the many-piled clouds of heaven with an awful way-cleaving, will approach and lend ear. The gods of earth, ascending to the tops of the high mountains and the tops of the low mountains, sweeping away the mists of high mountains and the mists of low mountains, will approach and lend ear.—From the *Norito* Shinto ritual.[2]

175. The land, people, and history.—Japan comprises a group of islands, partly mountainous, which lie off the eastern coast of Asia. They stretch in a curve from about 31° to 45° of north latitude. Two races, probably

---

[1] The name of an early Japanese minister of state.

[2] From W. G. Ashton, *History of Japanese Literature* (London, 1899), pp. 11 f.

both of Mongol stock (though ethnologists differ about it), occupied ancient Japan, the Ainu and the Yamato. The Ainu were first in the islands; the Yamato appear to have entered Japan by way of Korea. It has recently been shown that their language is closely akin to that of Korea, notwithstanding striking differences in vocabulary. Japanese mythology and legendary lore begin with the coming of the Yamato. They appear to have reached the central part of the main island in the early centuries of the Christian era. Japanese mythological chronology carries the time back to the sixth or seventh century B.C., but there seems little ground for regarding it as trustworthy.

By the third or fourth century of our era the Yamato had conquered the central portion of the main island of what was afterward to be Japan, and that slow evolution began which was to produce the Japanese nation. The people at this time lived in huts; there were neither cities nor temples. The huts were collected in rude hamlets. The chief occupations were hunting and fishing; some rude agriculture was practiced—chiefly the raising of rice; commerce was unknown; iron implements were used. The family was only partially organized. Marriage was only the open acknowledgment of a relation that had previously existed in secret. There was no definite distinction between marriage and concubinage, and not until centuries later was such a distinction established. A husband might have such wives as he pleased with families in different places. Marriages with half-sisters (children of different mothers) were not uncommon, and marriages with full sisters sometimes occurred.

From this state the evolution was slow; it was finally hastened by influences from China. Contact with China in the sixth century led to the introduction into Japan of the Chinese system of writing, and of Buddhism. It also brought a knowledge of the Confucian philosophy, which led to the formulation of Shinto, or the state religion. Supported by this the emperors, who were now believed to be descended from Izanagi and Izanami, the two primal deities who gave birth to all the other gods and to the islands of Japan, began a career of conquest and of vigorous government. The oldest chronicle of Japanese history that has come down to us was written in 712 A.D. From that time onward the record of events is fairly complete. Through the Nara epoch (710–94 A.D.), when the capital was changed with every sovereign, and through the Heian epoch (794–1186 A.D.) the empire continued to grow. The custom of making imperial offices hereditary in the same family prevailed.

With officeholders there was no distinction between public funds and their own private resources. Thus a powerful feudal nobility developed, which at the end of the Heian era the imperial power could no longer control. In the reign of the emperor Gotoba, 1186–99 A.D., the title of *seii-taishogun*, or generalissimo, was conferred upon Yoritomo, a powerful noble of Kamakura, who thus became the virtual ruler of the country. From that time until 1868, except for the brief period between 1339 and 1393, when the imperial government reasserted itself and once more controlled the land, the real government of the country was in the

¹ See K. Asakawa, *History of Japan* (Philadelphia, 1906), pp. 66 ff.

hands of nobles, who were called Shoguns, an abbreviation of the original title. From 1186 to 1339 the Shoguns resided at Kamakura; from 1393 to 1573, at Muromachi in Kyoto; from 1573 to 1868 a Yedo family held the Shogunate and resided in Yedo. In 1868 the imperial power was restored, and the modern Japanese era began.

The tradition of the descent of the emperor from the gods clothed him through all the centuries with such respect that, though the Shoguns did not hesitate to rob him of political power, none of them ever set him aside or put himself in place of an emperor. During the feudal period many wars were waged, and a class of knightly warriors called *samurai* was developed. The knightly code of this class, known as Bushido, represents Japanese ethics in its highest development.

176. The primitive religion of the Japanese was of the rudest sort. The conception of animate life entertained by the early Japanese was that men, animals, and gods (if gods they can be called) formed one society. In reality *kami*, often translated "god," means simply a marvelous or wonderful being. A Japanese scholar declares that *kami* "lies between super-man and super-human being."[1] *Kami* was applied to the sun, the heavens, the winds; but it was also applied to human beings, beasts, plants, trees, seas, mountains, and to all other things that excite wonder or fear. The *kami* of the earliest time are for the most part human beings, though the fox and serpent are also *kami*. The wolf and tiger were *kami;* it is also sometimes applied to peaches, jewels, and the leaves of plants. It thus

[1] See I. Nitobe, *The Japanese Nation* (New York, 1912), p. 123.

appears that the early Japanese conception of the divine was of a most rudimentary nature. Whatever excited wonder and fear they reverenced. To them, as to the Semites, the mystery of the propagation of life was most marvelous. Phallic emblems accordingly were widely employed as symbols of the divine. To them as to the primitive Semites the mystery of fatherhood and motherhood was the mystery of creation.[1] In reverencing the symbols of these they reverenced the divine in one of its most wonderful and beneficent forms. They put no wide difference between themselves and a transcendent creator, for their minds had not grasped the idea of such a creator. Among such primitive men these symbols cannot be regarded as obscene; they represented one of the most potent manifestations of the supernatural, and they excited in them as much reverence as they were capable of feeling toward anything.

The objects of worship of the early Japanese were, then, the mysterious processes of nature and her awe-inspiring phenomena—heavenly bodies, sky, mountains, and rivers. Of these they appear to have made no representations, for the originals were always with them. The one exception seems to be the mirror, the symbol of the sun-goddess, in which she was worshiped as though herself present.[2]

To these men the universe was small. Heaven was so near that it had been reached by an arrow which made

[1] See E. Buckley, *Phallicism in Japan* (Chicago, 1895); W. E. Griffis, *The Religions of Japan* (New York, 1895), pp. 27 ff.

[2] Compare G. W. Knox, *The Development of Religion in Japan* (New York, 1907), p. 31.

a hole in its bottom, from which objects fell to the earth, where they are still found. Heaven and earth were formerly connected by a bridge, but that had, unfortunately, fallen down. The underworld was a cavern in the earth, the entrance to which was formerly open, though now blocked by a large rock. Heaven is like the earth; the spirits that dwell in it gather in the dry beds of rivers for consultation. The underworld is, according to some legends, also similar to the earth; it contains meadows, rivers, and dwellings large and small.

Not in heaven, earth, or the underworld were the divisions between the orders of life fixed. "Fishes, beasts, birds, and serpents acted and spoke as men." "Crocodiles or sea-monsters became women, and men became birds, a rock fled before a man, the sun was at once the orb of day and a goddess who could be enticed from retiracy by an appeal to her vanity, while the moon and the storm were beings who acted like men."[1] There was no distinction between men and inanimate nature. A goddess is only a wonderful woman, but she gives birth to fire. The Japanese of this period recognized no distinction between body and soul. Man was man, and that was all. Many myths grew up to account for the facts of life as they knew it, but there is little of religion in it all. They betray no idea of a creator; the world was produced by natural generation from a god and a goddess, or a male and a female *kami*. No consciousness of sin can be detected, and consequently there was no conception of redemption. There was not even the idea of a soul. Such religion as there was consisted solely of awe in the presence of the marvelous.

[1] See Knox. *op. cit.*, p 18.

177. Shinto, or the "way of the gods," is the elaboration and organization of the primitive beliefs in the interest of the reigning house. The term "Shinto" is Chinese, and was employed by Confucius centuries before its adoption by the Japanese. Shinto was developed in the seventh or eighth century. By that time the dynasty that still reigns in Japan had obtained considerable power over the previously disorganized country. Intercourse with China had been established; Buddhism was coming in, and with it some knowledge of Confucianism. The mass of the people were, however, still imbued with their ancestral conceptions, and to bind them to the reigning family the old cosmogonic myth was retold and elaborated. According to this myth Izanagi, the primal male deity, and Izanami, the primal female deity, had by natural generation brought forth the other gods and the Islands of Japan. The genealogy was now extended so that it appeared that through a line of divine ancestors the imperial family (to use a later term) was descended from these same gods. Thus the natural reverence for the spirits in which their forefathers had believed was focused upon the reigning dynasty.

Along with this older worship there went as a natural development, under Chinese influence, an increased reverence for departed ancestors. This became possible because, under the stimulus of the Confucian reverence for the family, Japanese marriage became somewhat more regulated, the family attained greater cohesion, and ancestors were in time regarded with reverence. Little by little they took their places next to the *kami* and were reverenced also. Thus in Shinto doctrine man is in this life kindred to the divine, and after death joins the company of those who are to be reverenced. The deities of the Shinto pantheon range from the most insignificant gods, "whom pious spinsters respect as the spirits of sewing-needles or those to whom kitchen maids do homage as residing in the furnace, up to those who roar in thunder, or shine in lightning, or ride upon the whirlwind. Shinto is the most polytheistic of polytheisms."[1] The Shintoist does not "pray for forgiveness of sins, but for the sweet things of this life, for happiness, but not for blessedness."[2] The worshiper may be conscious that his heart is not of a divine quality of purity, but "he can of his own accord blow it off like dust, or wash it off like a stain, and regain purity."[3]

The shrines of Shinto are unusually simple. They are the plainest of wooden structures, "of an ancient form of architecture, unpainted and undecorated, usually in the shade of cryptomeria groves." The chief ministers of religion in Shinto belonged to particular families, upon whom the emperor often bestowed offices and titles. They married, dressed like others, and were in no way distinguishable from other men, except when officiating at Shinto rites. At some of the shrines there were virgin priestesses who acted as custodians.[4] Offerings, consisting of fruits, products of the soil, products of the sea, and fabrics of the loom,

[1] Nitobe, *The Japanese Nation*, p. 131.

[2] *Ibid.*, p. 124.

[3] *Ibid.*, p. 128.

[4] Griffis, *The Religions of Japan*, p. 84.

were made in ancient times. These are now often reduced to paper imitations.[1]

Shinto has little teaching for the conduct of private individuals. The god of Fujiyama is said to have enjoined upon his followers the following: "Ye men of mine, shun desire. If you shun desire you will ascend to the level of the gods. Every little yielding to anxiety is a step away from the natural heart of man. If one leaves the natural heart of man he becomes a beast. That men should be made so is to me intolerable pain and unending sorrow."[2] Such statements are, however, generally wanting in Shinto documents. Japanese ethics has been developed by other systems. The rituals consist largely of adoration and thanksgiving. Such prayers as it affords are national rather than individual. In the complete form of Shinto prayers the emperor appears as the high priest of his people. Just as the emperor of China worships heaven and earth, so the emperor of Japan intervenes between the *kami* and the nation.

The organization of the primitive beliefs into Shinto never took deep hold of the nation as a whole; it remained the religion of the few. It had sufficient power to sustain the imperial line as a figurative head of the nation during the centuries of feudal rule, and probably had some influence in bringing about the restoration of the imperial line to power in 1868. Since that time Shinto has called forth from its modern devotees some ingenious defenses. Men skilled in modern dialectics, and possessing some

[1] *Ibid.*, p. 83.
[2] Nitobe, *The Japanese Nation*, p. 134.

knowledge of science, have defended its stories and
its miracles.[1]

178. **Buddhism** was introduced into Japan in the
sixth century A.D.   Its coming was at first resisted by
the people, and the images of the Buddha were destroyed,
but in 584, when a plague of smallpox grew worse after
the image of Buddha had been thrown into a canal, the
image was rescued and set up with the approval of the
emperor.[2]   At first the Japanese were averse to it, but
the Buddhist priests declared that the Japanese *kami*
were Buddhas or Boddhisattwas, and the new faith was
reconciled to the old.   Buddhism thus became the pre-
dominant religion of the Japanese down to modern times.
The rapid assimilation of Buddhism, which was the
religion of all the civilized world known to the Japanese
(Korea, hoary China, and far-away India), was quite
analogous to the way in which in recent time Japan has
assimilated Western civilization and science because
they were the possessions of the civilized world.   Japanese Buddhism, brought from China by way of Korea,
was of the Mahayana type, called in Japanese *Daijo*.
This form of Buddhism established the belief that
Gautama passed through five periods of existence, in
the last of which he became identical with Absolute
Being.   It taught the doctrine of transmigration of the
soul, of heaven and hell, and of salvation by prayer.[3]
Its advent introduced the Japanese to a new world of
ideas.   Fostered by some of the emperors in the eighth
century, it rapidly attained a position of power.   "It

[1] Knox, *The Development of Religion in Japan*, pp. 70 ff.
[2] F. Brinkley, *A History of the Japanese People*, pp. 131–35.
[3] See above, pp. 174 f. and 218.

touched the very fountains of thought and set a-flowing
new currents of ideas. It sobered the light-hearted
nature worshipers. It furnished a deeper interpretation of ancestor worship. It created new notions of
nature and life. It invented a new vocabulary. It
gave rise to new arts, trades, and crafts. It initiated a
new policy of government. It changed the whole social
structure. Indeed there was nothing that was not
impregnated with the doctrines of Gautama." This is
the tribute of Professor Nitobe, but the doctrines of
Mahayana, which came to Japan, are as different from
the doctrines of Gautama as the philosophy of Hegel is
from the teachings of Jesus.

In the early part of the ninth century Japanese
Buddhism began to split into sects. The earliest of
these sects, the Tendai, or "Heavenly Command,"[1] was
founded by Saicho (also called Dengyo), a Buddhist
saint who visited China and there gained the inspiration which led to the founding of the sect. The metaphysics of this sect are thought by some to be more profound
than those of any other section of Mahayana Buddhism.
An attèmpt is made to combine the two opposites of
being and non-being. In this there may be discerned
the influence of Chinese Taoism as interpreted by
Kwang-tze. The aim of the sect is to lead its members
to the attainment of perfect Buddhahood through the
four stages of moral precept, meditation, secrecy, and
completion. The goal is completion. In the pursuit
of this end the leaders of the sect adapt their teachings
to the capacity of individuals, after the manner of
Ignatius Loyola, and have in consequence been called

[1] So Nitobe, *The Japanese People*, p. 141.

the Jesuits of Buddhism. One of the aims of the sect is to search out and reverence the Buddha in all his manifestations, and it has found such manifestations in Vedic gods, Hindu idols, and in Shinto *kami*. It thus came about that all Shinto was annexed by the Tendai. Its priests have intermarried with Shinto families in order to secure by heredity control of Shinto shrines.[1] The all-inclusive aim of the sect has resulted in its disintegration into several subsects.

Another sect, the Shingon, or "True Word," also dates from the ninth century. Its founder, Kukai (canonized as Kobo Daishi), also studied in China. According to this system the center of all things is Dai Nichi,

identified by the common people with the sun, and around him are four Buddhas of contemplation representing the highest abstractions, and around thèse group after group of significant genera and species, until the individual is reached. This is the "diamond" world, unchanging and real, while the phenomenal world is also grouped about Dai Nichi, who is represented, not now as the sun surrounded by four planets, but as the center of the lotus with eight Buddhas about him as petals. Thus he, or better it, is the center of all things, real and phenomenal, and correspondingly there are two ways of salvation, by meditation and knowledge, and by a righteous life. The end of the "Way" is reached when perfect knowledge is attained and the individual is absorbed in the Infinite. In popular language we become Buddha. Thus was the historic Buddha himself absorbed, and his individuality disappeared, so has his distinctive teaching and glory, for he remains in this system only as one of four Buddhas of contemplation, a symbol of abstraction, one of the last ideas which remain before all is swallowed up in the Absolute.[2]

[1] Compare Griffis, *The Religions of Japan*, pp. 244 ff.
[2] Knox, *The Development of Religion in Japan*, pp. 99 f.

The absorption of Shinto by the Shingon sect was even more easy and rapid than by the Tendai sect. Shinto did not altogether lose its identity, however, for at birth a child is taken to a Shinto temple for consecration and blessing, though at death the funeral is usually conducted by a Buddhist priest.

The Jodo, or "Pure Land" sect, founded in 1196 A.D. by Genkū, afterward called Hōnen Shonin, is an offshoot of the Tendai sect. Genkū, impressed by the evil of the world and the impossibility of doing right in it, and influenced by descriptions of the paradise of the West that had just reached Japan, held that it is not possible to reach Buddhaship here; one must first attain the "Pure Land." That land may be attained in another world, if one has faith in Amida, or Buddha the Savior. Blind faith in Amida, combined with ceaseless repetition of pious formulae (for faith must find expression in ritual), will lead to birth in Amida's Paradise after death. No change of heart is necessary here; but there one may have a chance at Buddhahood. The doctrine offered a cheap ticket to paradise and became very popular.

The Jodo Shin-shu, or "True Sect of Jodo," often called simply Shin-shu, was established in 1224 A.D. through the efforts of Shinran, a pupil of Genkū. This sect lays emphasis on faith alone. If faith saves, neither ritual nor works avail. One needs no knowledge of metaphysics, one need perform no acts of religious devotion, there is no need to keep a multitude of commandments, one need not leave home, renounce matrimony, or live by rule. Faith will accomplish all, if one worships Amida only, and prays for nothing that does not concern salvation. Whereas Jodo teaches that Amida will come only at death, Shin-shu holds that Amida dwells in the heart by faith now. In this teaching it has been said that Buddhism completed a cycle, denying everything that its founder affirmed, and affirming everything that he denied.[1]

A different line of development is represented by the Zen sect, founded about 1187 by Eisai, a monk who in 1168 had been in China to study. Zen is a Japanese translation of the Sanskrit *Dhyana*, "contemplation." Knowledge, Eisai held, can be transmitted without words. It may be reached only by contemplation. The essential thing is to find the Buddha in one's own heart. In order to find it, one must grasp the "fact of utter and entire void." The motto was in theory,

Oh to be nothing! nothing![2]

About 1223 two other teachers, after a visit to China, introduced into the Zen teaching the elements of scholarship and research. These together with contemplation were the way to the goal. Strange to say, this mystical sect became very popular with the *samurai*, or Japanese warriors. Its teachings stripped all things of their qualities to such a degree that death was robbed of its terrors, while its ritual of mere contemplation did not interfere with the activities of a soldier.

The Nichiren sect, named after its founder, Nichiren, who was born in 1222 A.D., embodies a violent reaction from the Jodo and Shin-shu sects. It alone of the Buddhist sects in Japan is intolerant. "Japan for the

[1] Knox, *The Development of Religion in Japan*, p. 133.
[2] *Ibid.*, p. 100.

Japanese" might well have been the motto of its founder.
He had been a student of the *Saddharma-Pundarîka*, or
the "Lotus of the True Law," from which he selected
various phrases, which were believed to constitute a
formula of salvation. He became a kind of Buddhist
evangelist, preaching this type of salvation to the common people. The true Buddha is the source of all
existence; he is the real moon in the sky; all other
states of being are like the moon reflected in the water.
The *kami* and all Japanese spirits are Buddhas. Indeed,
beasts, birds, and snakes are honored by this sect.
Nichiren denounced all other sects, characterizing the
Zen as a demon and the Shingon as national ruin.[1]
After a stormy career he ended his life in peace, but
bequeathed his contentious spirit to his sect. The sect
has made its founder an object of worship, embellishing
his life with many marvels; it worships his writings,
and has through all its history been intolerant and
violent.

179. Confucianism became known in Japan as early
as Buddhism if not earlier, and has had a profound
influence upon Japanese life. Japan has always been
ready to respond to the stimulus of a higher civilization
when once that stimulus has been felt, and such stimulus came to it from China in the sixth century of our
era. To the rude Japanese of that time China was a
land of hoary antiquity and of immemorial culture.
The civilization of China naturally became a pattern
to the Japanese. In China the whole organization of
the state and family was pervaded by Confucian ideals.
Though Confucius had sought only to regulate these,

[1] F. Brinkley, *History of the Japanese People*, p. 372.

and to stimulate reverence for them, a stable government presided over by a Son of Heaven and a well-organized family in which children reverenced parents, obeyed them, and sacrificed themselves for them, were fundamental to his system of thought. Such a state and family China presented to the Japanese as a model.

Under the influence of this ideal, Japan, as has already been pointed out, developed Shinto, to strengthen her ruling dynasty and to give the emperor in a purely Japanese system a place as exalted as that held by the Chinese emperor. The same influence led to a better organization of the Japanese family and the inculcation of filial piety. In Japan, however, this piety took on a different aspect and tone from that in China. China was on the whole a peaceful land; Japan was disturbed by continual strife. Filial piety in Japan assumed a martial coloring thoroughly in keeping with the Japanese environment and character.

In China the emperor ruled by virtue, and if he were not virtuous, Confucianism recognized the right of rebellion. In Japan he ruled by conquest, and no right of rebellion was recognized. The ethics of Confucius as understood in Japan were for a ruling race; for the common man there was left nothing but obedience. When the necessity of virtue in the ruler was no longer recognized, there was no restraint upon him, and tyranny naturally resulted. In the feudal age this Japanese interpretation of Confucianism as applied by the *samurai*, or warrior class, produced the ethical system of Bushido, or "military-knight ways," so attractively described by Professor Nitobe.[1] The ethics of

[1] I. Nitobe, *Bushido, the Soul of Japan* (Philadelphia, 1900)

Bushido, while they inculcate marvelous self-control, loyalty, chivalry, gentleness, and honor to those within one's circle, leave the warrior free to practice any deceit or fraud for the sake of overcoming an enemy.[1] There is in the conduct expected of the soldier a defect similar to the defect in that prescribed by Japanese Confucianism for an emperor.

In Chinese filial piety the family is the institution which demands the loyalty of children. The ideal Confucian son is one who labors and sacrifices to support needy parents. This idea was adopted in Japan, but was given a wider scope. It was made to apply to the state as well as to a family. It inculcated for all relationships of life the self-sacrifice of an inferior to a superior. This was carried to such lengths in the family that a daughter was commended for selling herself to a life of shame for the sake of supplying the wants of a needy father. Boys and men were in a similar way expected to sacrifice themselves for a superior and for the state. To endure the hardships incident to war—hunger, cold, fatigue—and to meet death without fear became the manly virtues that were most commended. In time loyalty to one's superior was thought to involve the refusal to live after that superior's death, hence the form of suicide known as *hara-kiri*, or disembowelment, was often commended. The emphasis led frequently to suicide for trivial causes. In such ways as these the fruits of Confucianism in Japan were very different from its fruits in China. In Japan it applied only to the upper classes; the peasantry was left with an ethical code almost as vague as in primitive times.

[1] Knox, *The Development of Religion in Japan*, pp. 151 ff.

There lived in China in 1130–1200 A.D. an exceedingly influential commentator on Confucius named Chu Hsi. In interpreting Confucius, Chu Hsi aimed at consistency, but he also taught that Confucius held man to be superior to spirits and demons. Chu Hsi accordingly denied that Shang-ti was a supreme ruler whom men must particularly honor. About 1604 his teachings were introduced into Japan and became the orthodox method of interpreting Confucius there. Probably the majority of educated Japanese at the present time are Confucianists of this type. Religion, whether of the primitive sort or of the Buddhistic variety, is regarded as superstition. The worship which a Confucianist performs before the tablet of an ancestor or a sage signifies little more than our lifting of the hat at the tomb of a hero or saint. For the rest Confucianist worship is adoration of the universe and the expression of gratitude to it.

Such has been the religious history of Japan. Buddhism was disestablished in 1872; Christianity, though now a power in the empire, has not yet been recognized by law as on an equality with the older systems. In conclusion, it may be observed that Japan has made no really great contribution to the world's religion. Her own religion was of the most rudimentary character, and the influence of Confucianism upon it, although it gave coherence and a system of ethics, nevertheless scarcely made the Japanese conceptions a religion. Buddhism alone has been creative, but its creative impulses have all been derived from China. The readiness with which Buddhism identified its Boddhisattwas with the Japanese *kami* led it to absorb the primitive Japanese superstitions. While Buddhism greatly stimulated Japanese thought, and was by far the most inspiring of the religions of ancient Japan, its sects either thought too much of the life to come, or were too anxious to be "nothing, nothing," to raise the present life to its highest potency.

SUPPLEMENTARY READING

CLASS A

On sec. 175: A. Asakawa, "Japan," in H. C. Lodge's *History of the Nations* (Philadelphia, 1906); or F. Brinkley, *A History of the Japanese People* (London, 1915); D. C. Holtom, "The Political Philosophy of Modern Shinto" in E. Kaempfer's *History of Japan*, III, 1–73, or J. B. Pratt, *The Pilgrimage of Buddhism*, New York, 1928, chaps. xxii–xxxi.

On secs. 176–79: G. W. Knox, *The Development of Religion in Japan* (New York, 1907).

CLASS B

G. F. Moore, *History of Religions*, I, chaps. vi, vii.

CHAPTER XIII

THE RELIGION OF GREECE

Io, Kuros[1] most Great, I give thee hail, Kronian, Lord of all that is wet and gleaming, thou art come at the head of thy Daimones. To Dikte for the year, Oh, march, and rejoice in the dance and song. . . . . For here the shielded Nurturers took thee, a child immortal, from Rhea, and with noise of beating feet hid thee away.—Fragment of a hymn of the Kouretes.[2]

They celebrate aegis-bearing Zeus, and majestic Hera, the Argive who treads proudly in golden sandals; and gleaming-eyed Athene, daughter of aegis-bearing Zeus; Phoebus Apollo; Artemis, arrow-queen; and earth-encompassing, earth-shaking Poseidon; august Themis; Aphrodite who shoots lively glances; and Hebe of the golden crown; and fair Dione; Eos[3] and the great Helios,[4] and the resplendent Selene;[5] Latona, and Iapetos, and wily Kronos; Ge,[6] mighty Okeanos, and dark Nux.[7]—HESIOD *Theogony.*

Ͻ Zeus, most glorious, greatest, shrouded in dark clouds, dwelling in the sky.—*Iliad* ii. 412.

> The air is Zeus, Zeus earth, and Zeus the heaven,
> Zeus all that is, and what transcends them all.
>
> —AESCHYLUS[8]

In God is no unrighteousness at all—he is altogether righteous; and there is nothing more like him than he is of us, who is most righteous.—PLATO *Theaetetus* 176.[9]

---

[1] An epithet of Zeus.

[2] From Miss J. E. Harrison, *Themis* (Cambridge, 1912), p. 7.

[3] Aurora.

[4] The Sun.   [6] The Earth.

[5] The Moon.   [7] Night.

[8] From E. H. Plumtre, *The Tragedies of Aeschylus* (New York), p. 343.

[9] From B. Jowett, *The Dialogues of Plato* (New York, 1887), III, 378.

180. **Greece and her people.**—As compared with great India, vast China, or even with insular Japan, Greece is insignificant in size. It is but a petty peninsula. "Its plains are deep narrow basins between high ridges and peaks." In place of rivers it has only rushing torrents incapable of floating a ship. Its soil is comparatively sterile, though its reddish color combined with the variety of hills and dales lends it a delightful charm. This is increased by the indentations of innumerable bays and inlets, which add the incomparable blue of Aegean water to the beauty of the landscapes. "No spot of the land is more than forty miles from the sea."

Long before the Indo-European Greeks came to this land it had been affected by the Aegean civilization. This civilization has been disclosed to us most completely in Crete, where excavations have revealed an outline of its history reaching back farther than 3000 B.C. Beginning there in the Stone Age, this civilization slowly evolved in a way as original as that of Babylonia, Egypt, or China. Scholars call the race that produced this civilization Minoan, from the myth of Minos of Crete. The early Minoan period of this civilization was contemporary with the Old Kingdom of Egypt; the Middle Minoan period, when the civilization reached its height, coincided with the time of Egypt's Middle Kingdom, 2000–1800 B.C.; while the Late Minoan period, contemporary with the Eighteenth and Nineteenth Egyptian dynasties (1600–1200 B.C.), though in parts a period of splendor, was on the whole a period of decline.[1] The Cyclades Islands, parts of Laconia, Argolis, Attica,

[1] See C. H. and H. Hawes, *Crete the Forerunner of Greece* (New York, 1909).

Boeotia, and Thessaly, as well as parts of Caria and the Troad in Asia, shared this civilization. Greece was thus a highly civilized land long before the coming of the Greeks.

At some time before the end of the second millennium B.C. the Indo-European Greeks began to enter the land from the north. They came in successive waves, Ionians, Achaeans, Dorians. They appear to have reached some degree of civilization before they separated from the Aryan branches of their race, the Persians and Hindus, for they worshiped some of the same deities as their eastern kinsfolk. On their way to Greece they had advanced farther in civilization, since they passed through the valley of the Danube and came under the influence of the Bronze Age civilization there.[1] When they reached Greece, however, they were far more backward than the men of the Mediterranean race whom they overcame, and it took time for the new race to absorb and transform the culture that they found. This period of absorption and transformation is reflected in the literature from the Homeric poems to the Peloponnesian War.

Two strains of ancestry are accordingly discernible in Greek religion, that of the Aegean civilization which had established itself at Mycenae, Athens, and elsewhere, and that brought by the Greek tribes. Here and there foreign influences, especially Semitic, may have been felt.

181. Minoan religion cannot be fully studied until the Cretan writing is deciphered. It is evident, however, from the artistic remains that the chief figure in

[1] See D. G. Hogarth, *Ionia and the East* (Oxford, 1909), pp. 33-41.

the cult of the island was a goddess. She is represented
in many ways, from Neolithic nude figures in the form of
an excessively fat woman (many primitive races have
regarded obesity as an element of feminine beauty) to
the goddess with a flounced skirt, tight-fitting waist,
and bare breast, of the Late Minoan period, who holds
serpents in her hands. The serpents apparently typify
her connection with the earth. Doves and lions were
often associated with her. She was, then, goddess of
the air and of wild animals. The bull was sacred to her.
He was most often offered in sacrifice, his horns adorned
her altars and temples, and ritual vessels were made in
his form. The goddess was served by priestesses, and
worshiped at times in wild dances.[1] As in other countries
that worshiped goddesses, she was thought to have a
son. Later Greek myths traced the birth of Zeus to the
Diktean cave in Crete, or to Mount Ida, where Rhea,
his mother, secretly brought him forth.[2] The myth is
reflected in the hymn quoted at the beginning of this
chapter. The son was thus identified in later time with
the Greek Zeus. Cyprus shared in the Aegean civilization, but Semitic colonies were also established there,
and the Aegean goddess was blended with the Semitic.
When Minoan civilization was dominant in Greece in
the Mycenaean age, the cult of the goddess was firmly
established in many parts of the land. She became
Rhea, mother of Zeus, Poseidon, and other deities. She
became Hera, goddess of Argos, Athena in Attica, and
Artemis in Attica and Arcadia. At Corinth, where
formative influences may have come from Cyprus, she

[1] See Hawes, *op. cit.*, pp. 135 ff.
[2] See Strabo x. 468, 475; Miss Harrison, *Themis*, p. 54, n. 5.

became Aphrodite.[1] The goddess, as among other primitive peoples, was apparently but the chief of an indefinite host of spirits that were feared. There is much evidence that in every part of the land there were many spirits, some of whom survived into the later religion. Throughout the whole Aegean area the pillar was sacred to this goddess[2] or to the male divinity associated with her. The deities were deities of fertility and the pillar had a phallic significance. As among the Semites, Hamites, and the early Japanese, the necessity of replenishing the food supply and the tribe led them to regard the power of reproduction as the divinest of qualities.

182. Greek gods.—The Greeks were monogamous and reckoned descent through the father. The one primitive Indo-European god whom the Greeks brought with them was Zeus, called "Zeus pater," etymologically identical with "Dyaush pitar" of the Vedas.[3] As with the Hindus, he was the god of the overarching sky. They appear also to have brought with them Apollo, the god who guided the wanderer through the trackless wild, perhaps originally a wolf-god, but later identified with the sun, who guides the wanderer on his way. Like their Aryan brethren of India, the Greeks worshiped Helios, or the sun, Ēos, or the dawn, and Ge, the earth. We cannot be sure that the worship of these gods goes back to primitive Indo-European days, for the names

[1] So Farnell in Hastings' *Encyclopaedia of Religion and Ethics*, VII, 396; *Higher Aspects of the Greek Religion* (New York, 1912), pp. 8 ff.

[2] So Gilbert Murray, *Four Stages of Greek Religion* (New York, 1912), pp. 74 ff.

[3] See above, p. 146.

by which the Greeks called them are not connected with the names given them in India. To these the Greeks added the worship of night and the ocean. The last-mentioned was added to the pantheon after the Greeks' entrance into a land bordering on a sea; possibly some of the others were developed in Greece.

183. The pantheon was formed by the fusion of deities from the Mediterranean race of the Aegean civilization and those of the Greek invaders. As the Greeks came southward in their victorious invasion, some of them settled in Thessaly. There Zeus was worshiped along with his female counterpart, Dione,[1] but Dione was forgotten by those who conquered Argos and Zeus was married to Hera. Thus the pre-Hellenic religion blended with the Hellenic. At Athens there was also a fusion, though here Zeus did not assume so important a rôle. Athena was, however, made his daughter, perhaps displacing Eōs. Artemis and Aphrodite were simply taken over by the Greeks. Artemis assumed different characters in different places. At Ephesus she was to the end the goddess of productivity. In some places the male god of the pre-Hellenes was absorbed by Apollo instead of by Zeus.[2] In time the pantheon was increased by the addition of other spirits, and by the personification of pure abstractions, such as Themis. One of the spirits that developed later into a god was that of the phallic post called a *Herm*. This post was placed above the graves of the dead as the symbol of the renewal of life. Its spirit came to be regarded as the means of communicating with the departed, hence in time this group of spirits or *Hermes*

[1] See Gilbert Murray, *op. cit.*, p. 75. [2] *Ibid* p. 69.

became the messenger god. Hermes was, however, represented by a post far into the artistic period.[1]

Zeus, who displaced or absorbed the pre-Hellenic gods, was said to have his abode on Olympus. There is an Olympus in Mysia, another in Thessaly, and still a third in Elis. Indeed, there are said to be more than twenty of them.[2] The Zeus of a place was supposed to inhabit the mountain that was nearest; they were only gradually merged. The gods of this time were worshiped with bloody sacrifices and such similar ceremonies as are found among early peoples.

184. The early poets.—(1) Homer: The poems that pass under the name of Homer were not all written by one hand or at one time. They were composed from the tenth to the seventh centuries, the oldest parts of the *Iliad* going back to nearly 1000 B.C. They represent a time in the development of the Ionian Greeks when they had come to regard themselves as of a higher degree of civilization than the surrounding barbarians. In the epics the gods are humanized; they are more personal and approachable. They are pictured as Hellenic aristocrats; they do not work; they only fight and indulge in amours. There is among them but one workman, Hephaestos, the metal-worker, perhaps of Aegean rather than Indo-European origin.[3] He is lame and is the sport of gods and poets. Just as the aristocratic heroes of Homeric story must have their weapons sharpened, but looked down on the non-fighting smith, so did their gods. Most of the gods

---

[1] See Gilbert Murray, *op. cit.*, pp. 74 ff.; Miss Harrison, *Themis*, p. 365.

[2] *Ibid.*, pp. 64 ff.

[3] Farnell, *Higher Aspects of the Greek Religion*, p. 14.

loved, hated, quarreled, intrigued, and fought, just as did their princely worshipers. Nevertheless, the artistic instinct banished from the poems much that was horrible in the earlier ceremonies and conceptions.

(2) Hesiod, a Boeotian farmer, who wrote about 750 B.C., was a very different person from the poets who sang at the courts of Asiatic princes. He was less gifted as an artist and his interests were those of the soil. He endeavored to arrange the Homeric gods into a pantheon. The effort took the form of a poetic genealogy, the *Theogony*. It is really an account of the origin of the world, a cosmogony, as well as an account of the origin of the pantheon. In it the past is idealized. The world is represented as growing steadily worse. The Gold Age was followed by the Silver Age, that by the Bronze Age. The present is the Iron Age, and deterioration is still in progress. What was noble in the past was glorified and its harsher features forgotten.

Hesiod's account of the origin of the universe begins with the emergence of Chaos. Earth next came into being, in the recesses of which was Tartarus. Then came Love. From Chaos were born Erebos and Night; from Night, Aether and Day; from Earth, the starry Heaven. From Earth and Heaven were born Okeanos, Thea, Rhea, Themis, and other goddesses.

In Hesiod's *Works and Days* the rules and taboos relating to agriculture are collected. It thus preserves many of the earlier customs and superstitions of the people. As the *Iliad* mirrors the religion of the aristocratic warrior, the *Works and Days* mirrors that of the peasant farmer.[1]

---

[1] See Gilbert Murray, *op. cit.*, p. 85.

185. Religion in the seventh and sixth centuries B.C.
—(1) *Conditions:* These centuries constitute a period of commercial expansion. In the seventh century Greeks were welcomed in Egypt by the kings of the Twenty-sixth Dynasty. The dynasty established by Gyges in Lydia eventually brought under its sway all of Asia Minor west of the Halys, and opened the country to Greek ideas and Greek enterprise. The Greek states themselves began to establish colonies in different parts of the Eastern Mediterranean, from the Black Sea and the Propontis to Cyrene in Lybia. They also swept westward and colonized Southern Italy and Sicily. This expansion created a fusion in religion and a new form of society. The colonies carried their home gods with them, but soon grafted on to the worship of these the local cults of their new homes. With the establishment of the colonies there came into being an extensive commerce, which soon created a class of wealthy merchants. Older Greek society had been agricultural; the aristocracy were the owners of large country estates. Little by little the wealthy city merchant took the place in popular esteem made vacant by the dwindling importance of the possessors of unproductive acres. The peasantry flocked to the cities, many foreign slaves were brought in, and the older social fabric was transformed.

(2) *Dionysos:* This transformation was accompanied by important religious changes. One of the most striking of these was the introduction and naturalization of the cult of the Thracian god Dionysos. In Thrace this god was a god of general fertility, not strikingly different from the deities of the old Aegean cult. He was worshiped at festivals with ecstatic orgies characteristic

of such cults. In Greece he became the god of the vine, but carried with him the festivals and orgies of his native land. The transfer of his cult to Greece, combined with the changing social conditions of the period, led to the introduction of a more personal element into religion. Gods had before been the deities of clans or cities in whose favor all members of the clan or city shared. The potency of the god had up to this time been confined to the present life. The underworld was a cheerless abode, such as is pictured in the *Odyssey*, Book xi, where the departed dragged out a shadowy existence. The cult of Dionysos as introduced into Greece held out the hope of a personal salvation. Individuals were initiated into its mysteries. Benefits unknown to others came to those so initiated, and those benefits extended to a happier life in the underworld. While a part of that world was peopled with terrifying monsters, there were in other parts delightful abodes for the initiated.[1]

(3) *Demeter:* Under the spur of the mysteries of Dionysos, those of Demeter at Eleusis developed into a similar cult. Demeter, though a Hellenic goddess, probably supplanted one that had her beginnings in Mycenaean times.[2] In Homer she appears as an earth-goddess whose daughter, Proserpine, who represents vegetation, was carried down to Hades. Demeter sought her daughter and brought her up again. At Eleusis she was the goddess of a minor tribe, but in competition with the cult of the foreign Dionysos her

[1] See Farnell, *The Cults of the Greek States* (Oxford, 1896–1909), V, chaps. iv–vii.

[2] Cf. *ibid.*, III. 11.

mysteries developed apace. People from outside the tribe became initiates; salvation was promised them, and the cult became popular. The Elysian fields of this cult were portrayed in more refined terms than those of the cult of Dionysos, and the cult appears to have appealed to a different class.

(4) *Orpheus:* Intermingled with these two cults were some that bore other names. The most important of these were the Orphic mysteries, which appear to have been in some way connected with those of Dionysos, but are found at Eleusis also. Orpheus was the half-mythical primitive poet who, by the power of his lyre, had brought his wife Eurydice back from the under-world. Verses of varying degrees of excellence were attributed to Orpheus and became the scriptures of the Orphic sect. Orphism endeavored to satisfy the human longing for a supernatural good, a foretaste of which might be enjoyed now. Among the doctrines prominent in the system was that of the transmigration of the soul. These mystery-sects offered to everyone a personal salvation that accorded with every taste and temperament. The mysteries of Demeter at Eleusis were stately and restrained; those of Dionysos were boisterous and ec-static. In the fourth century the Orphists sent missionaries about the country with drums and tambourines after the manner of the Salvation Army. They carried a donkey load of fawnskins, tame snakes, and other paraphernalia employed in the initiations.[1]

(5) *Philosophy:* The period which witnessed the rise of these personal religions witnessed also the rise of

---

[1] The description of this given by Demosthenes in his *De corona* 259 is very vivid.

philosophy. This began in Miletus, an Ionian city in Asia, where, in the sixth century, Thales, Anaximander, and Anaximenes sought, apart from religion, to explain the external world. They started speculations that lasted on through the fifth century, but which we may conveniently sum up here. They perceived the unity of the world, and each sought to find some one element that was original, the transformations of which would account for the phenomena of nature, for life and death. Thales believed the original element to be water, Anaximenes, air. Pythagoras of Samos, probably influenced by Babylonian mathematical lore, held that numerical relations explained all things. Other philosophers viewed the world from still different angles. Heraclitus of Ephesus held that all nature is in a state of flux; nothing is stable; the one permanent thing is change. Parmenides of Elea denied this view, holding that the one permanent thing is being. Empedocles held that there were four primal elements: earth, air fire, and water. Anaxagoras of Clazomenae taught that there were countless substances, that these substances were in confusion till mind came and set them in order. Democritus of Abdera hit upon an atomic theory of the universe that is strikingly similar to the atomic theory of modern physics. The only one of these philosophers whose theory appears to border on religion was Xenophanes of Colophon. He held that God is one and not like mortals; all things are one, and nothing comes into being or perishes.[1] The effect of these philosophical speculations was to undermine the faith of

[1] For a fuller statement of their views see Wilmer Cave Wright's *Short History of Greek Literature* (New York, 1907), pp. 145-51.

the more thoughtful in the old gods and the old religion.

186. The religion of poets and philosophers.— Greece's great contribution to the religious thought of the world was made through the great poets and philosophers, Pindar, Aeschylus, Sophocles, Euripides, Aristophanes, Socrates, Plato, and Aristotle. Aeschylus was born in 525 B.C., Pindar in 522, and Aristotle died in 322. The lives of these men accordingly extended across just two centuries. These writers were not religionists in any narrow sense. They were connected with no priesthood or religious order. The literature which they created was altogether of a secular character, but it was pervaded by conceptions that were so fundamentally religious that they have molded much of subsequent religious thinking in the Mediterranean basin, whether Greek, Jewish, Christian, or Mohammedan, and the religious thought of the rest of the world in so far as it has been subjected to Mediterranean influences.

(1) Pindar, who lived for a time at Syracuse in Sicily, wrote forty-four odes which have survived. He was devoutly religious. The old gods appear on his pages as on the pages of the *Iliad*, but they are more civilized. When Pindar is compared with Homer, his gods appear as much more refined than those of the epic as Homer's were more refined than those of primitive Greece. The passions of the gods are obliterated, their rule of the world is portrayed as righteous and just, and there is a tendency to exalt Zeus to a point where he embodies the moral order of the world.

(2) In Aeschylus this tendency appears in still greater clearness. He says in a fragment quoted at the

head of this chapter, the genuineness of which there is
no reason to doubt:

> The air is Zeus, Zeus earth, and Zeus the heaven,
> Zeus all that is, and what transcends them all.

If this language is more than the momentary utterance
of poetic feeling, it implies that Zeus is above and apart
from other gods, differing from them, not only in degree,
but in kind.   The same thought is expressed in various
ways in his tragedies.   It is not blind fate that brings
retribution in the wake of crime, but Zeus working his
supreme and just will.

(3) Sophocles stood nearer than Aeschylus to the
popular point of view.   In his plays no one god over-
shadows the rest of the pantheon.   He is more interested in portraying the possible benefits of suffering,
and depicts in such instances as Oedipus and Antigone
how character is purified in the crucible of life.

(4) Euripides, 480–406 B.C., manifested a very different attitude in his plays.   Aeschylus and Sophocles were
aristocrats who were interested in maintaining the old
religion and the old order; Euripides was a man of the
people.   He was a critic of the old religion—not the
kind of critic that a consistent thinker would be, but a
critic of artistic moods and poetic feeling.   For fifty
years he lived in Athens.   He is said to have written
ninety-two plays, only eighteen or nineteen of which
have survived.   In these he assumes toward religion
and the gods the various attitudes of a man who is, on
the whole, skeptical and yet possesses an artistic feeling
that is akin to religious emotion.   The myths which
attributed immorality to the gods repelled him, while

the conventions of his art compelled him to employ them. He took no pains to conceal the revolting aspects of these myths, though he took care so to portray them that they should prove unattractive to the crowd. Faithlessness, vengefulness, lust, and brutality were called by their right names when gods exhibited them. At times his characters express doubts as to the existence of the gods, though this usually occurs under circumstances such that the dramatic situation demands it. At times it is hinted that Zeus may be mere law. These plays undoubtedly did much to undermine the popular faith in the gods. Just at the end of his life Euripides spent two years in Macedonia, where he came in contact with the genuine Dionysian orgies. Those he had witnessed at Athens were but faint imitations. Under the spell of these he wrote his *Bacchae*. Some have found evidence in this that he who had been a skeptic all his life at last "found religion" and became a devotee of this cult. It is doubtful whether it is right to see in the play more than a complete artistic abandon to his theme. But even if his faith were awakened by the Dionysiac cult, he abated nothing of his lofty conceptions, for in this very play he exclaims:

It fits not that in wrath gods be as men.[1]

(5) Aristophanes, who died in 385 B.C., was the antithesis of Euripides, whom he disliked personally. He was an aristocrat, devoted to the old order of things. Aristophanes was a comic poet, whose aim was to catch the popular ear and raise a laugh. One of the surest ways to do this is to denounce the tendencies of one's

[1] *Bacchae* l. 1348.

own time. After allowance is made for this, there nevertheless remains in Aristophanes a genuine dislike of the tendencies of the age both in philosophy and in religion. His influence was, therefore, regressive.

(6) Socrates (469–399 B.C.) was a great critic of his age. His aim was to show men the shallowness of much of their pretended knowledge, to bring them to self-realization, to lead them to a philosophy of life that had been tested by experience. His method of doing this by drawing out the pupil with questions still bears the name Socratic. One should, Socrates thought, know himself, know whither he is aiming, and know the means that will bring him to his goal. Socrates believed he had a good spirit, a *daimon* he called it, that guided him. It told him when he was on the right track; it warned him when he was going wrong.[1] Xenophon calls this *daimon* a god, but probably it was thus that Socrates personified conscience.

Skeptic as Socrates was in practical matters, he nevertheless was a devout believer in the gods. Xenophon, his pupil, who knew him well, bears abundant testimony to this in the *Memorabilia*. Socrates devoutly offered sacrifices to the gods according to his means; he faithfully followed every intimation that he believed to be of the divine will; he "undervalued everything human, in comparison with counsel from the gods."[2] Xenophon reports a conversation that he heard between Socrates and Aristodemus in which Socrates argued for the reality of the gods, though they are unseen, from the reality of the mind in the body, which, though

[1] See the *Memorabilia* i. 1. 4.

[2] *Ibid.* i. 3. 4.

unseen, directs it.[1] He also employed an argument from design, based upon the wise adaptation of means to ends in the structure, of the bodies of animals and men. Reverent in religion, Socrates expended his dialectic, not in an attempt to explain the universe and nature, but in the endeavor to ascertain the best way of living. His philosophy was pragmatic rather than speculative. He believed that the gods knew all things, what was meditated in silence as well as what was done,[2] that the divine nature was perfection, and that to be nearest to the divine nature was to be nearest to perfection.[3] He lived a simple life, always helpful to the common people, and, when unjustly condemned to death, died bravely and cheerfully. Whether death was a dreamless sleep or an opportunity for converse with the heroes and sages of the past, he declared he did not know, but in neither case could it be an evil.

(7) Plato, born in 427 B.C., became a pupil of Socrates at the age of twenty, and enjoyed his instruction for eight years before Socrates was put to death. Plato lived until 337 B.C. His activity as an author extended over fifty years, and as a teacher over more than forty. Although he had studied the works of all preceding philosophers, his system was in reality a development of the basic principles of that of Socrates. "Socrates had explained that only the knowledge of concepts guarantees a true knowledge. Plato goes further, and maintains that it is only by reflection in concepts, in the forms of things, or 'ideas' that true and original Being can be attained." "From this point of view the reality of ideas becomes the necessary condition of the possi-

---

[1] *Memorabilia* i. 4.   [2] *Ibid.* i. 1. 19.   [3] *Ibid.* i. 6. 10.

bility of scientific thought. The same result follows from the contemplation of Being as such."[1] All things outward are subject to ceaseless change; only ideas are permanent. Plato was thus led to hold that ideas only are eternal. Sensuous existences have originated from attempts, only partially successful, to express an eternal idea. This lack of success is due to the nature of the second principle, matter, which enters into the structure of all sensuous things. This second principle Plato regarded as "unlimited, ever-changing, non-existent, and unknowable."[2] The soul, in Plato's view, stands midway between ideas and the corporeal world and unites both. "It is incorporeal and ever the same, like ideas, but spread abroad throughout the world, and moving it by its own original motion."[3] Plato "recognizes the true cause of the world in reason, in ideas, and the deity . . . . but the distinction of the creator from the ideas (or more exactly from the highest of the ideas)" is not very clear.

In Plato's conception "deity coincides with the idea of good, the belief in providence with the conviction that the world is the work of reason and the copy of the idea, while divine worship is one with virtue and knowledge."[4] He was a philosophical monotheist, and makes it clear that he regards the gods of mythology as creatures of the imagination.

In Plato's view the soul belongs to "the world above the senses, and in that only can find its true and lasting

[1] E. Zeller, *Outlines of the History of Greek Philosophy* (New York, 1890), p. 140.

[2] Zeller, *op. cit.*, p. 146.

[3] *Ibid.*, p. 149.   [4] *Ibid.*, p. 161.

existence; the possession of good or happiness which forms the final goal of human effort can only be obtained by elevation into that higher world. The body, on the other hand, and sensual life, is the grave and prison of the soul."[1] The mission of man is therefore to escape from this lower life into the higher world. This is accomplished "by the habit of the soul gathering and collecting herself into herself, out of all the courses of the body; the dwelling in her own place alone, as in another life, so also in this, as far as she can; the release of the soul from the chains of the body."[2] Plato did not, however, recommend the avoidance of the sensuous world as some oriental religions did; rather, sensuous phenomena were to be employed as a means of attaining to an intuition of the idea.

Plato's conception of the soul led him to adopt the Orphic doctrine of transmigration. As the idea is anterior to a soul, and a soul to a body, belief in the pre-existence of souls naturally followed. His conception of the soul gave a new meaning to life after death; a real doctrine of immortality was now possible. Plato also adopted the Orphic conception of hell, the terrors of the punishments in which were greatly intensified by his doctrine of immortality.

(8) Aristotle (384-322 B.C.) was a pupil of Plato, but when he attained to intellectual independence he differed from his master at many points. He found reality, not in the realm of ideas, but in things. He recognized that forms change, that individuals come into being and perish, but he noted that the genera or species remain. These correspond to the forms which make up our

[1] Zeller, *op. cit.*, p. 155.   [2] Plato, *Phaedo* 67 ff.

concepts. Individuals are to be referred to these concepts and are derived from them. Far more than Plato he confined his philosophy to natural science. The heavenly bodies and their movements led Aristotle to his conception of the world. The earth, he held, is in the center of a number of concentric spheres which revolve around it. These are moved by a Being who is apart and above them—a Being who is not material—who is Mind. The material world he distinguished from this Being even more sharply than Plato. Man is a creature intermediate between the material world and the eternal Mind, or God. Like several of his predecessors, he rejected the old mythology. He endeavored to put ethics on a scientific basis, and found the chief end of man in well-being. This well-being he found in the proper exercise of the specifically human faculties and the attainment of those virtues which constitute the distinctive human excellencies. He has nothing to say of the life after death.

These great Greek philosophers have profoundly influenced all subsequent philosophy and religion in the western world.

187. **Later philosophical development** took first the form of a reaction against the dualism of Plato and Aristotle. Passing by the Peripatetic school, of the doctrines of which little is known, this reaction found expression in the Stoic philosophy.

(1) The Stoic school was founded by Zeno of Citium in Cyprus, who died about 270 B.C. at the age of seventy-two. The Stoics elaborated the idea set forth by Heraclitus of Ephesus, that the world is penetrated by the divine *logos* or reason. In Stoic hands this became a

doctrine of the immanence of God. God was not a being outside the framework of the universe and apart from it, but One who interpenetrates its every part. The aim of the Stoics was purely ethical; their speculations accordingly revolved around the problems of life. Their great contention was that man should live according to nature. Nature was interfused with God; to live in accordance with nature was to live in accord with God. As God is the single causal force of the universe, one cause runs through all things and determines all. This view constituted the Stoic doctrine of fate. It was not a mechanical fate, but a fate directed by intelligence for wisest ends. The Stoics accounted for the presence of evil in a world pervaded by God on the theory that good cannot be perceived or even exist apart from its opposite. The Stoics held the soul to have a corporeal nature like the body, but its material is a part of the divine fire which descended into the bodies of men when they first arose out of the ether. It is a particle of God. Man is moved by brute impulses, but it is the business of the soul to pass judgment upon these and to bring them into subjection to reason. Stoic virtue is a battle with passions. They are irrational and must be eradicated. It is the duty of men to attain apathy, or freedom from passions. The virtuous man's happiness consists in "freedom from disturbance, repose of spirit, and inward independence."

The attitude of the Stoics toward the gods of mythology and the popular religion was one of tolerance. They were unwilling to deprive ordinary men of the ethical support afforded by religious beliefs, and it was possible to see in the gods different manifestations of the one philosophic God. By means of allegorical interpretation the myths were rationalized, philosophically interpreted, and the system justified.

(2) Epicurus was a contemporary of Zeno. Epicurean philosophy is at nearly every point the antithesis of the Stoic. Epicurus adopted the atomic theory of Democritus as to the composition of physical nature; in ethics he made the individual the aim of all action. In his view the only absolute good is the pleasure of the individual. He found pleasure, however, not in things low or base, but in virtue. It alone gives happiness. From this point of view a theory of society was worked out. The individual sought happiness in the society of others. Epicurus recognized the existence of gods, but their happiness required that they should not be burdened with the care of men. He also sought to relieve men from the oppression of fear of the gods.

188. **General results.**—The philosophies at which we have glanced were the most important ones which occupied men's thoughts up to the time when the life of Greece was merged into that of the Roman Empire. These philosophies attracted only the educated classes. Side by side with them the older beliefs survived. The common people had faith in the old gods, believed the old myths, offered the old sacrifices, and perpetuated the old mysteries. The philosophic systems were too tolerant to disturb the old religion; they were too coldly philosophical to be among the masses real substitutes for it. There was never such a sifting of the old from the new as the historical misfortunes of the Hebrews wrought for that nation, so that the primitive and the lofty existed side by side till the end. In this respect

the religious history of Greece finds a parallel in that of India.

SUPPLEMENTARY READING

CLASS A

On sec. 180: cf. J. H. Breasted, *Ancient Times* (New York, 1916), pp. 221–405.

On sec. 181:   C. H. and H. Hawes, *Crete the Forerunner of Greece* (New York, 1909), pp. 135–43; Nilsson, *History of Greek Religion* (Oxford, 1925), chap. i and chaps. iii and iv.

On secs. 182, 183: Hesiod *Theogony* (in translation).

On sec. 184: Gilbert Murray, *Five Stages of Greek Religion* (New York, 1925), chap. ii; or L. Campbell, *Religion in Greek Literature* (1898); or Nilsson, *ibid.*, chap. v.

On sec. 185: Farnell, "Greek Religion," § II, 9–11, in Hastings' *Encyclopaedia of Religion and Ethics*, VI; or Nilsson, *ibid.*, chap. vi.

On sec. 186: Farnell, *ibid.*, § II, 12—§ III, 6; and E. Zeller, *Greek Philosophy* (New York, 1890), pp. 101–221; or Campbell, *ibid.*

On sec. 187:   Zeller, *op. cit.*, pp. 228–73.

CLASS B

G. F. Moore: *History of Religions*, I, chaps. xvii–xx.

CHAPTER XIV

THE RELIGION OF ROME

Since there is nothing better than reason and since this exists both in man and in God, man's first communion with God is one of reason.—CICERO *De legibus* i. 7. 22 ff.

189. The Roman people belonged to that part of the Indo-European race which entered Italy and is, for that reason, often called Italic. At the beginning Rome was only an insignificant village community of Latium, the land of the Latins. The Italic stock were not the first inhabitants of Italy; they were preceded by the Mediterranean race whose presence in the Mediterranean basin is of unknown antiquity. The Italic stock was apparently scattered through the hills and valleys of Central Italy by 1000 B.C. or earlier. These people lived in huts and protected themselves as best they could. The beginnings of Rome consisted of collections of such huts. The site was selected because its seven hills could each be surrounded by palisades and be defended. Archaeological discoveries in the Forum seem to show that the site was occupied as early as 1000 B.C. About 800 B.C. that part of Italy now called Tuscany was invaded by a people from Asia, whom we call Etruscans. They were apparently kindred to the people of Lydia, for their art was similar to that of Lydia and they employed the same alphabet as the Lydians. The newcomers mingled with the Italic stock and formed the Etruscans of history. They were more civilized than the Italic population to the south of them.

The city-state of Rome came into existence about 750 B.C. During its early history it was one of the members of the Latin League, a number of kindred cities that were banded together. Representatives of these met yearly at Alba Longa. About 600 B.C. the Etruscans surged southward and conquered a good portion of Italy, submerging Rome also. An Etruscan line of kings occupied the Roman throne for about a century. Under these kings citizenship was made less exclusive and a strong military organization was developed. After the expulsion of this foreign line, Rome was ruled by an aristocracy, which, through the pressure of the populace from beneath and the vicissitudes of various wars, was transformed gradually into a republic. Little by little Southern Italy was conquered. It had been colonized by Greeks. Their sovereignty Rome swept away, and the struggle with Carthage for control of the western Mediterranean began. The story of the Carthaginian wars, of Rome's extension of power, the establishment of her colonies throughout the Mediterranean region, the transformation of the republic into the empire, 31–27 B.C., and the history of that great empire to its fall in 476 A.D., are too well known to be recounted here. Throughout their history the Romans were noted for their practical efficiency rather than for philosophical or speculative gifts.

190. The earliest religion of the Romans was of a simple, animistic nature. They were an agricultural folk to whom it was of prime importance to be on good terms with the spirits of the soil. Before their settlement on the land the clan, or gens, was the unit, but with the settlement in permanent abodes the family

emerged. To maintain the family was, after that, the main desire; it was for this that the fields were tilled. The spirits that presided over the procreative power of the family, over its dwelling, and over its nourishment were thus added to the spirits of the land as the objects of the earliest worship. Thus each individual man was believed to have a Genius and each individual woman a Juno, to whom each did homage. The Genius was the personified power of procreation; the Juno, of conception. The worship of these powers had for its motive the perpetuation of the family. Among many peoples the door or threshold has been regarded with reverence; its importance to the household as a means of entrance, exit, and defense is very great. Janus was the spirit of the door. The life of every household depends upon the hearth and centers about it; Vesta was the spirit of the hearth. The *penus* was the storehouse of the family; the *di penates* were the spirits who guarded the stores. Similarly the spirits which presided over agriculture were venerated. There were the *Lares*, originally the spirits of the family farm;[1] Faunus, who gave increase to the cattle; Pales who made the flocks breed; Saturn who presided over the sowing of seed; Robigo, who prevented mildew; Consus the protector of harvests, and many others. The departed members of a family or clan became spirits and were known as *Di Manes* who dwelt in the underworld. Each spirit was at once the object over which it presided, and more than the object. Thus Vesta was the hearth, but much more than the hearth.

[1] See Fowler, *The Religious Experience of the Roman People* (London, 1911), pp. 77 ff.

These spirits were apparently worshiped in festivals, though but little knowledge of the feasts has survived. One such was the Laralia, celebrated soon after the winter solstice, on a day set by the head of the family or the heads of families. 'All the family, including slaves, took part in it; it was free and joyous in character. Each family had its own altar on its own land. Some of the festivals were accompanied with singing and revelry. Marriage was a religious festival, for which a cake made of *far* was offered to Jupiter, the spirit of the sky. It is thought that the bride and groom partook of the cake as a sacrament.

Apart from the festivals the common daily life was attended by religious ceremonies. On every family table there was a salt-cellar and a salt cake baked by the daughters of the family. After the first course of the midday meal, which was the principal course, in a solemn silence a part of the salt cake was thrown on the fire from a sacrificial plate. This was a sacrifice to Vesta. Other spirits were doubtless propitiated in appropriate ways, so that religion pervaded life.

191. Religion of the city-state.—In course of time the exigencies of self-defense caused the agricultural communities to merge themselves into the city-state of Rome. Knowledge of the earliest religion of this state is obtained by studying the so-called calendar of Numa.[1] This calendar indicated the days on which it was "religiously permissible to transact civil business" and the days when to do so would be sacrilegious. There is reason to believe that the basis of this calendar antedates the coming of the Etruscans. The religious

[1] See Fowler, *Religious Experience of the Roman People*, chap. v.

ceremonies prescribed for each month show what the occupations in that month were. These ceremonies were designed to secure the blessing of the gods upon the work of the month. April was the month of agricultural beginnings. At the Fordicidia on the fifteenth a pregnant cow with her unborn calf was sacrificed to the Earth to insure fertility. On the nineteenth occurred the Cerealia, or festival of Ceres, the goddess of fruits. On the twenty-first, the Parilia, or festival of Pales, the tutelary deity of shepherds and cattle. On the twenty-third, the first Vinalia, or wine feast; and on the twenty-fifth, the Robigalia, or festival of the spirit that protects from mildew. The calendars of certain other months, when agricultural interests would naturally occupy the people, are in like manner agricultural. Thus there was a series of festivals in August that had to do with the harvest. Martial interests also occupied the attention of the state, for in March there were festivals for the consecration of implements of war before the beginning of the fighting season, and in October festivals for purification from the taint of bloodshed.[1] The agricultural feasts sought to maintain the life of the state; the martial feasts, to protect it.

In this period, as in the former, life was hedged about with numerous taboos, and religion was supplemented by magical practices.

192. Etruscan influence profoundly modified Roman religion. Tradition ascribed the occupation of Rome by the Etruscans to the sixth century before Christ, but their expulsion from the city may have occurred considerably later than the traditional date, 509 B.C.

[1] *Ibid.*, pp. 96 f.

Until the Etruscan period Rome had no wall; such fortifications as there were had been erected on the hilltops. The Etruscans gave the city both a military and a religious wall. The latter consisted of a furrow plowed in a circle outside the walls of the city. The plow was drawn by a bull and a cow yoked together and the furrow was turned toward the center of the circle. Inside this circle, called the *pomerium*, no gods except those of the state could be brought.

During the Etruscan period the Capitoline hill was crowned with a temple in which Jupiter, Juno, and Minerva were worshiped. These deities were essentially Italic rather than Etruscan. Jupiter had had a long history in Latium before he became supreme in Rome. Although he is the old Indo-European sky-god,[1] and was brought into Italy by the Italic immigrants from their primitive cradle-land, he did not hold the first place in the religious life of the primitive Romans. Janus took precedence of him. Juno and Minerva were also Italic deities,[2] each of whom had her separate cella in the temple on the Capitoline. The Etruscans worshiped them because they found them in the land into which they had come, and were compelled to propitiate them. As the Roman state developed, the figure of Jupiter far overtopped that of the goddesses and of all other deities. Success in war led the Etruscans at times to worship him as Jupiter Victor and to deify Victoria (Victory).

Another goddess that came to Rome in the Etruscan period was Diana. Originally she was a wood-goddess

[1] See above, p. 146.

[2] Cf. Fowler. *Religious Experience of the Roman People*, p. 238.

of Nemi who in time became the great goddess of Aricia, which was not far distant. Aricia afterward became powerful in the Latin League and Diana became the goddess of the League. The Etruscans accordingly erected a temple to her on the Aventine Hill and Diana came to Rome.

From the earliest times the Romans had practiced augury, but from the Etruscans they learned to draw certain imaginary lines in the heavens and to observe the flight of birds in relation to these. The earthly counterpart of the quadrangle thus created in the heavens was called a *templum* and became the ritual inclosure of a temple. The Etruscans also secured oracles by consulting the livers of victims. This they had learned, probably in some indirect way, from the Babylonians. This method of divination the Romans learned also from the Etruscans, though it never was completely naturalized among them. To the end they regarded it as a foreign art.

193. **The early republic,** or the period between 500 and 200 B.C., witnessed great changes in the Roman state and in its religion. At the beginning Rome was but one member of a league of city-states; at its close she was mistress of Central and Southern Italy, of Corsica, Sardinia, and Sicily, as well as of Spain. The struggles incident to this expansion and the commerce that followed in its train brought many new gods to Rome. The most important of these were of Greek origin. Greeks had colonized Southern Italy, but in the war with Pyrrhus, king of Epirus, early in the third century, Rome became mistress of the Greek territories. Even before this, trade had begun to bring Greek gods

to Rome, though the earliest of them were not recognized as Greek. Merchants brought the worship of Hercules to Tibur (Tivoli), and from there his worship spread to Rome as that of a native Italian god. Castor and Pollux, gods of the cavalrymen of Greeks in Italy, had established themselves at Tusculum in Latium. Afterward, thinking them native deities, the Romans welcomed them as such to their city. During this period the Sibylline oracles were introduced among the Romans. As these were consulted in times of difficulty, suggestions for appeal to other Greek gods were naturally received. Apollo was introduced from Cumae as a physician in the sixth century B.C. and given a place in the Campus Martius. Others came, but were kept outside the *pomerium;* such were Demeter, Dionysos, and Kore. They were given Latin names: Ceres, Liber, Libera. As knowledge of Greek deities increased, old Latin divinities of a shadowy nature took on the character of the corresponding Greek gods. Thus Mercury was understood to be Hermes, and Neptune, Poseidon. On account of a pestilence at Rome in 292 B.C., the worship of Aesculapius was introduced from Epidaurus. In 249 B.C. the worship of Pluto and Persephone was also established in the Campus Martius. They were called Dis and Proserpina.

Along with new deities came a knowledge of Greek mythology, which the Romans assimilated with great eagerness. They rapidly adapted their own deities to the conceptions of the new myths. Many of the Greek legends were taken over bodily, but all of Roman life was measured against a Greek background, and new stories concerning it were invented according to the

Greek pattern. It was thus that the story of the founding of Rome by Romulus came into existence.

The influx of foreign cults was accompanied by the influx of foreign immigrants. This fact, together with the experiences through which the Romans were passing, led to a great increase of the emotional element in religion. This new emotional element in its eagerness for satisfaction prompted the people to lay hold upon whatever promised to afford new experiences. Thus it happened that from this time to the end of the republic the Roman religion was characterized by what was called *superstitio*.

194. The later republic.—At the close of the Second Punic War Rome found herself a world-power. She was mistress of the western Mediterranean, and through her championship of the Greeks and her defeat of Antiochus III on Asiatic soil in 190 B.C., she assumed the position of arbiter of eastern Mediterranean affairs, which ultimately subjugated to her the countries of that region. It is often said that political expansion called into being ʻan extensive trade, and that Rome was gradually transformed from an agricultural to a commercial city. In course of time the character of its population was greatly changed. According to this view the change was effected by the influx of small farmers from the country and of foreigners from across the sea. A world-wide commerce is supposed to have created a capitalistic class. Before corporations were known there was little opportunity for such a class to invest surplus funds except in land. Many of the farmers found themselves in straits, for the invasion of Hannibal had destroyed the equipment of their farms, and they had little choice but to sell. In a land where all labor was performed by slaves, those who had lost their property could not work as laborers. They gravitated to Rome to swell the ranks of the unemployed. This view has recently been called in question, and it seems probable that, while there is no doubt about the change in the character of the population, it was brought about almost entirely by the importing of foreign slaves to Rome. These were set free and gradually formed about 90 per cent of the population.[1] In any event the dignity and sobriety of the populace of the older time was more and more replaced by the emotional and explosive qualities of oriental peoples. This composite populace possessed the ballot and each successful politician was compelled to gain its good will. In time, through the increase of luxury and lax standards, the family began to decay. Divorce became common, and many who were married avoided the responsibility of parenthood. These conditions produced profound religious changes.

The decay of the family led to the decay of the old family religion. The Genii and Manes of ancestors could not be worshiped when there were no descendants to perform that office. With the decay of the family an element of stability vanished from the state. The older priesthoods of Jupiter, Mars, and Quirinus were retained, as well as the *rex sacrorum* or the official who had taken over the priestly duties that in earlier centuries had been performed by the king, but all these were carefully excluded from political influence. When

[1] See T. Frank, "Race Mixture in the Roman Empire," *American Historical Review*, XXI, 689–708.

these officials were prohibited from touching the affairs of real life, popular interest in their functions waned. These cults accordingly became·in some degree ceremonial survivals from the past.

Along with the decay of the old, new forms of religion were introduced. The cult of Cybele, the Magna Mater of Phrygia, was brought in, in 204 B.C., to aid Rome in repelling invaders. Later the Egyptian Isis and other oriental goddesses were welcomed. The cult of the Thracian Dionysos was also introduced from Greece. The god was called Bacchus, and his orgiastic festivals were known as Bacchanalia. It was not at first recognized that this god was identical with Liber. The emotional character of the Bacchanalia accorded well with the growing emotionalism of the time. Cruder forms of Greek philosophy, such as that of the neo-Pythagoreans with its doctrine of the transmigration of the soul, were also taught. All this led to the production of very diverse states of mind in different people. Some regarded all religion as superstition; others, having lost faith in the old national forms, eagerly welcomed those of the foreign goddesses, hoping that they might find some source of supernatural help. Meanwhile the rulers, feeling that for the common people the forms of religion were necessary, rigidly supported the old national ceremonies.

The two systems of philosophy that were so powerful in Greece at this period found their way into Italy. Epicureanism became popular in Italy only in the last century B.C. In the Epicurean system the gods were really superfluous; the universe was mechanical. Nevertheless, many an Epicurean continued to worship in order that some subtle influence from the idea of each god might enter his soul. It is difficult to tell how far the practical Romans were capable of being influenced by such ideas. One of them, Lucretius, seems, however, while dissolving the old religious thought in the acid of his philosophy, to have attained a true mystic feeling for the Power unseen which manifests itself in nature.[1]

Stoicism, in some respects the most religious of the Greek philosophies, was introduced into Rome by Scipio about the middle of the second century B.C. Two great thoughts dominate Stoicism. The first is that the whole universe in all its forms shows unmistakably the working of reason and mind; the second is that man alone of all creatures shares with God the full possession of reason. Cicero, though an Eclectic, leaned to the Stoic school. In his *De natura deorum* he sets forth a view of God that is kindred to that of the eighteenth-century Deists. His conception of the relation of man to God is lofty, and his conception of human duty noble, but it is doubtful whether they had sufficient definiteness to grip the conscience of a Roman in his daily dealings with others.

In the face of the disintegration of the old religion which all these causes produced, Varro, the most learned of the Romans,[2] endeavored by learning to revive faith in the old religion. He interpreted its forms as parables of the Stoic philosophy, but the older faith was dead, and mere antiquarian erudition was powerless to bring it back to life.

---

[1] See J. B. Carter, *The Religious Life of Ancient Rome* (Boston, 1911), pp. 60 ff.

[2] He died in 28 B.C. at the age of eighty-nine.

195. **State religion of the early empire.**—One of the marvels of history is the religious revival wrought by the emperor Augustus.[1] Called to fight for his existence at the age of nineteen, he soon crushed his enemies, and proceeded to rule not so much by force as by tact. Augustus was gifted with insight to understand that no motive is so powerful in human affairs as the religious motive. He accordingly set himself to revive the cults that had been permitted to fall into decay. The temple of Jupiter on the Capitoline and that of Apollo on the Palatine rose again in renewed splendor, as did many others. He asserts, indeed, that he rebuilt eighty-two temples in and about the city of Rome. The priest-hoods were reorganized, purged of politicians, and taught their religious functions. The religious festivals were revived and were made by their splendor to appeal once more to the populace. The worship of the Lares at the corners of the streets, which Julius had sup-pressed because it had afforded opportunity for political intrigue, was revived, and with the Lares the Genius of the emperor was associated as an object of veneration. To a degree faith in the older religion came back, and loyalty to the emperor was fostered.

Augustus also gave to the whole empire a religion. Each of the many nations under his scepter acknowl-edged the sway of a different god. In order that there might be a common religious bond he organized emperor-worship. In the East it was no new thing to worship a king. Many kings had claimed, even while living, to be gods. In the West, however, this deification of the

---

[1] See Fowler, *Religious Experience of the Roman People*, Lecture XIX; Carter, *The Religious Life of Ancient Rome*, pp. 66 ff.

living man was more difficult. As the imperial religion demanded only the worship of the Genius of the living emperor, it was adapted to both East and West, though in the East the distinction between the Genius and the emperor was usually meaningless. Temples for the worship of the emperors grew up in the capitals of all the provinces, and in time in the smaller cities. To the temples organized priesthoods were attached. In time these grew into a hierarchy. The priests in metropolitan towns assumed authority over those in outlying districts.

At first sight the worship of Jupiter appears to be coextensive with the worship of the emperors, but this appearance is deceptive, for, while temples to Jupiter were found everywhere, they were temples to the local god under the Latin name.

196. Philosophies under the Empire.—The Stoic philosophy continued to influence a small but select circle. As the social religion of the family and the city-state had disappeared, and the empire was a vast agglomeration of different peoples, an individualism in religion arose. Men began to think of individual sin and of individual salvation. In Stoic circles, influenced by Seneca, Epictetus, and Marcus Aurelius, sin was ignorance; knowledge was salvation. The holy man was the wise man. It was assumed that he who knows the truth will do it. This philosophic gospel was, however, for the few.

Of far wider influence were the bands of wandering Cynic philosophers who on the street corners or on temple steps preached to the people the salvation of common sense and the return to nature. In the Cynic view knowledge is courage, justice, and wisdom. The content of virtue is one's will.   According to this teaching each one has the means to salvation in his own power. The satirist, Lucian, portrays these Cynics as preaching with earnestness and genuine enthusiasm, and even through his satire one detects a degree of respect. They sought to teach men the way of life, and exerted a wider influence probably on the masses than the aristocratic Seneca, or the imperial moralist, Marcus Aurelius.

Another philosophy of considerable influence in certain parts of the empire was the neo-Platonic.   Its precursor, if not its founder, was Plutarch, who was born in Greece about 50 A.D.   In philosophy he was eclectic, adopting some ideas from Plato, some from the Pythagoreans, some from the Stoics, etc.   He regarded the gods of the nations as different names for the one divine nature.   He held to a doctrine of demons which accounted for the evils of the world and even for the disgusting usages of some religions.   He regarded the gods as "our chiefest friends"; he coupled with faith in them the great "hypotheses of immortality"; he kept faith in an ultimate good.   He pointed the way which many, with deepening emotion, followed.   We call the way neo-Platonism.   It was a "strange medley of thought and mystery, piety, magic, and absurdity." It had little to do with Plato.

197. Mystery Religions.—In the quest for personal salvation, which was inaugurated by the emergence of individualism, oriental mystery-religions ultimately outstripped philosophy in popularity.   These religions appealed to the imagination on account of their great antiquity, their elaborate myths, their mystic rites,

their promises of regeneration and of salvation. Those that exerted a wide influence were three in number: the cult of Cybele of Phrygia, of Isis of Egypt, and of Mithra of Persia.

(1) The cult of Cybele had been introduced into Rome in 204 B.C. It was the cult of the Asiatic Phrygians. The goddess personified the fertility of the earth. She was supposed to have a son, Attis, who, like similar gods in matriarchal cults, was subordinate to her. In Phrygia it had been customary from time immemorial to mourn the death of the god during the winter, when vegetation languished. In the springtime, when it was reviving, the Phrygians celebrated festivals on wooded hilltops to the goddess and her son. These festivals were often orgies of wild excitement. Great emotion was experienced because the god now lived again. Sacrifices were offered to the two deities; men cut themselves that their own blood might mingle with that of the sacrifice; they even sacrificed their virility, and became priests of the goddess. Such was the religion that unwittingly the sedate Romans of the republic admitted to their midst. As soon as its character was known, it was hedged about by laws which prevented its spread among the people. It did not become popular until the time of the empire. Claudius is said to have bestowed imperial sanction upon the Phrygian cult, and thereafter it spread rapidly. It seems from the beginning to have sought to bring the worshiper into harmony with deity by ecstatic and mystic ceremonies. One of these was the *taurobolium*. A pit was dug, the initiate was placed in it, the opening was covered with planks, and a bull was slaughtered above. Through the crevices

of the planks the blood dripped down upon the novice.
He received it on his face, in his ears, his eyes, his
nostrils; he even let it touch his palate and swallowed it.
Of course it flowed over his body. When he emerged he
was congratulated as one who had put away his old
nature and been united in life to the goddess. Revolting as the ceremony was, many sought salvation in this
way, and the cult was introduced into most of the
provinces of the empire.[1] In time, however, the bar-
baric character of the ceremonies and the revolting
nature of the myths connected with the cult—features
that even allegory could not render attractive—caused
it to lose its hold upon the people.

(2) Another mystery-religion that became popular
was that of Isis. This goddess was the Egyptian mother
of fertility, of immemorial antiquity, who, with her son
or husband Osiris, was worshiped throughout Egypt.
Her worship in early Egypt had been attended with
ceremonies which had set forth in a crass way the idea
of the propagation of life, but these features had been
greatly toned down in the time of the Ptolemies. In the
religious establishment brought about by Ptolemy Lagi,
Osir-Api (corrupted to Serapis) had taken the place of
Osiris, and a ritual in the Greek language had been
established. While the Egyptians quickly recognized
in Serapis their old god Osiris, the older features of the
cult which were repugnant to Greek sensibilities were
eliminated.

During the Ptolemaic period the cult of Isis spread
through the Mediterranean world. Temples to her

[1] See F. Cumont, *The Oriental Religions in Roman Paganism*
(Chicago, 1911), pp. 46–72.

were built in Syria, Asia Minor, Greece, the Aegean islands, and even in Italy. Though the grosser features of early Egyptian days had been suppressed, Isis was still regarded as a patron of illicit love. These features of her worship were repugnant to the sturdy Romans, and of the devotees of such cults the followers of Isis only suffered persecution. In 48 B.C. the chapels of Isis were demolished, and in 28 B.C. it was forbidden to erect her altars within the *pomerium*. Aversion to her worship appears to have waned under the empire, for Caligula about 38 A.D. erected a great temple to Isis on the Campus Martius, of which Domitian later made one of Rome's splendid monuments. About 215 A.D. Caracalla built the goddess a temple still more magnificent. The third century marks the climax of the power of Isis in the empire. The Serapeum at Alexandria was destroyed by the patriarch Theophilus in 391, yet the processions of Isis were witnessed on the streets of Rome as late as 394 A.D.

It is difficult at this distance to understand the exact features of the Egyptian cult which made it so popular. Egyptian theology, or rather mythology, was always in a fluid state, and it appears that during the centuries of her worship by the Romans Isis lost her early character and became the chaste protector of virginity. It seems probable, however, that the great attraction of the cult lay in its conception of the life to come. In the older Egyptian religion Osiris had become the judge of the dead; each person, after death, must pass an examination before Osiris before entering upon his career in the other world. Serapis had taken the place of Osiris, and in a period when the other life was very real, men sought

eternal salvation in a cult that especially prepared
them for the great assize of the judgment day. Like all
early religions, this cult had its ceremonial purifications
and ablutions. These in time came to have a deep
significance. They were regarded as having power to
wash away the stains of sin and to purify character.
Thus the cult of Isis came to be popular among those
who were earnestly seeking personal salvation.[1]

(3) Perhaps even more popular than these was the
cult of Mithra. Mithra was an old Aryan sun-god.[2]
His cult was a survival of those heathen elements of
Persia which Zoroaster had been unable to suppress.
As it developed on Persian soil, it took on the dualistic
tendencies of later Zoroastrianism—the belief in Ahriman, and in angels and demons, together with the idea
of perpetual strife between the good and the evil. By
the time the cult reached the West it had been deeply
penetrated by Babylonian influences. It had absorbed
the Babylonian sidereal conceptions, as well as its
systems of conjuration. Mithraism also brought from
Persia the general features of Zoroastrian eschatology.
Its devotees believed in a very real heaven and hell. It
developed a rich liturgy, with initiations, sacraments,
and love-feasts.[3] It recognized in an emphatic way the
evil of the world with which men were impressed in the
early centuries of our era, and offered a plausible explanation of it; it confronted the individual with the

[1] See Cumont, *The Oriental Religions in Roman Paganism*, pp. 73–
102; T. G. Tucker, *Life in the Roman World of Nero and St. Paul*
(New York, 1910), pp. 372 ff.

[2] See above, p. 121.

[3] Cf. Cumont, *Oriental Religions in Roman Paganism*, pp. 135–61;
The Mysteries of Mithra (Chicago, 1903), *passim*.

alternative of a happy heaven or an endless hell; and it offered mystic means of grace by which heaven could be secured. Moreover, the cult was very adaptable. In Babylonia, Mithra was Shamash under another name; in Rome he was Jupiter; in Syria, Baal. Wherever it spread it adapted itself to the local surroundings and absorbed the important features of the local cult.

The introduction of Mithraism into Rome dates from her conquests of Asia Minor and Mesopotamia. Though there is said to have been a congregation of Mithra's votaries in Rome in the time of Pompey in 67 B.C., the real diffusion of his mysteries began with the Flavians in the last quarter of the first century A.D. Mithraism became more important under the Antonines in the second century, and still more so under the Severi in the third. At the beginning of the fourth century Mithra seemed on the point of eclipsing all rivals, for in 307 A.D. Diocletian, Galerius, and Licinius met at Carnuntum on the banks of the Danube and dedicated a sanctuary to Mithra, "the protector of their empire."[1] Indeed, when Constantine accepted the sign of the cross, as told in the well-known legend, it is doubtful whether he was able to distinguish between the cross of the Galilean and the wheel-like sun disk, the symbol of Mithra.

Of all the mystery-religions the cult of Mithra was the purest and most austere. It contained no impure ceremonies and nothing ethically repulsive. It exceeded the others in moral elevation, and was well calculated to gratify the imagination, appeal to the heart, and stimulate the moral instincts. Soon after the famous meeting of Diocletian, Galerius, and Licinius, Constantine gave

[1] See Cumont, *Oriental Religions in Roman Paganism*, p. 150.

to Christianity that imperial patronage which helped to make Christianity dominant. After that the history of the religion of the Roman Empire is merged in the history of Christianity.

198. Summary.—The religion of Rome began in a vague worship of spirits—as vague as that of the Japanese. This worship had for its center the family and the perpetuation of the family. The struggle for existence merged this family religion in course of time into the religion of the state. Both were restrained, ethical according to the standards of the time, and devoted to practical ends. As the city-state expanded into the empire the social and commercial changes created conditions which undermined the old religions, and foreign influences and manners found a ready welcome. Decay of faith, and a growth of superstition and skepticism followed. Augustus called into existence the state religion, to which many in the empire responded, but the rise of individualism with the thirst for personal salvation opened the door to the mystery-religions of the East, and also to Christianity, which ultimately triumphed over them all.

SUPPLEMENTARY READING

CLASS A

On sec. 189: cf. J. H. Breasted, *Ancient Times* (New York, 1916), pp. 484–713.
On secs. 190–195: W. Warde Fowler, *The Religious Experience of the Roman People* (London, 1911), Lectures IV–XIX.
On sec. 197: F. Cumont, *The Oriental Religions in Roman Paganism* (Chicago, 1911).

CLASS B

G. F. Moore, *History of Religions* (New York, 1913), chaps. xxi, xxii.

CHAPTER XV

THE RELIGION OF THE CELTS AND TEUTONS

He was their god,
The withered Cromm with many mists . . . .
To him without glory
They would kill their piteous wretched offspring,
With much wailing and peril,
To pour their blood around Cromm Cruaich.
Milk and corn
They would ask of him speedily
In return for a third of their healthy issue.
Great was the horror and fear of him.
To him the noble Gaels would prostrate themselves.

   —LEABHAR LAIGNECH, *Book of Leinster* (London,
1880), 213b[1]

High blows Heimdallr, the horn is aloft;
Odin communes with Mimir's head;
Trembles Yggdrasill's towering ash;
The old tree wails when Ettin is loosed.

   —From the Prose Edda.[2]

Wroth stood Röskva's Brother,
And Magan's Sire wrought bravely:
With terror Thor's staunch heart-stone
Trembled not, nor Thjalfi's.

   —Song of Eilifr.[3]

[1] Quoted by J. A. MacCulloch, *The Religion of the Ancient Celts* (Edinburgh, 1911), p. 79.

[2] A. G. Brodeur, *The Prose Edda by Snorri Sturluson* (New York, 1916), p. 80.

[3] *Ibid.*, p. 108.

Bravely Thor fought for Asgard
And the followers of Odin.
—Song of Gamli.[1]

Many a fearless swordsman
Received the Tears of Freyja
The more the morn when foemen
We murdered; we were present.
—Song of Skuli Thorsteinsson.[2]

Then up and down the river he sought some ferryman;
He heard a splash of water; to hearken he began.
'Twas made by elfin women within a fountain fair;
Who fain to cool their bodies were bathing themselves there.
. . . .
They floated like to sea-birds before him on the flood,
It seemed to him their foresight must needs be sure and good.
—The Lay of the Nibelungs.[3]

199. The Celts, a name of uncertain derivation, is applied to the Welsh, Irish, the Highlanders of Scotland, the people of Brittany, and those who speak, or have spoken, languages kindred to theirs. "The earliest Celtic kingdom was in the region between the upper waters of the Rhine, the Elbe, and the Danube, where probably in Neolithic times the formation of their Celtic speech as a distinctive language began. Here they first became known to the Greeks, probably as a semi-mythical people, the Hyperboraeans—the folk dwelling beyond the Ripoean Mountains, whence Boreas blew—with whom Hecateus in the fourth century identifies them. . . . . The name generally applied

[1] A. G. Brodeur, *The Prose Edda by Snorri Sturluson*, p. 109.

[2] *Ibid.*, p. 148.

[3] A. Horton and E. Bell, *The Lay of the Nibelungs* (London, 1898), ll. 1533, 1536.

by the Romans to the Celts was 'Galli,' a term finally confined by them to the people of Gaul. Successive bands of Celts went forth from this comparatively restricted territory, until the Celtic 'empire' for some centuries before 300 B.C. included the British Isles, parts of the Iberian Peninsula, Gaul, North Italy, Belgium, Holland, and a great part of Germany and Austria. When the Graman tribes revolted, Celtic bands appeared in Asia Minor, and remained there as the Galatian Celts."[1]   Later, by the coming of the Teutons and other races, the Celts were gradually confined to Brittany, Wales, Ireland, and Northern Scotland.

200. **Celtic animism.**—The Celts down to the coming of Christianity attributed to everything a spirit or a "personality," as personality was then understood. Many of these "personalities," such as the earth, sun, moon, sea, wind, rivers, wells, and certain trees and plants, were worshiped. Thus inscriptions from the Pyrenees tell of the Fagus Deus, or divine beech.[2] An old Irish glossary gives *daur*, "oak," as an early Irish name for god.[3]   It has been argued that the holy object within the central triliths at Stonehenge was an oak.[4] "The Irish *bile* was a sacred tree of great age, growing over a holy well or fort. . . . . Another Irish *bile* was a yew described in a poem as 'a firm strong god.' The other *bile* were ash trees."[5]   The Druids held nothing more sacred than the mistletoe. When it was found growing on a tree it was thought to show that that tree had been selected as the object of especial divine favor.

---

[1] From J. A. MacCulloch, *op. cit.*, pp. 18 f.
[2] *Ibid.*, p. 198.   [4] *Ibid.*, p. 200.
[3] *Ibid.*, p. 199.   [5] *Ibid.*, p. 201.

It was cut by a Druid, clad in white, with a golden sickle; it was caught in a white cloth, and two white bulls were sacrificed beneath the tree.[1]

Evidence of the sacredness of waters—lakes, rivers, and wells—is also abundant.   In inscriptions the names of rivers are preceded by a divine epithet, such as *dia* or *augusta*.   St. Columba is said to have routed the spirits of a Scottish fountain which was worshiped as a god.   A yearly festival, three days in length, was held at Lake Gévaudan.   Animals were sacrificed, and garments, food, and wax were thrown into the waters.[2] St. Patrick found the pagans of his day worshiping a well called *slan*, "health-giving," and offering sacrifices to it.   *Slan* occurs in the names of many wells, a goodly number of which are venerated to this day. Sometimes the well itself is still venerated, though it is more often its saint.   As in other parts of the world, offerings were thrown into sacred wells.[3]

Out of these natural objects of worship many deities were formed.   The names of river or fountain deities are not infrequent.   Such are Acionna, Aventia, Bormana, Brixia, Carpundia, Clutoida, Divona, Sirona, Ura—well-nymphs; and Icauna (the Yonna), Matrona, and Sequana (the Seine)—river-goddesses.   The moon seems to have been the most important object in nature to the early Celts.   Festivals of growth began, not at sunrise, but in the evening when the moon arose.   The Celtic moon-goddess was sometimes equated with Diana.[4]   If we may believe the Christian missionaries, the ancient Celts did not always distinguish between the

---

[1] *Ibid.*, p. 205.
[2] *Ibid.*, p. 181.
[3] *Ibid.*, p. 194.
[4] *Ibid.*, pp. 177 f.

natural object and the god. Among them a sun-hero held a prominent place.[1] There are indications that originally certain animals were sacred to the Celts, and that totemism existed among them. In historic times this had declined, and animals were regarded mainly as symbols or attributes of divinity.[2]

201. Celtic gods.—Julius Caesar in his *Commentaries on the Gallic War* gives a list of the gods of the continental Celts, equating them after Roman fashion with Roman deities. He declares that their principal divinity was Mercury, whom they held to be the inventor of the arts and the guide on roads and journeys, and to have especial power in the matter of acquiring money and in commercial transactions. His images were especially numerous.[3] A Gallic god identified with Mercury was Ogmios. Lucian, a Greek who traveled and wrote in the second century of our era, identified him with Heracles.[4] Another Celtic god identified with Mercury was Moccus, a swine-god. A similar god was worshiped in England, for an inscription from Yorkshire is dedicated to "the god who invented roads and paths." Another local god of roads, also identified with Mercury, was called Cimiacinus.[5] Caesar's "Mercury" was in reality several local gods of agriculture, commerce, and culture.

Caesar mentions next Apollo, who wards off diseases. As in the case of Mercury, many local gods were identified with Apollo. In an inscription found in Cumber-

---

[1] Cf. John Rhys, *The Origin and Growth of Religion as Illustrated by Celtic Heathendom* (London, 1898), Lecture V.

[2] Cf. MacCulloch, *op. cit.*, chap. xiv.

[3] vi. 14.   [4] Lucian *Herakles* i f.

[5] MacCulloch, *op. cit.*, pp. 24 ff.

land Apollo is called Maponus, a name connected with the old Welsh *mapon*, a boy or child.   A boy Apollo was worshiped by Celts as far from England as Transylvania.[1]   Another god, or group of gods, identified with Apollo was called Grannos.   They were gods of thermal springs.   In eastern Gaul and the Rhine provinces a goddess, Dirona or Sirona, was associated with Grannos. She too was a water-spirit or an earth-goddess.   Belenos was another Celtic Apollo.   The name is derived from a root that means "shining one."   Belenos was accordingly a sun-god.[2]   Caesar next mentions the war-god Mars.   Some sixty names or titles of Celtic war-gods are known.   They are probably local tribal deities. Some of the names show that the gods were thought of as valiant warriors: thus we have Caturix, "battleking," Albiorix, "world-king."   In Britain a common name was Belatu-Cadros, meaning perhaps "comely in slaughter."[3]

The next god mentioned by Caesar is Jupiter.   At least three different deities have been identified with him—a god with a hammer, Taranis, a crouching god called Cernunnos, and a god called Esus or Silvanus. These gods are often represented with hammers—to early men a symbol of power—and were thought to be thunderers.[4]

Caesar lastly mentions Minerva, who taught the beginnings of the arts.   In Ireland such a goddess was called Brigit.   What the name of the corresponding Gallic goddess was it is impossible to say.   The Celts had many goddesses, some worshiped as individuals.

[1] Rhys, *op. cit.*, pp. 21 f.   [3] *Ibid.*, pp. 27 f.
[2] MacCulloch, *op. cit.*, pp. 24 f.   [4] *Ibid.*, pp. 29–39.

generally as the consorts of male deities, others—and these were much more numerous—worshiped as group-goddesses.[1] In connection with their worship phallic symbols appear at times to have been employed.[2] There were numerous local divinities and tutelary deities. Those that have been mentioned, while the most important, are representatives of classes. They thought of their deities as like men but much more powerful. The most interesting way to indicate the likenesses and differences of conception among the different Celtic nations without going into wearisome detail is to glance at the different national mythological cycles. It appears from these myths that, as among other peoples of similar development, there was believed to exist between gods and men a class of demigods or heroes. There is evidence of a cult of the dead among the Celts, and some of their deities may have been deified mortals.

202. Irish myths.—Three cycles of divine and heroic myths are known in Ireland, one telling of Tuatha Dé Danann, another of Cúchulainn, and the third of Fionn. They are distinct in character and contents,[3] though the gods of the first cycle often help the heroes of the later cycles.

(1) Tuatha Dé Danann means "the tribes or folk of the goddess Danu."[4] The name appears to have been given because the goddess had three sons, Brian, Iuchar, and Iucharbar. These sons, in the hands of annalists and poets, are sometimes three kings and some-

---

[1] Cf. MacCulloch, *op. cit.*, pp. 40 f.

[2] Cf. R. C. MacLagan, *Scottish Myths* (Edinburgh, 1882), pp. 84 ff., 214 ff.

[3] *Ibid.*, chap. x.   [4] Cf. MacCulloch, *op. cit.*, chap. v.

times three gods. They are associated with hills and
mounds which were resting-places of the dead. They
figure in many a tale. In later times they were regarded
as gods in exile, as extraordinary fairies, and sometimes
as demons. Danu is in the mythology more important
than her sons. She is, like Ishtar, called the mother of
the gods. At times she is identified with a goddess of
culture and the arts, called Brigit, who, like Vesta, was
in some localities a goddess of fire. Brigit was too
popular to be suppressed by Christianity, and survives
in Christian worship as Saint Brigit. Other goddesses
remembered in the traditions are Cleena, Vera, and a
river-goddess, Clota. Though the Irish gods were
fighters, there were special war-gods. More prominent
than these were the war-goddesses Morrigan, Neman,
and Macha. Badb sometimes takes the place of one
of these. Women as well as men fought in ancient
Ireland, so their goddesses were naturally warriors.
With Danu and Brigit were associated other goddesses
of fertility, together with their sons. The pre-eminence
of goddesses in Ireland has led some to believe that early
Irish society was matriarchal.

(2) The second group of myths consists of a cycle of
stories of one Cúchulainn, a kind of demigod.[1] The
tales are preserved in the *Book of the Dun Cow* and the
Book of Leinster and must have attained their present
form in the seventh or eighth century. The tales are
supposed, however, to relate to a time synchronous with
the beginning of the Christian Era. Cúchulainn was
the son of Dechtire, a goddess. One form of the story
makes his father the god Lug; in other forms his father

[1] *Ibid.*, chap. vii.

was Sualtaim or Conchobar, a brother of the goddess. He possessed great strength and skill when very young. One of his early exploits was the slaying of the watch dog of Culann, the smith. To appease Culann's anger he offered to act as guardian in the dog's place; hence he gained his name Cú Chulainn, "Culann's hound." At the age of seven he overcame three mighty champions. As he grew up he was unrivaled in strength, wisdom, and skill. Everywhere women fell in love with him. After his death it is said that "thrice fifty queens had loved him." He begat many children. For ten years he was the champion of Ulster. He fought many battles. His love affairs and his struggles form the subject-matter of the tales. He has been compared to Herakles and is regarded by some as a solar hero.

(3) The Fionn saga has to do with the exploits of Fionn, a mythical hero of Leinster, his father Cumal, and his son and grandson. While Cúchulainn has been the saga of the literary class, Fionn has been the saga of the people. It has received constant additions, some of them as recently as the eighteenth century. The stories, like those of all sagas, have to do with hunting, fighting, and love-making. They embody the Celtic characteristics, vivacity, valor, kindness, tenderness, boastfulness, and fiery temper. Some of the details, such as cooking game on red-hot stones wrapped in sedge, reveal the primitive character of the age in which the cycle began. MacCulloch believes that the saga was inherited by the Celts from their non-Celtic predecessors in Scotland and Ireland. As there must have been much aboriginal blood in the veins of the common people of these countries, he accounts in this way for

the fact that among the common people the saga of Fionn was more popular than that of Cúchulainn.

203. Myths of the Brythons.—The myths of the Celtic inhabitants of England are now chiefly found in Welsh sources. The chief of these is the *Mabinogion*, a collection of tales, four of which belong to the cycle of King Arthur. Two others are attributed to the same period, and the rest are independent of Arthurian influence. The name *Mabinogion* signifies "instruction for the young." Other sources are poems such as the *Triads* and the *Taliesin*, and, for the names of the gods, ancient inscriptions. The Brythons had their own gods and cycles of myths, though the forms assumed by the myths in the later poets (some of the sources were written or interpolated in the twelfth century) may have been due to Irish Influence.

A goddess Dôn, the equivalent of Danu, a goddess of fertility, was the mother of the deities Gwydion, Gilvæthwy, Amæthon, Govannon, and Arianrhod, with her sons Dylan and Llew. Llew is the Welsh form of the Irish Lug. In the myths these deities, like the gods and goddesses of Homer, figure in amours, quarrels, trickery, and broils. Another group of gods in the *Mabinogion* circles about Llyr, whose name is connected with the Irish Ler, a sea-god. They are apparently opposed to the group of Dôn. Into the stories of this group elements from the Teutons and Norsemen have probably filtered, though it is barely possible that the features in question were native to all three peoples. In Geoffrey and the chroniclers Llyr became a king whose story was immortalized by Shakespeare. These and many other deities and demigods figure as men in Welsh tales. Their loves and hates, their rivalries and strifes, are told in various forms after the manner of early sagas. One of these deities was Taliesin, a god of poetic inspiration, often confused with a sixth-century poet who bore the same name.[1]

204. Celtic priests and cult.—The most venerated priests among the Celts were the Druids. It has been thought by some that they were a pre-Celtic priesthood of Britain[2] that was adopted and honored by the Celts. The theory appears, however, to be without foundation. They were a native Celtic priesthood. Druid means "the very knowing or wise one,"[3] and the druids were thought to possess the key to all knowledge and magic. They exercised authority in the selection of rulers and took precedence of kings. Magical power to give or withhold rain or sunshine, to cause storms, to make women and cattle fruitful, to make objects invisible, to produce magic sleep, etc., was attributed to them. No sacrifice was complete without one of them. They seem to have been distinguished by some kind of a tonsure. At the mistletoe rite they were dressed in white, but at other times they wore scarlet and gold-embroidered robes and golden necklets and bracelets.[4] The priestly office was by no means confined to the Druids, though they were most honored. In the cults of the mother-goddesses priestesses were especially prominent.

The Celtic year was originally an agricultural year, and their festivals were connected with the agricultural

---

[1] Cf. MacCulloch, *op. cit.*, chap. vi.

[2] Cf. *ibid.*, pp. 294 f., for details and references.

[3] So *Ibid.*, p. 293.   [4] Strabo iv. 275.

seasons.   The year was ushered in on the first of November by the feast of Samhain.[1]   This was apparently a threshing festival.   Possibly when the Celts lived in more southerly lands it had been a harvest festival. At this festival new fires were brought into each house from a sacred bonfire, kindled probably by friction of pieces of wood.   The putting away of old fires expelled the spirits of evil; the new fire, obtained in this sacred way, assured the ritual purity necessary for a festival. Forecasts by divination, to learn the fate for the coming year, were also made.   Animals were slaughtered for winter consumption.   Samhain was also a festival of the dead; their ghosts were fed at this time.   As winter came on the powers of growth were suffering eclipse, and men sought by magical means to aid them.   This they did by means of a bonfire, from which brands were carried about and new fires lit in every house.   In North Wales people jumped through the fire.   There was a sacrifice at Samhain and there is some reason to believe that in early times it was a human sacrifice.   Caesar bears witness that in his time human sacrifices were offered by the Druids to avert sickness and to secure victory in battle.[2]

Beltane was a spring festival celebrated on the first of May.   It was a festival of the sun shining in his strength and was intended to promote fertility.   Bonfires were kindled, often on hills, lighted by friction from a rotating wheel.   The house fires were extinguished. Cattle were driven through fires, or between two fires, to keep them in health during the year.   Sometimes the fire was made beneath a sacred tree or pole,

[1] MacCulloch, *op. cit.*, pp. 258 f.   [2] *Commentaries* vi. 14.

which has survived in the Maypole. Connected with the festival was a May king or queen or both. These represented the fertile powers of nature. Probably there was a considerable amount of sexual laxity, permitted for the magic purpose of assisting the productivity of nature. The ritual marriage of the king and queen of the May had the same intent. Sacrifices were offered. Probably at times a human victim was included.[1]

Lugnasad, celebrated on the first of August, took its name from the god Lug. Its ritual did not differ materially from that of Beltane. Bonfires were lighted to represent the sun, and people danced around them. Burning brands were carried through the fields to assist the ripening of the crops. Marriages were also arranged at this feast, and promiscuous love-making occurred. Like Beltane, its purpose was to secure a plenteous harvest.[2]

The Celtic temples were sacred groves. From the allusions of many writers we know that they had altars. These were probably rude heaps of stones. They represented their gods by images, and certain weapons, as the hammer and axe, were also symbols of gods.[3]

205. The soul and the hereafter.—No people except the ancient Egyptians have had such a real faith in the life after death as the Celts. They did not believe simply in the survival of the soul apart from the body, but they expected the dead to live again in bodies identical in form and needs with those which they had already inhabited. There are almost no Celtic ghost

[1] MacCulloch, *op. cit.*, pp. 264 ff.
[2] *Ibid.*, pp. 268 ff.   [3] *Ibid.*, chap. xix.

stories. When the dead appear, it is in bodies like the living. Their burial customs and literature all attest their strong faith in another life. They believed that the souls of heroes and demigods could migrate to birds, animals, and the bodies of other men, but they entertained no general doctrine of transmigration for all. They had a keen and persistent faith in an elysium, but it was for deities and heroes. Ordinary men were to live their future life here on the earth. The insular Celts held that this elysium was situated on an island in the Western Sea, and their poets never tired of singing of the magic beauty of this "sweet and blessed country."

206. **The Teutons,** like the Celts, belong to the Indo-European race. They came into Western Europe later than the Celts and pushed the Celts gradually to the extreme western regions which they now occupy. The Germans had reached the region of the Rhine before 58 B.C., for Caesar found them there. Other waves of Teutons came later, the Goths, East Goths, and Vandals surging westward as late as the fourth and fifth centuries. Caesar's information concerning the Germans was of the vaguest sort.[1] Tacitus, who lived at the end of the first and the beginning of the second century A.D., and who was at one time a Roman official among the Germans, knew them much better, and his *Germania* is our oldest extended source of information concerning them. The Germans, as described by Tacitus, consisted of various tribes that often made war on one another. They were not savages but lacked many institutions found among peoples of more advanced culture. They lived from the chase and from their flocks, though

---

[1] Cf. *Commentaries* i. 1 and vi. 21 ff.

agriculture was not unknown to them. The names of
the tribes known to Tacitus have long since disappeared.
Even in his day, however, the Germans treasured in
songs, of which they were very fond, the deeds of their
heroes.

207. **The religion of the Teutons,** as reported by
Tacitus, centered, like that of the Celts, in sacred groves,
in which the silence of the forest seemed to bring them
especially near to the divine. According to Tacitus
their chief god was Mercury. It was thus that he desig-
nated Wodan (Odin), a god of the wind, of agriculture,
and of poetry. Tacitus was probably led to regard
Wodan as the principal deity because the Romans were
accustomed to identify the chief Celtic god with him.
To Wodan human victims were offered on certain days.
The next god mentioned by Tacitus was Hercules.
Some of the gods identified with Hercules were Celtic
or Roman, but among some of the Teutons the Hercules
mentioned in inscriptions was Donar or Thor, the god
of thunderstorms, who was regarded as a god of fertility.
The Mars, whom Tacitus next mentions, was Tiu
(Ziu, Tyr), a sky-god who was also a god of war. The
name is held by many scholars to be identical with Zeus
and Dyaush. Tacitus also mentions a goddess Isis,
whom he believed on inadequate grounds to be Egyptian. She was probably Frija, a mother-goddess common to all the Teutons. He also mentioned that the
northern Germans worshiped Mother Earth as a goddess
called Nerthus. Perhaps it was in connection with the
worship of this mother-goddess that they reverenced
woman, attributing to her a spirit of augury and prophecy that was regarded as celestial.

The Teutons continued in contact with the Romans for more than five centuries. It is impossible, however, to learn that their religion was influenced by this contact. Inscriptions to gods, probably Teutonic, were set up in many places, but the Roman soldiers called the Teutonic deities by Roman names. It is a matter of conjecture what gods were intended in each case. Isolated facts come to light here and there. These confirm the picture drawn by Tacitus. The human sacrifices of the Teutons seem to have particularly impressed the Romans.

208. The Teutons and Christianity.—The nominal conversion of the Teutons to Christianity did not at first radically modify either their ideas or their morals. "The West-Goths were converted in the fourth century, about 375; then the East-Goths and Vandals; early in the fifth century the Burgundians, later the Franks; in the sixth, Alamannians and Lombards; Bavarians in the seventh and eighth; Frisians, Hessians, and Thuringians in the eighth; Saxons in the ninth. This is for the Continent. Anglo-Saxons were converted about 600 and took the lion's share in converting their Continental brethren. Scandinavians accepted Christianity in the tenth and eleventh centuries."[1] Most of the Teutons embraced the Arian form of Christianity. At first the Christian religion seems to have been carried by missionaries, like Ulfilas, or by prisoners of war. Later, for military or political reasons, whole tribes went over to Christianity in a body. The classical example of this is the conversion of Chlodowech (Clovis), king of the Franks, who was baptized on Christmas

[1] F. B. Gummere, *Germanic Origins* (New York, 1892), p. 19.

Day, 496 A.D., and whose conversion was followed by the profession of Christianity on the part of many Franks. An even better example of rapid conversion is afforded by the Burgundians, who were baptized by a Gallic bishop after having been instructed for a period of only one week.[1] Such conversions did not immediately eradicate the old religion, and in the complaints of Christian writers of the practices of Teutonic Christians we learn something of Teutonic heathenism. Thus a missionary found among the Alamanni both heathens and Christians taking part in a beer sacrifice to Wodan.[2] Three goddesses, probably survivals from the Celtic occupation of their country, were also worshiped by this tribe.[3] Among the Thuringians a complaint was made as late as the eighth century that Christian priests offered sacrifice to heathen divinities, and that, on the other hand, heathens administered baptism as a magical charm.[4] The Frisians, who occupied a strip of land extending from the North Sea in Flanders to Sleswick, retained their sacred groves, sacred springs, and temples, and stored their treasure in them. They had several temples on Helgoland. They retained the worship of heathen gods, among whom Thor, Tiu, and Frija are mentioned.[5] Charlemagne in the eighth century subdued the Saxons and compelled them to accept Christianity only with the greatest difficulty. They worshiped Thor, Wodan, and a national god, Saxnot. We hear also of a sacred wooden pillar of unusual size

---

[1] P. D. Chantepie de la Saussaye, *The Religion of the Teutons* (Boston, 1902), p. 116.

[2] *Ibid.*, p. 120.

[3] *Ibid.*

[4] *Ibid.*, p. 121.

[5] *Ibid.*, p. 122.

among them, called Irminsul.[1]   As among other peoples
religious ideas and customs were hard to eradicate, and
many of these were taken over with Christian names and
Christian interpretations into Teutonic Christianity.

209. The German heroic sagas.—The best known
of the sagas is the *Nibelungenlied*, but there are several
others—the Saga of the East Goths, the *Hartungen
Saga*, and the *Hildebrand Lay*. The beginnings of
these sagas go back to the period of migrations in the
fourth and fifth centuries. In particular the heroes
who struggled against the inroads of the Huns are
celebrated. The sagas themselves took shape much
later. The *Nibelungen*, for example, was, in its present
form, written in Christian times. Its heroes and heroines
are baptized and attend mass. Space forbids an analysis
of these poems or an outline of their story. Like all the
heroic poems of early peoples they celebrate the deeds
of heroes. In the lapse of time the doings of a god or a
mythological being were added to the deeds of a hero.
The importance of a study of these sagas for the history
of religion is that a discriminating analysis enables the
student to learn the type of nature-myth that was
current among the ancient Teutons.[2]   Thus it is believed
that the Saga of the East Goths and the *Hartungen
Saga* have been influenced by a myth of the Dioscuri
(Castor and Pollux). The *Hildebrand Lay*, the story
of a hero who, condemned to be slain, is cast out, grows
up among strangers, becomes a wanderer, and fights
dragons, contains elements kindred to the story of Odys-
seus, the Celtic Cúchulainn, and similar stories among
other nations. The similarity of these stories is thought

[1] *Ibid.*, p. 123.   [2] *Ibid.*, chap. vii.

by some to indicate that they reflect, in part, a nature-myth.

The *Nibelungenlied* tells the story of Siegfried, a hero who grew up in a forest without knowledge of his parents, but under the care of a cunning smith. In combat with a dragon he came into possession of a boundless treasure. He then rode through fire and liberated a maid on a mountain, whom he awoke from magic sleep. Later, under the influence of a draught of oblivion, he forsook her and came under the influence of a race of demons, the Nibelungen, whose sister he wedded, and through whom he lost his treasure, his former bride, and finally his life. The tale deals undoubtedly with many historic characters, but Siegfried is believed by many to be a purely mythical sun-hero. Whether he represents the day, who rides through the light of dawn to awaken the sun, and finally dies in night; or summer, who through the light of spring awakens life on the earth, only to die in winter, is regarded as uncertain. The sagas thus help us to see what sort of nature-myths mingled with the Teutonic conceptions of gods and heroes. They also reveal to us the world of dragons, demons, and giants in the midst of which the Teutons believed themselves to live.

210. **The Anglo-Saxons,** or Saxons, who penetrated England in the fourth and fifth centuries, at first held fast to their heathenism, although Christianity had found a home among their Celtish predecessors in Britain as early as 200 A.D. For a hundred and fifty years they maintained their ancestral rites until they were converted to Christianity after the middle of the

sixth century. The literature they have left us is all
Christian, but, as in the case of the Continental Teutons,
they brought into Christianity so many of their ancestral
ideas and customs that some glimpses of their ancient
heathenism may be discerned. They worshiped the
Saxon god Saxneat (Saxnot), the gods Wodan, Thor
(called by them Thunor), Tiu, and Bældæg, the Norse
Baldr. Nicors or water sprites were also reverenced.
Mother Earth was tilled with all manner of symbolic
rites and formulas that were supposed to promote
fertility. Running water was believed to possess
magic power for healing sickness. Rheumatic pains
were thought to be brought into the limbs by gods,
elves, or hags. They were cast out by incantations in
which more powerful spirits were invoked.

In the epic *Beowulf*, completed in its present form
not later than the eighth century, a number of sagas
contemporaneous with the immigration of the Anglo-
Saxons are gathered up. There is in the epic something
of history and something of myth, as well as later
Christian elements. The poem relates how a Danish
king, Hrothgar, built a splendid hall, Heorot. A
monster, Grendel, carried off from this hall every night
thirty thanes. No one was able to hinder it until
Beowulf, a Geat, slew Grendel and afterward, in the
depths of the sea, Grendel's mother. Enriched with
spoils Beowulf returned to his native land and became
king of the Geatas. After a long and glorious reign
he undertook to fight a dragon who guarded a great
treasure. He was slain, but not until he had slain the
dragon. He died satisfied that he had won a great
treasure of gold for his people. It is believed by some

scholars that there are in this story the same elements of a sun-myth that they find in the tale of Siegfried.[1]

211. The Scandinavians.—Our sources of knowledge for the Scandinavian religion are the so-called Eddas. These consist of the Elder or Poetic Edda, a collection of thirty-two poems composed at different periods from the ninth century onward; and the Younger or Prose Edda composed by the Icelander Snorri Sturluson in the thirteenth century. The authors of the Eddic poems, though born in Norway, were deeply affected by conceptions, stories, and poems from the British Isles.[2] In these works Teutonic heathenism appears in a purer form than in any other literary sources. The Scandinavians worshiped Odin (Wodan) as All-Father, Tyr (Tiu), Bragi, a god of poetry, Thor, Frigg (Frija), who as Freya appears at times as a separate goddess, and Baldr, a god of light. A masculine form of Frigg, called Freyr, also bore the name *Sviagodh*, "god of Sweden." A mother-goddess, Nerthus, and her masculine counterpart, Nǫrdhr, were also widely worshiped outside of Sweden. Loki often appears in the poems as a divine name, but it is uncertain whether he was a real god or was fabricated by poets. Other deities, many of them late in appearing, and developed perhaps by epithets from older gods, were Forsete, Heimdallr, Hœnir, Ullr, Vidharr, Vali, and the goddesses Sif and Idunn.

Those most widely worshiped among the Teutons were Odin, Thor, Tyr, and Frigg, though, as already

[1] P. D. Cantepie de la Saussaye, *The Religion of the Teutons*, chap. viii.

[2] See S. Bugge, *The Home of the Eddic Poems* (translated by W. H. Schofield, London, 1899), p. xvii.

noted, their names in Germany had slightly different forms. The characteristics of these deities have already been indicated.

212. Spirits.—In addition to the gods there was a widespread belief, which existed from the earliest times, though it underwent special development in the later literature, in groups of female spirits known as Walkyries, Swan-maidens, and Norns. The word *Walkyrie* is found only in Norse and Anglo-Saxon, but belief in these spirits as Swan-maidens is found in Germany also. They are the spirits that give victory in battle. They themselves took part in battle. They were supernatural heroines. The Norns were similar beings, who determined fate. Often they cannot be distinguished from the Walkyrie. The world was also thought to be peopled by elves, dwarfs, and giants, beings that figure in many a Teutonic tale.

213. Temple, priesthood, and cult.—The sacred places of the Teutons in the time of Tacitus were groves. In Germany this continued to be the case down to the introduction of Christianity. Indeed a number of these continued to be venerated long after the introduction of Christianity and were suppressed by the church only with the greatest difficulty. In the grove the gods dwelt; to it sacrifices were brought; it was approached with feelings of reverence and awe. Temples are sometimes also mentioned, but their form is uncertain. In Scandinavia and Iceland we hear of many temples. At least four large temples existed in Denmark; over a hundred are known to have existed in Norway and several in Sweden. That at Upsala was wholly equipped with gold. In Iceland the old religion was thoroughly

organized. The country was divided into districts, each one of which was furnished with a certain number of temples, making thirty-nine in all. The Norwegian and Icelandic temples consisted of two buildings, an oblong structure in which the festivals were held, and a semicircular building at one end of this and separate from it, which contained the images of the gods and the altar.

Tacitus declares that the Germans did not make images of their gods, but in later times they certainly employed them. The use of images among them can be traced back to the fourth century. The Teutons had priests and priestesses, though there appears to have been no organized priesthood among them like that of the Druids among the Celts. The priesthood appears to have been exercised by a sort of nobility. It exerted a powerful influence from the time of Tacitus onward. Customs varied in different localities. The goddess Nerthus had a male priest, while the god Freyr at Upsala was attended by a priestess.

Sacrifices were offered to the Teutonic gods, but, as far as our information goes, these were determined by necessities of state rather than by an elaborate ritual. Human sacrifices appear to have been not infrequent. Prisoners of war especially were often reserved to be offered to deities.

The early Teutons possessed no calendar, and their feasts do not appear to have been as thoroughly systematized as those of the Celts. Sometimes we read of two gatherings each year, sometimes of three, sometimes of four. These were held in different localities at different times. When there were two festivals one

was held about the first of May and the other in the
autumn at Martinmas. Scandinavian sagas mention
three festivals, all held in the winter. The great festival
of Scandinavia was Yuletide, the mid-winter feast.
This is, however, thought not to be ancient. Among the
Danes we hear of a great festival, the Thietmar, which
occurred once in nine years. While it is probable that
these feasts were originally connected with the agricultural divisions of the year or the course of the sun, it
is not possible to trace a connection as close as in the
case of the Celtic feasts.[1]

214. Cosmogony, the soul, and eschatology.—Only
in the Norse mythology is there a complete theory of
the origin of the world. There is some evidence through
Christian sources that other Teutons were interested
in the subject, but we have no means of knowing just
what their ideas were. According to the Norse conception there was, at the beginning of things, a yawning
abyss, on the south of which was Musspellsheim, the
home of heat, and on its north Niflheim, the home of cold
or mist. Sparks from the former crossed the abyss and
fell on the ice fields of the latter. They melted some of
the ice and the result was a living giant Ymir. A cow
also came to life, from whose milk Ymir was nourished.
From Ymir's flesh the earth was created; from his
bones the mountains, from his skull the sky, and from
his blood the sea. Other giants multiplied, and from
them the gods descended. The idea that the world
was formed from a giant's body is found in India[2] as
well as in many parts of the world. The world was

[1] See S. Bugge, *The Home of the Eddic Poems*, chaps. xix and xx.

[2] See *supra*, pp. 148 ff.

divided into nine districts. Asgard and Jötunheim (home of the giants) had been appropriated by gods and demigods, but the middle part of the world (Midgard) the gods had prepared as a home for man. Beneath it was situated Hel, the abode of the dead. This was at least a later view. At one time Hel was located in Jutland.

The Teutons all believed in life after death. Their belief was of the common animistic type. Apparently after a while the dead faded away. They thought of the soul as existing apart from the body. Among them no such conception of the resurrection of the body was entertained as is found among the Egyptians and Celts. Among the Norse a man was believed to have a sort of second ego, or *fylgja*. It was thought that this was identical with his soul, which dwells in his body and leaves it at death, but during his lifetime was believed to lead an independent existence. In the earlier time the dead were believed to reside in the lower world or Hel. In the thought of later Norse and Icelandic poets, however, souls were believed to be wind. The sighing and howling of the wind, especially at night, were thought to be the cries of departed souls. The dead at times were thought to come to life again. Souls could not only come back into bodies again but could change their forms and take the shape of animals or birds. This is the substance of the belief in werewolves and the Norse bersekers.

In the Viking period there was developed in the North belief in a Walhalla, or heroes' paradise. Into it those who had fallen in battle were admitted and there led a life of feasting and joyous combat.

In the later Edda it is declared that a time will come when there will be a Fimbul-winter (three winters without an intervening summer). The ship Naglfar (nail ship), built from the nails of the dead, will come from the land of the giants. It will bring Hrymr to the final conflict. Tyr and the dog Garm will kill each other, vengeance will be taken on the Fernis-wolf, and after this a new earth and a rejuvenated race of gods will arise from the waters. These conceptions of final struggle and a new earth were undoubtedly shaped under the stimulus of Christian eschatology.

215. Summary.—The religions of the Celts and Teutons, like those of Babylon and Egypt, were religions of peoples emerging from a primitive state to a period of literary expression. They have contributed to the literatures of Western Europe many a character, literary theme, and illustration. They have given to our race and kindred peoples their May Day festivals and to Halloween and some festivals such as All Saints Day, Martinmas, and Christmas a number of their characteristic customs. They have contributed to the calendar of saints other names than St. Brigit. It is in ways such as these that these religions have made to our civilization a contribution such that no educated person can afford to be ignorant of them. To the vital religious ideas of the modern world they have offered no important contribution.

SUPPLEMENTARY READING

CLASS A

On **secs.** 199–205 read J. A. MacCulloch, *The Religion of the Ancient Celts* (Edinburgh, 1911).

On secs. 206–214 read P. D. Chantepie de la Saussaye, *The Religion of the Teutons* (Boston, 1902), supplementing this for sec. 214 by A. Johnson's "The Religion of the Teutons" in *Religions of the Past and Present*, edited by J. A. Montgomery (Philadelphia, 1918).

CLASS B

The articles "Celts" and, when published, "Teutons," in J. Hastings, *Encyclopaedia of Religion and Ethics* (New York, 1908).

CHAPTER XVI

CHRISTIANITY

For the Son of Man came to seek and to save that which was lost.—Luke 19:10.

Christ the power of God and the wisdom of God.—I Cor. 1:24.

And the Word became flesh and dwelt among us (and we beheld his glory, glory as of the only begotten from the Father), full of grace and truth.—John 1:14.

216. Jesus was born in Palestine in the reign of Herod the Great shortly before the year 1 of our era. The exact year of his birth is unknown.[1] His mother was the wife of a carpenter in Nazareth, and he was brought up to the same trade, which he followed until about thirty years old. Shortly before he reached that age John the Baptist had begun to preach that the Kingdom of God[2] was near and to baptize men in token of their desire to be ready for its coming. Jesus went to be baptized of John, and as he was coming out of the water a voice from heaven spoke in his soul declaring that he was the Son of God—the expected Messiah. He had been reared among those who shared the messianic expectations of his people, and probably had shared in the belief in such a Messiah as that portrayed in Enoch, chaps. 46 and 48. The conviction that he was to fulfil

[1] For a discussion of the data see G. A. Barton, *Archaeology and the Bible* (5th ed., Philadelphia, 1927), Part II, chap. xxix.

[2] See above, chap. v, sec. 90.

these messianic expectations overwhelmed him, and he withdrew to the wilderness to think out what it meant. The story of his struggle there is embodied in the narratives of the temptation.[1] From this struggle he came forth with a new conception of the messiahship and the Kingdom of God. He had put the political ideal definitely behind his back. That ideal involved the establishment of a rule over the bodies of men by force of arms; he chose to do the will of God in establishing a rule over men's hearts by self-sacrifice and love. He still held to a messianic mission, but it was as a king of the spiritual and not the political realm. He chose as his self-designation the term "Son of Man," a term that had been employed in a messianic sense in Enoch,[2] but which in the dialect employed in Galilee also means simply "man." In his teaching concerning the Kingdom, Jesus taught that it is every man's privilege to come under the direct personal guidance of God. The Kingdom was no longer simply a monarchy with God as a far-off sovereign; it was a family, of which God is the loving Father. All men are brethren. The parable of the Prodigal Son gives us the heart of his message. In his person Jesus exhibited the ideal of one who enjoyed to the full personal relations with the Father. He was thus a fitting Messiah of the Kingdom which he proclaimed.

He chose twelve peasants to be his disciples and companions, and spent some fifteen months or a little more, traveling here and there in their company, preach-

---

[1] For a fuller interpretation of the temptation, see G. A. Barton, *Jesus of Nazareth* (New York, 1922), pp. 117–25.

[2] In Enoch 46: 2, 4; 48: 2.

ing and healing.[1] Not until toward the end of this period did he disclose even to them that he claimed to be the Messiah, and even then they did not understand how his conception of messiahship differed from current Jewish conceptions. His uncompromising denunciations of sham, his emphasis upon personal righteousness, the light value that he set upon ceremonial, and his popularity with the poor set the hierarchy against him, and they accomplished his crucifixion about 28 or 29 A.D. On the third day after this his disciples were convinced by experiences that came to several of them that he was still alive; they were filled with joy, and formed a little group of Jews who held that the Messiah had come in the person of Jesus of Nazareth.

Jesus himself wrote nothing. His matchless discourses and parables, in which he revealed the depth of his penetrating insight into the nature of man and God, were treasured in the memories of loving disciples. Perhaps memory was aided here and there by hastily made notes, but the Gospels were not written until later.

217. The early Jewish church.—The little band of followers that Jesus left had no thought that loyalty to him demanded a separation from their fellow-Jews. They believed that Jesus was the Messiah, but, in accordance with the messianic expectations[2] of some of their Jewish brethren, they believed that he had been caught up to heaven to be revealed in power at some future time. Christians differed from their Jewish

---

[1] This is the chronology of Matthew, Mark, and Luke. As these were composed considerably earlier than John, they are generally thought to be more authoritative sources in matters of history.

[2] Apoc. of Baruch 30:1.

brethren simply in believing that Jesus of Nazareth was the Messiah, and that, when the Messiah was revealed, he would be their loved Master. In their thought of him and his Kingdom the spiritual conceptions which he had taught and which they had only half understood fell into the background. The current Jewish apocalyptic expectations took their place. Among Christians the Kingdom of God took on a wholly Jewish coloring. The Jewish belief in a Paradise for the righteous and a Gehenna for the wicked, which Jesus had confirmed, assumed the form given to it in the Jewish apocalypses. Christianity was for a time a Jewish sect. Its leaders punctiliously observed Jewish ritual.[1]

218. Paul, whose Hebrew name was Saul, was born in Tarsus in Cilicia. His family appears to have settled there when the city was reconstructed by Antiochus Epiphanes in 171 B.C.,[2] and probably obtained Roman citizenship in the transition from the republic to the empire. Saul was sent to Jerusalem to be educated, and was trained by Gamaliel in the liberal wing of Pharisaism. Later he returned to Jerusalem to live. His logical mind led him to attempt to eradicate Christianity as a curse to Judaism. He connected the crucifixion of Jesus with the statement in Deut. 21:23, that he that is hanged is cursed of God, and that the curse might spread to the land. In his view all who became Christians shared the curse of Jesus.[3] Then he

[1] See Acts 3:1 ff.

[2] See W. M. Ramsay, *The Cities of St. Paul* (New York, 1908), pp. 180 ff.

[3] See Gal. 3:13 and its interpretation in Barton, *Studies in New Testament Christianity* (Philadelphia, 1928), pp. 86–93.

had a vision which convinced him that Jesus had risen from the dead. His whole rabbinical education led him, in consequence of this, to regard Jesus as a man especially honored of God. God did not honor liars; Jesus must, accordingly, be the Messiah, as he had claimed. Paul thus became a Christian. Moreover. he recognized that Jesus occupied a place where, in spite of the ceremonial curse of the law, God bestowed his favor. Paul concluded, then, that all who identify themselves with Jesus shared this favor, even though they did not keep the Jewish law.[1] He accordingly became the Apostle to the Gentiles, and by a stormy ministry of more than thirty years broke the Jewish bonds. During this period there was evolution in Paul's thought. For a long time he continued to think of Jesus as the Jewish Messiah and to accept the Jewish apocalyptic.[2] In time, however, contact with the world of Greek thought, and especially the necessity of combating incipient Gnosticism, led him to discard apocalyptic views, and to regard Jesus as the incarnation of the creative power by which God had made the world, and the World-Soul that holds all things together.[3] This was the first step in that development of thought about Jesus that led to the formation of the Christian doctrine of the Trinity.

Throughout his entire career Paul was a profound mystic. He held that the believer may be so filled with Christ—so united to him in fellowship—that he is one with Christ; what the believer does Christ

[1] Barton, *Studies in New Testament Christianity*, pp. 88 ff. and 127 ff.
[2] Cf. I Thess. 4:13 ff.; II Thess., chap. 2.
[3] Cf. Col. 1:15-17.

does.[1] Paul found Christianity a Jewish sect; he left it a religion universal in its scope.

219. The Gospel of John was composed about 100 A.D., probably at Ephesus in Asia Minor. The purpose of its author was so to tell the story of the life and teaching of Jesus as to commend the Christian religion to the complex thought of his time. Gnosticism, incipient in the time of Paul, was now more thoroughly developed. At its base lay the late Zoroastrian conception of two gods, a god of good and a god of evil. Matter was the creation of the evil god. Judaism was by this time in open opposition to Christianity, and it was necessary to repulse its attacks. The disciples of John the Baptist still formed a separate sect that sought to rival Christianity. In the church itself there was a tendency to lay too great stress upon organization and the magic influence of the sacraments. In his endeavor to meet this situation the writer of the Gospel of John took up and elaborated Paul's idea of Jesus as the World-Soul. This he expressed by the term *Logos*, or Word— a term that had played a great rôle in Greek thought from Heraclitus[2] down, and had also been prominent in Hebrew thought. Philo[3] had made considerable use of it. Gnostic thought was squarely met by the statement that the Word was God,[4] and that the Word became flesh and dwelt among us. This conception of

Cf. Barton, *Studies in New Testament Christianity*, pp. 124–30.

[2] See above, sec. 185.

[3] See above, sec. 95.

[4] John 1:1. A more accurate translation of the Greek would be, "the Word was divine." It means that the Word belonged to the same order of being as God, not that he was identical with God.

Jesus as the Word underlies the whole portrait of Jesus in this Gospel, although the term "Word" does not occur after the preface. Jesus is portrayed throughout as superhuman. His temptation is omitted. The dovelike descent of the Spirit occurred for the benefit of John the Baptist.[1] Jesus knew what was in man;[2] at the grave of Lazarus he gave thanks to the Father, not to meet any need in himself, but for the sake of the people.[3] Jesus is represented as proclaiming his messiahship at the beginning of his ministry to a perfect stranger,[4] and as debating it publicly with the Jews on many occasions.

In thus portraying Jesus the fundamental conception of Gnosticism was combated, and his discourses with the Jews were made the vehicle of combating the leaders of that religion. John the Baptist was made to bear witness to the superiority of Jesus and the conquering power of Christianity,[5] while, to meet the overemphasis on the Eucharist, all record that Jesus established such a rite was omitted. Instead of it the account of Jesus washing the disciples' feet was introduced in chapter 13, while in chapter 6, in a discourse on eating his flesh and drinking his blood, Jesus, we are told, declared that the flesh is of no profit, but that his words are spirit and life.[6]

In the Gospel the thesis is set forth that Christ is Jesus, and that the disciples may be one with him and with God. They are to be sent into the world as Christ was sent into the world.[7] In the First Epistle of John,

[1] John 1:33.
[2] John 2:25.
[3] John 11:42.
[4] John 1:48 f.
[5] John 1:15; 3:27-30.
[6] John 6:63.
[7] John 17:18.

in which his thesis is that Jesus is the Christ, the union of the believer with Christ is powerfully set forth. This writer gave Christianity its three best definitions of God, the metaphysical, the moral, and the religious. They are: "God is spirit";[1] "God is light";[2] and "God is love."[3]

220. **Christianity in the second century** was influenced by its conflict with Gnosticism and its contact with Greek culture. In this conflict it developed its episcopal form of government, its tendency to rely upon written creeds, and it placed the New Testament books on a par with those of the Old Testament. It also developed some writers of wide breadth of vision and culture, whose views of Christianity exhibit great philosophic insight. There were also reactions against these developments.

(1) Gnosticism manifested itself in many sects in a great variety of forms. As Docetism it reduced all the facts in the life of Christ to illusions. In antagonizing it Ignatius of Antioch (112–115 A.D.) proposed the monarchic episcopate as the government of the church— a view that ultimately prevailed. Valentinus, Basilides, and Marcion, though they differed radically from one another in doctrine, referred to alleged apostolic writings in proof of their views. Marcion made a canon consisting of one gospel and ten epistles. By silent processes which we cannot now trace, a list of New Testament books was agreed upon by 170 A.D., as the Canon of Muratori[4] bears witness. In combating Marcion the church at Rome adopted a baptismal formula about

---

[1] John 4:24.   [2] I John 1:5.   [3] I John 4:8, 16.

[4] See B. W. Bacon, *An Introduction to the New Testament* (New York, 1900), pp. 50 ff.

150 A.D., which afterward grew into the symbol now called the Apostles' Creed.

(2) The best fruits of the combination of Christianity and Greek culture appear in the Epistle to Diognetus and the writings of Clement of Alexandria. These men recognized that God had not made the Hebrew people his only channel of revelation; that Greek philosophy was also a vehicle by which his truth was transmitted. Clement held that God is immanent in his world; that man is akin to God; that sin has marred the divine image in man, but has not effaced it; that God has always been educating man; that Christ came to complete the education by revealing clearly to man's consciousness the God who has always been here.

(3) Certain Jewish elements of Christianity withstood all this advance and gradually separated from the church. Such were the Ebionites, the Nazarenes, and the Elkasites. They maintained that Christianity should be simply a reformed Judaism. Paul was the object of their especial dislike, and in the so-called Clementine Homilies, Recognitions, and Epitome Paul is roundly denounced under the name of Simon Magus.

221. The Eastern church and the councils.—While the church rejected Gnosticism, it was profoundly affected by it. The idea that matter is inherently evil gradually permeated Eastern Christendom. As early as 200 A.D. it began to drive men to the desert. Marriage was an indulgence of the flesh; life's ordinary occupations were a snare to the soul. The common life of man was, they thought, beyond redemption. They would be free; they would save themselves from the wreck of the world. Little by little the number of anchorites increased. They were gradually organized into monasteries.

The Eastern church was fond of definitions; it cast its faith in the terms of thought. During the third century two great schools of Christian thought and learning developed—one at Antioch and one at Alexandria. At Antioch they taught that God dwells apart from his world; at Alexandria, that he interpenetrates it. At Antioch they held that the Son was created by the Father, not begotten of him; that he is not of the same substance as the Father, but only of like substance. About 318 A.D. Arius, a disciple of the school of Antioch, began to teach in Alexandria. His teachings seemed heretical to the Alexandrian Christians, and he was deposed. Immediately all the East was aflame.

Constantine, who had become nominally Christian in 312 A.D., without, perhaps, clearly understanding the difference between Christ and Mithra, became sole master of the Roman Empire in 324. He desired to employ the church to bind together his empire, but found it rent by the Arian controversy. He accordingly summoned in 325 A.D. the Council of Nicaea, the first of the ecumenical councils. To it came bishops and others from many parts of the church, and after long deliberations it adopted the Nicene definition of the nature of the Son, declaring that he is of one substance with the Father. Although the Alexandrian view prevailed in the council, much of the church was Arian, and the controversy raged for fifty years. When it had about spent itself, Theodosius I called the First Council of Constantinople in 381 A.D. It reaffirmed the Nicene declaration as to the Son's nature, and declared that the Holy Spirit proceeds from the Father.

Early in the next century another controversy arose between the school of Antioch and that of Alexandria. The Antiochians held that Christ had two natures, a divine and a human; the Alexandrians, that, after the incarnation, the two natures became one divine nature. These last delighted to call Mary the Mother of God. The third ecumenical council, called by Theodosius II, met at Ephesus in 433 A.D. to settle this matter, but the difference of opinion ran so high that the council separated into two, each of which condemned the other. The Council of Chalcedon, in 451 A.D., sought to solve the difficulty by declaring that he possesses two natures, which, unmixed, unconverted, undivided, were combined into one person, but its definition satisfied neither of the extremes. The Monophysites, who believed in one nature, separated from the church. These form the Egyptian (or Coptic), the Abyssinian, and the Armenian churches to the present time. The radical Dyophysites, who believed in two natures, also separated and formed what is known as the Nestorian church. For some centuries they flourished, spreading eastward to Turkestan and China, but have now dwindled to a small remnant in Persia.

The main body of the Eastern church accepted the decree of Chalcedon and kept on its way. In 553 A.D. in the reign of Justinian at the Second Council of Constantinople, the works of Theodore of Mopsuestia, the real thinker of the Dyophysite party, were condemned. The Third Council of Constantinople was held in

680 A.D., which, in logical sequence from the Council of Chalcedon, declared that Christ had two wills. The last of the ecumenical councils, the Second Council of Nicaea, in 787 A.D. sanctioned the use of pictures and images in churches.

The act of this last council indicates to what extent the church had absorbed the customs of pre-Christian heathenism. Old gods were in many places christened as Christian saints, and their cults were maintained under a Christian name. By the year 800 A.D. the main lines of the Eastern church were fixed.

222. The Western Church.—From the beginning the genius of the West was different from that of the East. The East was given to speculation and definition, the West to organization and administration. In the West practical problems absorbed men's minds; here the doctrines of tradition and the church were worked out. The doctrine of tradition had been stated in substance in the Pastoral Epistles, written probably from Rome before the end of the first century. In them the true faith is something committed to a disciple by an apostle, which the disciple is to guard and hand on to others.[1] This doctrine was revived at the end of the second century by Irenaeus,[2] who held that the true doctrines of the church were left by the apostles as a "deposit" with the bishops whom they appointed, and that these bishops had passed the "deposit" on to their successors, withholding no part of it. Thus the true "deposit" was still to be found in the faith of the churches in the large cities, where any deviation from apostolic standards

[1] See I Tim. 6:20; II Tim. 1:13, 14; 2:2.
[2] Cf. his work *Against Heresies* iii. 3.

would be quickly detected. This argument, he held, applied with especial force to the church at Rome, since Rome was the capital of the empire and any variation from the "deposit" at Rome would be detected more quickly than elsewhere. This argument concerning tradition was elaborated by Tertullian of Carthage, a younger contemporary of Irenaeus, and became the basis of the claim of Rome to the right to rule the church.

Cyprian of Carthage developed the doctrine of the bishopric, as Irenaeus had that of tradition. He held that the bishop is the representative of Christ, and as such he possesses over his congregation the same authority that Christ has over the church universal. Christ was a priest; he offered himself in sacrifice. The bishop is a priest who at the celebration of the Eucharist repeats the sacrifice of his Lord. Christ can remit sins; hence his representative can remit sins. The views of Cyprian ultimately prevailed and transformed the Christian ministry into a priesthood.

The foundations of the theology of Latin Christianity were completed by Augustine of Hippo (d. 430 A.D.). Augustine's thought was developed through three controversies, that with the Manichaeans, that with the Donatists, and that with the Pelagians. The Manichaeans denied that the church is the sole depositary of the truth; the Donatists, that the church has a right to rule the conscience; the Pelagians, that human nature needs such a church as the Western Fathers believed in. In the course of these controversies Augustine set forth the doctrine of original sin, holding that man has been completely separated from God. It was this that gave the church its reason for existence. The divine image can, he taught, be renewed in man only by the rite of baptism; in the act of baptism regeneration occurs, if it can occur at all.   Christ had come to establish the church, and had gone away again to the distant heavens, leaving the church to rule.   There was no salvation outside her, but not all within her will be saved, for salvation depends upon the will of God and is granted only to the elect.   This was the form of Christian thought which ruled Western Europe for a thousand years.

The personal piety of Augustine reflected in his "Confessions," the greatest religious autobiography ever written, is wonderfully attractive.

223. The early Middle Ages formed a period of increasing ignorance.   The coming of the barbarians gradually submerged the finer characteristics of the earlier time.   In a rude way these barbarians were gradually Christianized, though many of their old beliefs and customs were continued under Christian names.   By 800 A.D. the pope at Rome was able to assert his authority over the civil power, and the church became in name at least supreme.   With the decline of culture crude doctrines sprang up.   One of these was the doctrine of purgatory.   Until this time the almost universal belief of antiquity, that the dead reside in a subterranean cavity, still prevailed.   To this had been added the Jewish-Christian faith that before the Judgment Day the dead will be raised.   Little by little it had come to be held that this period of waiting would be occupied with expiatory sufferings, and that whether these sufferings were to be long or short depended upon the will of the priesthood.

Another doctrine that emerged in this period was that of trans-substantiation—the doctrine that at the consecration of the elements of the Eucharist the bread and wine are miraculously transmuted into the body and blood of Christ. Alchemists at the time believed that lead could be transmuted into gold, if one could only find the secret, and theology traveled in the same path.

224. The later Middle Ages began with the eleventh century. The second migration of the barbarians (the later Huns, Northmen, Danes, and Saracens) had caused extended suffering. This suffering, together with the widespread expectation that the end of the world would occur in the year 1000, sobered and deepened the life of Europe. After the year 1000 it was a more religious world; its happy, thoughtless childhood had passed. Gothic cathedrals began to express the aspirations and longings of the age.

It soon became an age of intellectual activity. The leaders of this activity were the "schoolmen," who occupied themselves in justifying to the intellect the dogmas of the church. Anselm (1038–1109 A.D.), the first and greatest of the schoolmen, gave to the church its first worthy doctrine of the atonement. It had been held from the beginning that the death of Christ somehow accomplished the salvation of men, but how it accomplished this had not been definitely explained. Some had taken Christ's figure of a ransom[1] literally, and held that God gave his Son to Satan in order to redeem men from his grasp. Anselm changed all this. He explained the death of Christ on the analogy of feudal

[1] Matt. 20:28.

law. Man owed God a fealty which he had failed to pay; the debt was infinite because God is infinite. Man could not pay the debt because he is finite. He was accordingly doomed to endless woe. But if man perished, God's love would be thwarted. The infinite Son of God accordingly became man, in order to die and satisfy God's honor. According to this view the sacrifice of Christ was a sacrifice of God's love to God's justice.

Not all schoolmen were so considerate of the Latin church. Abelard was led to hold many of the views of the Greek theology, and became a martyr for his independence. With the dawning of new intelligence several sects sprang into existence, the adherents of which sought greater satisfaction for the soul than the church afforded. The church took alarm and in 1229 closed the Bible to the laity, and in 1232 invented the inquisition to enforce the decision. Thomas Aquinas (1227–74) propounded a little later the doctrine of two kingdoms, the kingdom of nature and the kingdom of grace, which for a time gave the church an intellectual triumph also. According to this view nature is a kind of hierarchy, rising through the lower orders of life to its culmination in man. Rising above this is the kingdom of grace, which has its outward embodiment in the church, and is continued by the angels in heaven. It culminates in the throne of God. In the kingdom of nature the thought of man was said to be free to act; in the kingdom of grace man must accept what God reveals.

These measures and doctrines were not, however, permanently successful. In the fourteenth century Wycliffe (1324–84) translated the Bible into the vernacular for the people and preached an evangelical

doctrine. In Germany in the same century Eckhardt
(d. 1329), Tauler (d. 1361), and Thomas à Kempis
(1380–1471), while they remained in the church, taught
the possibility of a direct union with God, a view which
was contrary to what had come to be regarded as
fundamental doctrines of the church. John Huss in
Bohemia, an evangelical preacher of the same type as
Wycliffe, held to liberty of conscience, and died a
martyr's death in 1415. After the conquest of Constantinople by the Turks in 1453 many Christians from
the East fled to Italy. They brought with them the
Greek Testament and a knowledge of classical learning,
which created such a ferment that a new type of Christianity was created.

225. The Reformation was a declaration of the
liberty of the individual conscience, and a shift of the
basis of authority from the church to the Bible. While
it presented great varieties of form, the forms which
attracted most adherents did not differ radically from
the Catholics as to the transcendence of God, the
depravity of man, and a standard of authority external
to the conscience. Luther (1483–1546), the first pro-
tagonist of the Reformation, made much of the doctrine
of justification by faith. He was not a consistent
theologian. His system retained many features and
conceptions of the church, while departing from it in
other respects. Zwingli (1484–1531) departed more
widely from the Latin church in thought. He revived
from another point of view Augustine's doctrine of
election. John Calvin (1509–64) formed the most complete system of theology, giving to Protestantism its
fighting armor. To him as to Augustine God was an

absent sovereign.   He differed from Augustine in finding
the will of God expressed in the Bible rather than in the
church.   Menno, Schwenkfeld, Arminius, and others
took positions that departed in many respects more
widely than those of Luther and Calvin from the positions previously occupied by the church.   Many founded
sects or parties in Protestantism which continue to the
present day.   The period of the Reformation was the
period of expanding knowledge, when our modern world
was born.   The religious impulse of the Reformation
lasted through the sixteenth and seventeenth centuries.
It produced many types of thought and of Christian
organization, varying from the Anglican church, which
retains the Episcopal organization, but discards five of
the Roman sacraments, to that of the Friends or followers
of George Fox (d. 1690), who dispensed both with an
ordained ministry and with all outward sacraments.
The most widely accepted theology was, however, that
of John Calvin, in which man is regarded as a totally
depraved being, whose sins were vicariously borne by
Christ.   Christ, however, did not, according to Calvin,
redeem all of humanity, but the elect alone.

In countries where the Reformation gained sufficient
power, as in England and Scotland, a state church was
substituted for the Roman church.

226. The eighteenth century was one of religious
reaction.   This was in part due to the fact that the
enthusiasm of the Reformation had spent itself, and in
part to the trend given to philosophy by John Locke.
According to this philosophy everything was to be
tested by the understanding, and the effort to make
religion not mysterious reduced it at times to a cold

intellectual system. This century saw, nevertheless, the evangelical revival inaugurated by John Wesley. This revival stood quite apart from the thought of the century in which it occurred. The philosophy of the time thought of God as far away; those who participated in the Methodist revival held that he is near and that everyone can approach him.

227. **The nineteenth century** was in many ways the most remarkable century since the first in the history of Christianity. Intellectually Christianity had to find itself in the midst of new systems of thought. The philosophies of Kant and Hegel were especially influential with Christian thinkers. Never in the history of man had scientific knowledge been so rapidly acquired. Nearly all our sciences were born in the nineteenth century. But along with new explanations of Christian theory, and in spite of doubts raised by new knowledge, Christian life had never been more intense or more vital. With an enthusiasm unknown since the Apostolic Age, efforts were undertaken to convert the world to Christ, and were successfully prosecuted. Though modern methods of studying history were applied to the Bible itself—methods which revealed its history in aspects hitherto unsuspected—though the basis of faith was shown to be wider than was formerly thought, the adjustment was made in many quarters, and Christ appeared to his followers secure as Master in the realm of religion.

In parts of Protestantism, but especially in the Church of Rome, there have been reactions. One of these led to the proclamation in 1870 of the dogma of the infallibility of the Pope. This was but natural.

The Roman church stands for the mediaeval form of Christianity and is bound to carry to a logical conclusion the principles that were formulated in the Middle Ages.

228. **Modern Christian thought** in Protestantism is still endeavoring to adjust itself to the new intellectual universe called into being by modern science. The adjustment is not fully accomplished and there is, consequently, much variety. Certain tendencies may be noted. God is now conceived as the Infinite Soul of a universe that surpasses the limits of human imagination. He is still defined as Spirit, Light, and Love. He dwells, not apart from the universe, but interpenetrates it. Man has "felt after" God in all the religions of the world. God has been manifest in the religious experience of all peoples. The great religious teachers, Amos, Hosea, Isaiah, Jeremiah, Zoroaster, Gautama, Lao-tze, Confucius, Socrates, Plato, Mohammed, have each in their degree grasped more than their fellows of truth about God or life, and have helped men to larger knowledge or larger experience of God, or to both. Jesus is the greatest of all teachers. He knew so much more of God and truth and the soul than they that he stands supreme in the religious sphere. None has revealed God as he did. The Christian doctrine of the Trinity is seen by many to stand for a truth, the eternally social nature of God—that nature which makes it possible for God to be eternally knowing and eternally loving. It is in this fundamentally social nature of God that there is found a basis of faith for the realization of the social aspirations of man for a perfect social state—the Kingdom of God.

For a time the doctrine of evolution seemed to destroy the ancient doctrine of the fall of man into sin. It now appears that the third chapter of Genesis and the stories of a Golden Age are human recollections of the way the world of man's innocence seemed to him to be destroyed, when his brain had developed to such a degree that he could imagine how his acts affected others, and conscience was born. It was then that sin began. The suffering of the good for the bad, especially the suffering of the Christ, is thought to be the divinely appointed means of awakening, in accordance with psychological laws, the spirit of man to recognize his sin, the goodness of God, and his own possibilities. Righteousness is conceived to be the highest ethical life lived in companionship with God by one who is doing God's will in the world—who is seeking to establish God's Kingdom of peace and righteousness. Such a religion has in it the capabilities of satisfying the aspirations of the most cultured, and of becoming universal.

229. Summary.—There are three main divisions of Christendom: the Eastern churches, the Roman church, and Protestantism. The Eastern churches crystallized at the beginning of the Middle Ages and have since contributed little to Christian progress. The Roman church crystallized at the end of the Middle Ages and adjusts itself to modern progress with the greatest difficulty. Protestantism presents the greatest variety. Some sections of it have not passed beyond the semi-mediaeval point of view of the early Reformers, while other sections of it have welcomed the new knowledge and in its light see light. To these last the great religious truths seem more beautiful and more fundamental than ever.

Of all the religions we have studied three aim at universality—Mohammedanism, Buddhism, and Christianity. Without disparaging or underestimating either of the others, it must be said that in spite of all the un-Christian things that have marred its history, and its failure to realize its ideals in life, the best hope of the world lies in the possibility that Christianity may come to have universal influence. This is because the Christian conception of God is capable of becoming adequate to the needs of man's expanding knowledge of the universe, while it satisfies the highest personal and social aspirations of man; it is also because the ethical standards of Jesus, combined with the Christian conception of God, afford the best basis for a universal brotherhood; and also because it was the aim of Jesus to make the whole world such a brotherhood—one family.

SUPPLEMENTARY READING

CLASS A

On sec. 216: Cf. Burton and Mathews, *The Life of Christ* (revised edition, Chicago, 1928); or G. A. Barton, *Jesus of Nazareth* (New York, 1922).

On sec. 218: B. W. Robinson, *The Life of Paul* (Chicago, 1920).

On secs. 219–27: G. B. Smith, editor, *A Guide to the Study of the Christian Religion* (Chicago, 1916).

On sec. 228: G. A. Barton, *The Heart of the Christian Message*, 2d ed. (New York, 1912), chap. viii.

CLASS B

G. A. Barton, *The Heart of the Christian Message*, 2d ed. (New York, 1912).

CHAPTER XVII

THE UNFOLDING OF THE IDEA OF GOD IN THE RELIGIONS OF THE WORLD

230. God revealing himself.—There are people to whom home never appears at its real value until they have traveled abroad. In religious matters we are all somewhat provincial. We come back, if we are wise, from a world-wide survey of religion with a new appreciation of the "depths of the riches" of our Christian faith. One cannot, as our ancestors used to do, regard the non-Christian religions as works of the devil. If God is good he has been seeking to impart to all men a knowledge of himself ever since man was man. Just as the success of a teacher depends in part upon the degree of mental ability possessed by his pupils, so the success of the Great Teacher has depended upon the mental, ethical, and spiritual powers of the races of men. In the process of the evolution of the human race these powers have unfolded gradually. They have varied with climate, environment, and the progress of civilization. Viewed from the human side we may rightly speak of the evolution of the idea of God. Viewed from the divine side we may speak of the progress of revelation. The two ways of speaking are not contradictory. He who speaks from the human standpoint does not necessarily deny the theological standpoint; he who speaks from the theological, does not, if wise, deny the human facts. In reality, what man discovers is identical with what God reveals. Always God would reveal more if human weakness and ignorance could grasp it.

The study of the religions of the world is, then, a study of the processes by which God has revealed himself. It may be wise before laying aside our study to recapitulate some of the facts of the process of this revelation or evolution and to attempt to classify them. It will help us to a new appreciation of Christianity.

In every study of this kind it is necessary to guard against a pit into which many crude thinkers fall. We must not make the mistake of thinking that because we can trace an idea or an institution to a humble origin we have thereby discredited it. Not its origin, but the present truth and function of an idea, are the test of its value. Science leads us to believe that man was created by evolution from a lower order of life. At first this seemed to degrade man, but in reality it has done nothing of the sort. Whatever his origin, man, with all his powers and possibilities, is what he is. In reality the scientific view has placed man in a new position of honor and dignity. Similarly it seems to some that to know that Yahweh was once the tribal god of an obscure Semitic tribe, hardly distinguishable from any other Semitic deity of that time, forever discredits "supernatural" religion. In reality it only helps us to disentangle from the conceptions that have come down to us that which is "of the earth earthy," and to help that which is really supernatural to stand out in all its beauty and power.

231. Primitive conceptions of God.—Savage men— and all men were once savages—have no unified conception of the world of spirits. Each one of them is conscious that he has a spirit, and he supposes that every bush, crag, rock, hill, mountain, stream, star, as well as the sun, moon, and wind, have similar spirits. These are believed to be more powerful than man—they can help him in time of need, if they will—but no one of them is omnipotent. Man attributes to these all his own passions. They are jealous, bloodthirsty, revengeful, quarrelsome, and savage. The words of Genesis tell us that "God made man in his own image"; all savage men make their gods in their own image. It is this that gives to the savage religions their revolting cruelty and in some instances bestiality. It has sometimes happened that primitive savage notions of the gods survive into periods of high culture. Many are familiar with the ethics fostered by the primitive Semitic mother-goddess,[1] and how they survived far down into historical times in all the Semitic nations of antiquity. Every reader of the Old Testament remembers how strenuously the Hebrew prophets were compelled to denounce the abominations of Ashtoreth. One marvels as he looks back that they succeeded in leading the people to firm faith in a God of purer ethics. A similar instance of savage survival is found in the case of the Vedic god Indra. The Hindus of the Vedic period were exceedingly fond of intoxicating Soma. Under its influence they forgot the painful past and the hard present. They felt that they were themselves gods. In time Soma was worshiped as a god. He was thought to give the other gods their immortality. Just as he exalted the spirits of men, so he did the spirits of gods. Thus

[1] See *supra*, pp. 9 and 61–67.

it comes about that hymn 119 of Book X of the Rig-Veda is, as generally understood, an utterance of the god Indra when intoxicated![1] Indra was the blusterer among their gods, but here he outdoes himself. He has all the exaltation and loquacity of the drunkard at a certain point of his exaltation. It is the earliest known attempt in literature to embalm in immortal verse the boastful babblings of a drunkard—and all this is told of a god of the famed and vaunted Veda!

Savage kings sometimes in their successes exalted themselves not only over men but over the gods. A classic instance of this, already noted in chapter iii, is found in the oldest religious text that has come down to us from Egypt. The text was inscribed on the walls of the tomb of Unis, the last king of the Fifth Dynasty, who ruled about 2655–2625 B.C. One will recognize in the following quotation a number of savage and even cannibalistic traits, in addition to some peculiar conceptions of the relation of a man to his gods:

> King Unis is the one who eats men and lives on gods,
> Lord of the messengers, who dispatches his messages;
> It is the "Grasper-of-Forelocks" living in Kehew
> Who binds them for king Unis.
> It is the serpent "Splendid Head"
> Who watches them for him and repels them for him.
> It is "He-who-is-upon-the-Willows"
> Who lassoes them for him.
> It is "Punisher-of-all-Evil-doers"
> Who stabs them for king Unis.
> He takes out for him their entrails,
> He is the messenger whom he (king Unis) sends to punish.
> Shemsu cuts them up for king Unis

[1] See *supra*, p. 145.

And cooks for him a portion of them
As his evening meal.

. . . .

He has taken the hearts of the gods;
He has eaten the Red,
He has swallowed the Green.
King Unis is nourished on satisfied organs,
He is satisfied, living on their hearts and their charms.

. . . .

Their charms are in his belly.
The dignities of king Unis are not taken away from him;
He hath swallowed the knowledge of every god.

. . . .

Lo their (the gods') soul is in the belly of king Unis,
Their glorious ones are with king Unis.
The plenty of his portion is more than that of the gods.

. . . .

Lo their soul is with king Unis.[1]

When a king is superior to the gods, can send his
messengers to capture them, can have his attendants
cut them up and cook them for his evening meal, and
thus by a kind of cannibalistic[2] communion store away
in his person their superior charms as an addition to his
own, it is clear that the conception of the gods held by
his people is not very exalted. Faith in such gods can
give birth to no lofty religion. If noble ethics develop
among such a people, as actually happened in ancient
Egypt, they develop in spite of religion.

[1] From Breasted, *A Development of Religion and Thought in Ancient
Egypt*, pp. 128 ff.

[2] Archaeological evidence of Egyptian cannibalism has been found
in Egypt; cf. W. M. F. Petrie and J. E. Quibell, *Naqada and Balas*
(London, 1896), p. 32, and Petrie, Wainwright, and Mackay, *The
Labyrinth, Girzeh and Mazghuneh* (London, 1912), pp. 8-15. The
authors call it a "ritualistic" dismemberment, but ritualism had its
origin in this case in a reality.

This Egyptian view of the gods is not unique. One finds it everywhere in antiquity, if one searches far enough. Thus in the best known of the Babylonian accounts of the Flood, in the part that describes the great flood-producing storm, we read:

> The gods were frightened at the deluge,
> They fled, they climbed to the highest heaven;
> The gods crouched like dogs, they lay down by the walls.

Fine, brave gods these! They were "touched with a feeling of human infirmity" but were of little use in an emergency like the deluge. These gods too were dependent on men. While the flood lasted no sacrifices were offered, and the gods became hungry. When the deluge subsided and the Babylonian Noah, once more on dry land, offered sacrifice we read:

> The gods smelled the savor,
> The gods smelled the sweet savor,
> The gods about the sacrificer collected like flies.

Among the early Romans and Japanese the gods were but vaguely defined spirits. We would hardly call them gods at all. In the earliest Roman religion Jupiter scarcely appears at all. Instead various spirits of the household and the farm were worshiped. The Genius of the man, the Juno of the woman (the powers of procreation and conception), Vesta, the spirit of the hearth, Penes, the spirit of the storehouse, Lares, the spirit of the fields, together with many spirits of the flocks, herds, grains, fruits, etc., were the objects of their worship. Their personality was but ill defined. Vesta was the hearth and more than the hearth; Penes was the storehouse and more than the storehouse; and so with the others. This stern, practical, warlike people, that afterward conquered the world, had little imagination for the divine. It worshiped the spirits that were supposed to aid in practical living, but its conception of these was most vague.[1]

The Japanese, like the Romans, possess many practical characteristics. They also resemble the Romans in their vague conceptions of the divine. The Japanese language has no real word for God. The word generally employed, *Kami*, means something wonderful, awe-inspiring. It designates something between superman and superhuman being. Foxes, trees, mountains, rivers, volcanoes, the sun, flowers, and fruits were all *Kami*. When, under the stimulus of the Confucian philosophy, the primitive beliefs and myths of Japan were shaped into a loose system in support of the reigning dynasty, a system known as Shinto, or the way of the gods, this tendency to call everything wonderful *Kami* and to give it a sort of reverence was continued. Notable men, ancestors, benefactors, and heroes have been added to the list of *Kami* or gods.

These ancient conceptions of gods and spirits find their parallels, with many variations, among the savages of Africa, Australasia, and Polynesia today. From such humble origins all later conceptions of God have developed. From such beginnings one can trace the evolution of four different types of conception of deity.

232. Pantheism.—The first of these is a kind of philosophic monism or pantheism. This developed in the latest stratum of the Vedic literature, the Upanishads, written between 800 and 500 B.C. According to this view the universe is composed of one supreme

[1] See *supra*, pp. 266 f.

impersonal substance, variously called *Atman*, "breath," and *Brahma* or *Brahman*, "holy thought."[1]   *Atman*, or breath, like the Semitic *nephesh*, also meant "soul" or "self."   This supreme impersonal substance was in time conceived as the supreme self.   Individuals were but partial manifestations of the universal *Atman*, just as every part of the universe was also an expression of IT.   It was a pantheism 2,500 years before Spinoza. All that is is *Brahman* or *Atman*.

However impossible it may seem that such a view could inspire ethical enthusiasm or religious devotion, yet some passages of the Upanishads set forth the lofty ideal that every act should be performed for the self and gains its value only as this is done.   Thus we read:

Verily a husband is not dear, that you may love a husband; but that you may love the Self, therefore the husband is dear.

Verily a wife is not dear, that you may love the wife; but that you may love the Self, therefore the wife is dear.

Verily sons are not dear, that you may love the sons; but that you may love the Self, therefore sons are dear.

Verily wealth is not dear, that you may love wealth; but that you may love the Self, therefore the wealth is dear.

Verily cattle are not dear, that you may love cattle; but that you may love the Self, therefore cattle are dear.

.   .   .   .

Verily the worlds are not dear, that you may love the worlds; but that you may love the Self, therefore the worlds are dear.

Verily the gods are not dear, that you may love the gods; but that you should love the Self, therefore the gods are dear.

Verily the Vedas are not dear, that you may love the Vedas; but that you may love the Self, therefore the Vedas are dear.

[1] See *supra*, p. 155.

Verily creatures are not dear, that you may love creatures; but that you should love the Self, therefore creatures are dear.

Verily everything is not dear, that you may love everything; but that you may love the Self, therefore everything is dear.

Verily the Self is to be seen, to be heard, to be perceived, to be marked, O Maitreyi! When the Self has been seen, heard, perceived and known, then all this is known.[1]

Much more of a similar strain follows. It is an expression of a lofty philosophico-religious ideal—to value the part for the whole, and to love the universal self. It never led, however, to the redemption of any great part of Indian life. It was too intangible, and it contained the seeds of pessimism. According to this doctrine man is but an evanescent bubble on the surface of the Infinite Self. The Upanishads were introduced into Persia in the early centuries of the Christian era. Omar Khayyam was steeped in their philosophy. Their legitimate fruit may be studied in his charming, but hopeless, poems. It will be noted that, in the passage from the Upanishads just quoted, the existence of the old gods is not denied. They are taken for granted as a part of the world, but, like men and cattle, are regarded as partial expressions of the Infinite Self.

233. Gods caught in the meshes of the universe.— According to a second evolution from the primitive type of thought the gods or spirits remained as they had originally been conceived, and the conception of the universe was enlarged so that the gods, like men, were thought to be entangled in its meshes, and men ceased to look to the gods for their salvation. At least five systems of religious thought, two in India and three in China, came into existence in consequence of this

[1] *The Sacred Books of the East*, XV, 182 ff.

general view of the universe and the gods. In the
Indian systems the gods ceased to be worshiped; in
the Chinese a sort of secondary reverence was still paid
to them; but in both countries, in the systems referred
to, something else than the gods took the chief place
in human thought. As many millions (at least a third
of the population of the globe) profess religions today
that were born from this conception of the divine as
profess Christianity.

The monistic philosophy of the Upanishads was not
the only one that had grown up in India before the year
500 B.C. There was another, called later the Sankhya
system,[1] according to which the universe was dualistic.
On the one side was the primary substance, matter,
eternally active, productive, the source and seat of all
change. On the other an infinite number of individual
souls. These souls were caught in the meshes of the
material universe. To this philosophy the doctrine
of transmigration was added. Death brought no release
from the pain of material enmeshment. It was begun
again in a rebirth. Indeed, the doctrine of transmigration was by this time common to all India, and not the
property of any one philosophy. Along with these
conceptions the doctrine of *karma*, or the "deed," had
been accepted, according to which one's next migration
depended upon his conduct. If one acted like a pig he
would be born next time as a pig. If he acted like a
Brahmin (the highest caste) he might be born into that
caste next time. This was the state of Indian thought
when, about 567 B.C., Gautama, afterward called the
Buddha, or the "Enlightened," was born.

[1] See *supra*, p. 181.

(1) The first of the five religions that accepted our second conception of the gods is Buddhism. Gautama held to the Sankhya or dualistic philosophy. To him the gods were simply spirits caught like men in the meshes of the material universe. Gautama did not, therefore, appeal to the gods for help. His theory of salvation—that which came to him at the time of his illumination—was simply a system of ethical culture. As the basis of the theory were the Four Noble Truths: (a) All that exists is subject to suffering. (b) The origin of suffering is human desires. (c) The cessation of desires releases from suffering. (d) The path that leads to the cessation of existence and accordingly to the cessation of suffering is the Noble Eightfold Path. This Eightfold Path, which constituted the fourth of the noble truths, consisted of right views (free from superstition or delusion), right aspirations (high and worthy of an intelligent man), right speech (kindly, open, truthful), right conduct (peaceful, honest, pure), right livelihood (bringing hurt or danger to no living thing), right effort (in self-training and self-control), right mindfulness (the active, watchful mind), right rapture (in deep meditation on the realities of life).[1]

Three of the truths are philosophical assumptions. The fourth is an ethical path out of the pain of existence. He who followed it attained Arahatship—a kind of consciousless, passionless, pure character—and so passed into Nirvana and escaped the burdens of existence. He did not become a saved soul, for Gautama did not believe in an immortal soul. The soul was, in his view, only a bundle composed of desires, as a chariot is

[1] See *supra*, pp. 158, 163, and 164.

composed of wheels, axle, pole, etc. Take these away and there is no chariot. So take away desires that cause suffering, and there is no soul. So reasoned the Buddha. Here was, and for our present purpose is, the important point, a way of salvation that had no use for gods, or God.

(2) Almost contemporary with Gautama (perhaps even a little earlier) there lived another Indian prophet, Vardhamana, more often called Mahavira, the great hero. Like Gautama, he accepted the doctrine that the gods were helpless spirits caught in the network and pain of the universe. He too held the doctrine of transmigration and the belief that matter and soul are distinct. Like Gautama, he sought a way of release from the agony of material existence. Gautama at the beginning of his search had, like many of his countrymen before him, tried asceticism but had given it up in despair, when, having reduced his physical strength almost to zero, he found himself no better. Mahavira, on the other hand, pursued the ascetic path for twelve years, when he announced himself the *Jain*, or the "victorious." As Gautama became the apostle of enlightenment and of ethical culture, so Mahavira became the apostle of victory by means of asceticism. He founded the Jain sect, which still persists in India.[1] Like Buddhism, it is a system of salvation by human effort. Had Mahavira spoken in biblical phrase, he would have sung:

> Mine own right arm hath gotten me the victory.

(3) Passing to China, while we find the same general conceptions of spirits and gods, we find quite a different

[1] See *supra*, pp. 175 f.

development. The oldest books of the empire teach that the universe consists of two souls or breaths, *Yang* and *Yin*. *Yang* represents light, warmth, productivity, life; *Yin*, darkness, cold, death. The *Yang* is subdivided into an indefinite number of good souls called *Shen*; *Yin* into an indefinite number of demons and specters called *Kwei*. The world is full of these spirits, especially of *Kwei*. Man himself has in him a *shen* that accounts for his good qualities and a *kwei* that accounts for his bad. Belief in a multiplicity of spirits has persisted through all the centuries of Chinese civilization to the present day.[1] Sometimes even Christian missionaries to China catch the belief in demons.

In the Chinese state religion as represented in the Chinese classics, which were old even in the days of Confucius, 500 B.C., the worship of the emperor is centered mainly, though not exclusively, upon Heaven and Earth. Sacrifices are also offered to certain hills and rivers. To this day Heaven is worshiped at the winter solstice in a sacred park south of Pekin, and the Earth at the summer solstice in a sacred park to the north of the city. Heaven and Earth are thus regarded as the chief objects of worship. Other spirits are appealed to, but in this system it is implied, though perhaps not fully thought out, that the other gods are inferior to the great material universe. The system simply betrays a tendency.

(4) This tendency is seen at its maximum in Taoism, founded by China's earliest sage, Lao-tze, born about 600 B.C. To him the great thing in the universe was *Tao*, a word that may be variously translated "way,"

[1] See *supra*, p. 204.

"road," "path," "nature," "power," etc. Probably on the lips of Lao-tze, Tao meant "the way the universe goes," or "nature." To come into harmony with the Way was, according to him, salvation. Like the early Christians, he was an apostle of "the Way." He did not make his chief appeal to gods or spirits. Nature was superior to them. To come into harmony with the Tao was the supreme aim. He sought to accomplish this by a kind of mystic quietism. Here are some of his sayings:[1]

The Tao that can be *tao*ed is not the enduring and unchanging Tao (or, The way that can be walked is not the enduring and unchanging way). Again:

> The grandest forms of active force
> From Tao come, their only source.
> Who can of Tao the nature tell?
> Our sight it flies, our touch as well.
> Eluding sight, eluding touch,
> The forms of things all in it crouch;
> Eluding touch, eluding sight,
> There are their semblances all right.
> Profound it is, dark and obscure;
> Things' essences all there endure.
> Those essences the truth enfold
> Of what, when seen, shall then be told.
> Now it is so; 'twas so of old.
> Its name—what passes not away;
> So in their beautiful array,
> Things form and never know decay.

Again: "How pure and still the Tao is, as if it would ever so continue! I do not know whose son it is. It might appear to have been before Shang-ti."

[1] From the *Sacred Books of the East*, Vol. XXXIX; cf. *supra*, 214 f.

Shang-ti is the chief of the Chinese spirits. Legge translates the term "God." When Lao-tze says that the Tao might have been before Shang-ti he expresses the thought that nature is at least coeval with, if not superior to, gods and spirits.

(5) The fifth system of thought that grew up from the conception of the divine that we are considering was Confucianism. Confucius was a younger contemporary of Lao-tze, was born 551, and died 478 B.C. Confucius was not an originator of new systems of thought, nor a religious reformer. He was rather a practical systematizer of the conduct of life. That his system has become a sort of religion in China is one of the curious developments of the Chinese national genius. Confucius venerated the past, and built on the foundation of the state religion; consequently, for him also, Heaven and Earth were superior to gods and spirits.

234. God a philosophic Absolute.—A third fundamental conception of the divine grew out of northern Buddhism, called Mahayana Buddhism, or Buddhism of the Great Vehicle, because its sacred books or Bible contain so much more than those of southern Buddhism, which is called Hinayana Buddhism, or Buddhism of the Little Vehicle. Northern Buddhism developed largely outside of India in Nepal, Thibet, China, and Japan. While in India the Buddha came in a little while to be worshiped as an incarnation of the supernatural, the whole system of thought remained tolerably near that of the founder. In northern Buddhism, however, belief in a wonderful system of pre-existent Buddhas and Bodhisattwas soon arose. According to one of these systems, which flourished in China and Japan, all things are comprehended in a Being who is a kind of philosophical Absolute. He is in all things and comprehends them all. He cannot be set forth in words but has been incarnated in successive Buddhas. In this system Gautama occupies a subordinate place. There have been many Buddhas. Salvation according to this system consists in first attaining Buddhahood, and then in being absorbed in the Absolute.

235. Monotheism.—From these developments, the first and third of which are coldly philosophical, and the second theologically abortive, one turns with satisfaction to monotheism. Of the four monotheistic religions, the monotheism of Judaism and Zoroastrianism was separately and independently developed; that of Christianity and Mohammedanism was derived from Judaism.

236. Jewish monotheism.—Monotheism made its appearance as a permanent force in history in the teachings of the Hebrew prophets in the eighth century B.C.[1] The earlier attempt of Amenophis IV of Egypt to establish the worship of one god came to nothing. His was not a spiritual monotheism. His one god was the physical sun-disk. The Yahweh, whom Amos, Hosea, and Isaiah proclaimed as the one God, developed though

[1] About the eighth century B.C. the mind of man began to be sufficiently developed to grasp spiritual religious ideas. During the next four hundred years, from China to Greece, men moved away from inherited conceptions toward positive and spiritual views. The Hebrew prophets, the authors of the Upanishads, Zoroaster, Gautama, Lao-tze, Confucius, Socrates, and Plato all lived during this period. Such a world-wide movement of great minds away from the material toward the spiritual is indicative of the beginnings of spiritual adolescence in the human race.

he was out of an earlier national and tribal god, was nevertheless to these prophets primarily spiritual and ethical. He was chiefly interested in the social welfare of his people; he demanded justice between man and man. The best sacrifice one could offer to him was "to do justice, to love mercy, and to walk humbly." He was to his people as a loving husband. He was a God who was near at hand, who communed freely with his people. "Surely Yahweh-God will do nothing, except he reveal his secret to his servants the prophets" (Amos 3:7).

Through the adoption of the Deuteronomic law, the ministry of Ezekiel, and the adoption of the priestly law, the religion of the prophets was transformed into Judaism. The monotheism of the prophets was retained, but the nearness of Yahweh was lost. God became transcendent. The Judaism of Palestine developed in time the deism that characterizes Judaism through most of its history. The Judaism of the Dispersion, especially Alexandrian Judaism in the person of Philo, developed a philosophical conception of God and his Logos (i.e., Reason or Word), through which God reveals himself in the world. This view was taken up later by Christianity in a modified form, and, perhaps largely because of this, it ceased to be fostered by Judaism. The legalistic, deistic conceptions of Pharisaism prevailed, and Judaism became what it has been through the centuries—a national religion, incapable of reaching to any considerable degree beyond its racial boundaries, ethical without emotion, devoted to monotheism without passion. Its God has been the one God, but he has been cold and far away.[1]

[1] See *supra*, chap. v.

237. Zoroastrian monotheism.—Zarathustra, or Zoroaster, the Prophet of Persia, was a contemporary of the prophet Jeremiah. He is believed to have died in the year 583 B.C. at the age of seventy-seven years. His genuine teaching is presented in a body of psalms known as the Gathas. To these Gathas there are added some centuries later the Yasts and the Vendidad, the ceremonial books of Zoroastrianism. These are the Book of Leviticus of that religion, and bear about the same relation to the teachings of Zoroaster as the Book of Leviticus does to the teachings of Hosea. Later still by a thousand years or more is the Bundahishn, which bears about the same relation to the earlier literature that the Talmud does to the Old Testament, or the Patristic literature to the New.

From the Gathas and Assyrian sources we learn that Zoroaster did for a Persian god named Mazda, called Ahura Mazda, or "Lord Mazda," what Amos did for Yahweh. He lifted him out of his local environment and made him the God of the world. Zoroaster was a pure monotheist. In his thought Ahura Mazda is everything. He scarcely mentions the prince of evil, Angra Maynu, later called Ahriman. It was only in the later literature that Ahriman became a god coequal with Ahura Mazda who almost successfully contests the sovereignty of the world with him. The development of Zoroastrianism is paralleled in this respect by some sections of Christianity, where Satan is regarded as almost as powerful as God.

To return to Zoroaster, he was a pure monotheist, earnest, ethical, practical. As compared with Hebrew prophets his thought was abstract and at times vague.

He personifies "Good Thought," "Perfect Righteousness," "Health" or "Salvation," "Immortality," and
"Bad Thought" until they are subordinate supernatural
beings. As one reads him he is strongly reminded of
the vocabulary of Christian Science.[1]

Perhaps it was because of this abstractness that
Zoroastrianism did not succeed until King Vishtaspa
was converted and began to propagate it with the
sword. At all events there is in the use of the sword
something of a parallelism between Zoroastrianism and
Islam.

For some reason the monotheism of Zoroaster never
won many converts outside of Persia. It took up into
itself after the prophet's death many heathen elements,
but so did the religion of the prophets in becoming
Judaism, and so did Christianity. Nevertheless, as in
Judaism, the bonds of race held it. Once the religion
of a mighty people, Zoroastrianism holds today the
devotion of but some 100,000 descendants of the old
Persians, of whom about 90,000 are resident in India.

238. Mohammedan monotheism.—Mohammedan-
ism derived its monotheism from Judaism. It was the
stories of Abraham and the patriarchs, orally heard and
imperfectly understood, that shaped Mohammed's conception of God. Islam yields to no religion in the world
in its emphasis upon the divine unity and its intolerance
of the worship of anything other than the One God. The
God of Islam out-deists deism. He is remote. He is
absolute, incomprehensible, exalted. He is said to be
merciful and compassionate, but his mercy is extended
only to believers; for unbelievers he has only the literal

[1] See *supra*, chap. vii.

fires of a very material hell. He is without real love.
The three or four passages in the Koran which speak of
the love of Allah refer, as the context shows, to his
approval of certain kinds of conduct and of men. Like
Yahweh, Allah is once called "holy," but his holiness
is a freedom from the violation of taboos rather than the
possession of ethical perfections. Allah, according to
the Koran, is crafty; he can outwit tricky men in plot-
ting. He was an ideal Arab of the seventh century
made infinite.

Perhaps the dominant characteristic of the Mohammedan conception of God is his absolute rule of the
world. So absolute is this rule believed to be that he is
declared to be the author of evil as well as of good. In
this respect Mohammed but perpetuated and emphasized
a phase of the conceptions held by the Hebrew prophets
concerning Yahweh.

This God, the Mohammedan believes, rules the world
like an oriental despot. He demands of his followers an
ethic of the rude sort that Arabia had reached in the
seventh century A.D. Islam means "to submit." Islam
is the religion of submission to the will of God. His
will rules the world as blind fate. He demands no
sacrifice; he asks no atonement for sin. All men can
do is to throw themselves on the divine mercy and trust
Allah. True, Allah promises paradise to those who
believe and to those who die fighting for Islam.

Like a wise despot he rewards those who advance the
limits of his dominions.

While it is true that the Shiites by their doctrine
of Imams practically modify this view of God, and that
Mutazilites have doubted it, such is in brief the mono-

theism of Islam over all the Mohammedan world. It was developed in barbarism; it appeals to barbarism, and since the world is still barbarous Islam is the religion of about one-sixth of the human race. In East Africa, for example, it is winning converts far more rapidly than Christianity.[1]

239. Christian monotheism.—The full religious richness of monotheism is found only in Christianity. Things that are precious are a long time in the making. This is true of the Christian conception of God. That God is One and that he demands social justice had been the great message of the eighth-century prophets. Hosea and Jeremiah had taught that God loves like a fond husband and tender parent. These great truths, somewhat dimmed in the development of Jewish legalism, were not only revived but surpassed in the teaching and life of Jesus Christ. "Since Jesus lived God has been another and nearer Being to Man," Dr. Fairbairn said. Dr. Fosdick writes: "Jesus had the most joyous idea of God that ever was thought of." "That joyous sense of God he has given his followers," declares Glover, "and it stands in vivid contrast with the feelings men have toward God in the other religions."[2] He gave new vividness to the fatherhood of God. His all-embracing love, his tireless service to the down-trodden and suffering, gave a new depth and a new catholicity to love. After he lived men dared to believe that God was like him. The nearness of God, his human interest,

[1] For a more complete statement see the chapter on the Mohammedan and Christian conceptions of God contributed by the writer to James L. Barton's *Christian Approach to Islam* (Boston, 1918).

[2] T. R. Glover, *The Jesus of History* (New York, 1917), p. 87, where Fairbairn and Fosdick are also quoted.

his tireless and unchanging love, came back into human life at a higher tide than ever·before.

Decades passed and the great, nameless religious genius whose works pass under the name of John gave new and deeper significance to Philo's doctrine of the Word. By applying that term to Jesus Christ he transformed and transfigured its meaning. The Logos, or Word, was no longer a vague philosophical abstraction; it glowed and palpitated with the life and love of Jesus.

This writer too, catching from Christ truth before unbelievable, gave us our best definitions of God: "God is Spirit"; "God is Light"; "God is Love"—perfect metaphysically, morally, religiously. Men need new faculties before they can appreciate definitions of God better than these. The Fourth Gospel also tells us that Jesus had spoken of the Holy Spirit in personal terms as the Comforter, and that he had declared that this Comforter was his representative.

As the first Christians recalled their contact with Jesus Christ they were convinced that God had in him come into human life in a unique way. After the lapse of centuries, when the Arians were denying that God had come into human life, the Nicene Fathers enunciated the doctrine of the Trinity in order to maintain the faith that God had really come into the life of man. It is doubtless true that the Nicene creed lacks the glow of the apostolic experience of God, but faith expressed in a formula is better than a faith lost. In reality the Fathers of the Oecumenical Councils were feeling after an important truth when they formulated the Christian doctrine of God in Trinitarian terms.

Different minds assume different attitudes toward the conception that God is a Trinity. Some doubtless have conceived the divine existence in a fashion hardly distinguishable from tritheism; others have regarded it as a revealed mystery, incapable of rational comprehension by the mind, but a mystery before which one must worship; still others have regarded it as a mathematical impossibility to be rejected as a figment of the pious imagination. Others (and among them are some of the keenest of modern educated men) have perceived that the idea that God is a Trinity stands for a great and necessarily eternal fact of the divine nature—a fact that no creed necessarily expresses in its completeness, but which is nowhere even hinted at in non-Christian monotheistic conceptions of God.[1]

Intelligent life as we know it on the earth is rich in its power to know, to sympathize, and to love. As no fountain can rise higher than its source, all this rich life must have its counterpart in God. No knowledge is possible without a knowing subject and a knowable object. Unless the nature of God is sufficiently manifold so that he contains in himself both subject and object, his knowledge is not eternal. It is easy to think back to a time, on that supposition, when God knew nothing. Unless the nature of God embraces realities corresponding in some degree to differences in personality, God's love could not be eternal. Love, unless it is hateful self-love, is a social product. Its existence presupposes

[1] It was set forth by John Caird in *The Fundamental Ideas of Christianity* (Glasgow, 1899), Lecture III; by George A. Gordon in *The Ultimate Conceptions of the Faith* (Boston, 1903), pp. 370 ff.; and adopted by the writer in *The Heart of the Christian Message* (New York, 1912), p. 202, and in chapter ix of J. L. Barton's *Christian Approach to Islam.*

a lover and a beloved. If God be a lone monad it is not difficult to think back to a time when in all the universe, even in God, noble love was unknown. Before the beginnings of creation such a God was not the eternally blessed One, but the eternally wretched One. Such a conception of God fails utterly to account for the richness of the intellectual and social life of mankind. If God be only such a One as this, all that is best in human life is an exotic product foreign to the nature of the universe; the brutal powers of which must inevitably some day blot it out. If, on the other hand, God is in himself a social Being, as the Trinitarian doctrine declares, he is not only Eternal Wisdom and Eternal Love but the guaranty that wisdom and love are bound to triumph over ignorance and brutality. If all this is true "the stars in their courses" fight on the side of the social ideal. If all this is true it is of the very nature of God that "he so loved the world that he gave his only begotten Son, that whosoever believeth on him might not perish." It is for this that the doctrine of the Trinity stands. It may not express the whole truth. God may be multitarian for aught we know, but, however rich in diversities his nature may be, the faith that God is after all an essential unity, that in purpose and in love as well as in essence all his richly diversified nature is a unity, prevents Christianity from deserting the ranks of monotheistic religions. It is the flower of monotheism as monotheism is the flower of all that had gone before.

We cannot really know even a neighbor, if we forever misunderstand him, and this is no less true of God. When the supernatural hosts are conceived as bloodthirsty and savage, without unity or ethical purpose, men cannot know God as he is. When these hosts are conceived as too impotent to help man—when man passes them by and relies on his own unaided efforts— men cannot know God so as to let him illuminate life and heart. When God is conceived as an unknowable Absolute, when he is regarded as so weak that Satan is easily his rival, when he is thought of as an arbitrary and capricious despot, the deeper riches of the inner life, the highest joys of the human heart, are not called forth. When we pass in review the poverty of the nations, when we view in comparison the riches of the gospel of the "God who was in Christ reconciling the world unto himself," inevitably the obligation of the Great Commission rests upon us with a new emphasis: "Go ye, therefore, and make disciples of all the nations."

SUPPLEMENTARY READING

For supplementary reading on the topics treated in this chapter the student is referred to the bibliographies at the end of chapters i, iv, v, vi, vii, viii, ix, x, and xv, and in Appendix I.

APPENDIX I

ADDITIONAL BOOKS FOR THE USE OF THE TEACHER

ETHNOLOGY

Keane, A. H. *Ethnology.* Cambridge University Press, 1896.

Brinton, D. G. *Races and Peoples.* New York, 1890.

Hutchinson, Gregory, and Lydekker. *The Living Races of Mankind.* New York, 1902.

Ripley, W. Z. *The Races of Europe.* New York, 1889.

SAVAGE RACES

Spencer and Gillen. *The Northern Tribes of Central Australia.* London, 1904.

Howitt, A. H. *The Native Tribes of South-East Australia,* London, 1904.

Dahl, Knut. *In Savage Australia.* Boston, 1927.

Dowd, Jerome. *The Negro Races.* New York, 1907.

Haddon, A. C. *The Head Hunters.* London, 1901.

Gomes, E. H. *Seventeen Years among the Sea Dyaks of Borneo.* London, 1911.

Codrington, R. H. *The Melanesians.* Oxford, 1891.

Rivers, W. H. R. *The History of Melanesian Society.* Cambridge, 1904.

Skeat, W. W., and Blagden, C. O. *Pagan Races of the Malay Peninsula,* London, 1906

Skeat, W. W. *Malay Magic,* London, 1900.

Mills, J. P. *The Ao Nagas.* London, 1926.

Brown, J. L. *Among the Bantu Nomads.* London, 1926.

Lopez, V. F. *Les Races aryennes du Pérou.* Paris, 1871.

Payne, E. J. *History of the New World Called America.* 2 vols. Oxford, 1899.

Reports of the Cambridge Anthropological Expedition to Torres Straits, chaps. xiii and xiv. Cambridge University Press, 1908.

Frazer, J. G. *The Golden Bough*, 3d ed. London, 1914.

———. *The Belief in Immortality*. London, 1913.

———. *Lectures on the Early History of Kingship*. London, 1905.

———. *Totemism and Exogamy*. 4 vols. London, 1910.

Webster, H. *Primitive Secret Societies*. New York, 1907.

Lang, Andrew. *The Making of Religion*. London and New York, 1900.

Morris, M. "The Influence of War and Agriculture upon the Religion of the Kayans and Sea Dyaks of Borneo," *Journal of the American Oriental Society*, XXV, 231–47.

Conard, L. M. "The Idea of God Held by the North American Indians," *American Journal of Theology*, VII, 635–46.

Chamberlin, A. F. "Haida," in Hastings' *Encyclopaedia of Religion and Ethics*, VI, 469–77.

Gray, L. H. "Iroquois," *ibid.*, VII, 420–22.

Alexander, H. B. "North American Mythology," in Gray's *Mythology of All Races*, Vol. X. Boston, 1916.

Dixon, R. B. "Oceanic Mythology" in Gray's *Mythology of All Races*, Vol. IX. Boston, 1917.

Scott, J. G. "Indo-Chinese Mythology" in Gray's *Mythology of All Races*, Vol. XII. Boston, 1918.

RELIGIONS IN GENERAL

Jevons. F. B. *Introduction to the History of Religion*. London, 1896.

———. *Comparative Religion*. Cambridge University Press, 1913.

Toy, C. H. *Introduction to the History of Religions*. New York, 1913.

Paterson, W. P. *The Nature of Religion*. London, 1925.

Menziez, A. *History of Religion*. New York, 1895.

Carpenter, J. E. *Comparative Religion*. New York and London, 1912.

Brinton, D. G. *The Religion of Primitive Peoples*. New York, 1897.

King, I. *The Development of Religion, a Study in Anthropology and Social Psychology.* New York, 1910.

Moore, George F. *The History of Religions.* 2 vols. New York: Scribner, 1913–19.

——. *The Birth and Growth of Religion.* New York: Charles Scribner's Sons, 1923.

Whitehead, A. N. *Religion in the Making.* New York, 1926.

Robinson, T. H. *Outline Introduction to the History of Religions.* London, 1922.

Morris, M. "The Economic Study of Religion," *Journal of the American Oriental Society*, XXIV, 394–426.

Religions Past and Present, A series of lectures delivered by members of the Faculty of the University of Pennsylvania. Edited by James A. Montgomery. Philadelphia, 1918.

Hopkins, E. W. *The History of Religions.* New York, 1918.

——. *Origin and Evolution of Religion.* New Haven, Conn., 1923.

Otto, R. *The Idea of the Holy.* Oxford, 1925.

Rohrbaugh, L. G. *The Science of Religion.* New York, 1927.

Morgan, W. *The Nature and Right of Religion.* Edinburgh, 1926.

Paton, L. B. *Spiritism in Antiquity.* New York, 1921.

Jayne, W. A. *The Healing Gods of Ancient Civilizations.* New Haven, 1925.

Sneath, E. H. *The Evolution of Ethics.* New York: Macmillan Co., 1927.

——. *Religion and the Future Life.* New York, 1922.

Hume, R. E. *The World's Living Religions.* New York, 1924.

Maynard, J. A. *The Living Religions of the World.* Milwaukee, 1925.

SEMITIC RELIGIONS

Smith, W. R. *The Religion of the Semites*, 3d ed. New York, 1927.

Barton, G. A. *A Sketch of Semitic Origins, Social and Religious.* New York, 1902.

Curtiss, S. I. *Primitive Semitic Religion Today.* New York, 1902.

BABYLONIAN AND ASSYRIAN HISTORY

King, L. W. *History of Sumer and Akkad.* London, 1910.

————. *A History of Babylon.* London, 1915.

J. B. Bury, S. A. Cook, and F. E. Adcock. *The Cambridge Ancient History,* Vols. I and II. New York, 1924–26.

Rogers, R. W. *History of Babylonia and Assyria,* 6th ed. New York, 1915.

Jastrow, M., Jr. *The Civilization of Babylonia and Assyria.* Philadelphia, 1915.

Olmstead, A. T. E. *History of Assyria.* New York, 1923.

Smith, Sidney. *Early History of Assyria to 1000 B.C.* London, 1928.

BABYLONIAN AND ASSYRIAN RELIGION

Jastrow, M., Jr. *Religion of Babylonia and Assyria.* New York, 1898.

————. *Religion Babyloniens und Assyriens.* 2 vols. Giessen, 1905, 1912.

————. *Aspects of Religious Belief in Babylonia and Assyria.* New York, 1911.

————. *Hebrew and Babylonian Traditions.* New York, 1912.

Rogers, R. W. *The Religion of Babylonia and Assyria.* New York, 1908.

King, L. W. *Babylonian Religion and Mythology.* London, 1899.

Hehn, J. *Die biblische und babylonische Gottesidee.* Leipzig, 1913.

Jeremias, A. *Handbuch der altorientalischen Geistkultur.* Leipzig, 1913.

Mackenzie, D. A. *Myths of Babylonia and Assyria.* London, 1915.

Meissner, B. *Babylonien und Assyrien.* 2 vols. Heidelberg, 1920–25.

TRANSLATIONS OF BABYLONIAN RELIGIOUS TEXTS

Harper, R. F. *Assyrian and Babylonian Literature,* pp. 282–460. New York, 1901.

Langdon, S. *Sumerian and Babylonian Psalms.* Paris, 1909.

————. *Sumerian Liturgies and Psalms* (in Publications of the Babylonian Section of the University Museum, Vol. X, Nos. 1, 2, 3, and 4). Philadelphia, 1915–19.

Langdon, S. *The Babylonian Epic of Creation.* Oxford, 1923.

Rogers, R. W. *Cuneiform Parallels to the Old Testament.* New York, 1912.

Barton, G. A. *Archaeology and the Bible*, Part II, 5th ed. Philadelphia, 1927.

Thompson, R. C. *Reports of the Magicians and Astrologers of Nineveh and Babylon*, II. London, 1900.

———. *The Devils and Evil Spirits of Babylonia.* 2 vols. London, 1903, 1904.

The Epic of Gilgamish, London, 1928.

King, L. W. *The Seven Tablets of Creation*, Vol. I. London, 1902.

Jastrow, M., Jr. *Babylonian and Assyrian Birth-Omens.* Giessen, 1914.

Barton, G. A. *Miscellaneous Babylonian Inscriptions*, Part I, Sumerian Religious Texts. New Haven, 1918.

EGYPTIAN HISTORY

Breasted, J. H. *History of Egypt*, 2d ed. New York, 1909.

———. *History of the Ancient Egyptians* (condensed). New York, 1908.

Petrie, W. M. Flinders. *History of Egypt.* 3 vols. New York, 1895–1905.

Budge, E. A. W. *History of Egypt.* 8 vols. London, 1902.

Weigall, A. *A History of the Pharaohs.* Vol. I. New York, 1925. Vol. II, 1927.

Mahaffy, J. P. *The Empire of the Ptolemies.* London, 1895.

Bevan, E. *A History of Egypt under the Ptolemaic Dynasty.* London, 1927.

Budge, E. A. W. *The Literature of the Egyptians.* London, 1914.

Erman, A. *The Literature of the Ancient Egyptians.* London, 1927.

EGYPTIAN RELIGION

Erman, A. *Handbook of Egyptian Religion*, translated by A. S. Griffith. 1907.

Steindorf, G. *Religion of the Ancient Egyptians.* New York, 1905.

Petrie, W. M. Flinders. *Religion and Conscience in Ancient Egypt.* New York, 1898.

Naville, E.   *The Old Egyptian Faith,* translated by C. Campbell. London and New York, 1909.

Breasted, J. H.   *Development of Religion and Thought in Ancient Egypt.*   New York, 1912.

Mackenzie, D. A.   *The Myths of Egypt.*   London, 1914.

Budge, E. A. W.   *The Book of the Dead.*   London, 1898.

——.   *The Gods of the Egyptians.*   London, 1904.

——.   *The Teaching of Amen-em-apt.*   London, 1924.

——.   *The Literature of the Egyptians.*   London, 1914.

Reisner, G. A.   *The Egyptian Conception of Immortality.*   Boston, 1912.

Müller, F. Max.   "Egyptian Mythology," in Gray's *Mythology of All Races,* Vol. XII.   Boston, 1918.

L. Speleers.   *Les Textes des Pyramides Egyttiennes.*   Bruxelles, 1923.

THE RELIGION OF THE ANCIENT HEBREWS

Carpenter, J. E., and Harford-Battersby, G.   *The Hexateuch.*   London: Longmans, Green & Co., 1900.

Addis, W. E.   *The Documents of the Hexateuch.*   London, 1898.

Kent, C. F.   *The Student's Old Testament.*   New York, 1910–27.

——.   *The Historical Bible,* Vols. I–IV.   New York, 1908–13.

Driver, S. R.   "Leviticus," W. H. Bennett, "Joshua," and G. F. Moore, "Judges," in P. Haupt's *Sacred Books of the Old Testament.*   New York: Dodd, Mead & Co., 1898, 1899.

Nowack, W.   "Richter, Ruth und Bücher Samuelis," and R. Kittel, "Die Bücher der Könige," in Nowack's *Handkommentar zum Alten Testament.*   Göttingen.

Box, G. H.   *The Book of Isaiah.*   New York, 1909.

Budde, K.   *The Religion of Israel to the Exile.*   New York, 1899.

Addis, W. E.   *Hebrew Religion to the Establishment of Judaism under Ezra.*   New York, 1906.

Marti, K.   *The Religion of the Old Testament.*   New York, 1907.

Smith, H. P.   *The Religion of Israel.*   New York, 1914.

Peters, J. P.   *The Religion of the Hebrews.*   Boston, 1914.

Badè, W. F.   *The Old Testament in the Light of Today.*   Boston, 1914.

Barton, G. A.   *The Religion of Israel,* 2d ed.   Philadelphia, 1928.

Noyes, Carleton. *The Genius of Israel.* Boston, 1924.

Torrey, G. C. *The Second Isaiah.* New York, 1928.

Smith, J. M. P. *The Prophet and His Problems.* New York, 1914.

———. *The Moral Life of the Hebrews.* Chicago, 1923.

———. *The Religion of the Psalms.* Chicago, 1922.

Fowler, H. T. *The Origin and Growth of the Hebrew Religion.* Chicago: The University of Chicago Press, 1916.

Wallis, Louis. *Sociological Study of the Bible.* Chicago, 1912.

Kay, David M. *The Semitic Religions, Hebrew, Jewish, Christian, Moslem.* Edinburgh, 1923.

Gray, G. B. *Sacrifice in the Old Testament.* Oxford, 1925.

Bertholet, A. *The Civilization of the Hebrews.* London, 1926.

Pedersen, J. *Israel, Its Life and Culture.* London, 1926.

Simpson, D. C. *The Psalmists.* Essays edited by D. C. Simpson. Oxford University Press, 1926.

Peters, J. P. *The Psalms as Liturgies.* New York, 1922.

Robinson, T. H. *Prophecy and the Prophets in Ancient Israel.* New York, 1923.

Gordon, A. R. *The Prophets of the Old Testament.* New York, 1917.

———. *The Poets of the Old Testament.* New York, 1912.

JUDAISM

The Jewish Encyclopedia. New York, 1901–6.

Montgomery, J. A. *The Samaritans.* Philadelphia, 1907.

Herford, R. T. *Christianity in Talmud and Midrash.* London, 1903.

Lauterbach, J. Z. *Sadducees and Pharisees.* London, 1913.

———. *The Pharisees.*

Abrahams, I. *A Short History of Jewish Literature.* New York, 1906.

Schürer, Emil. *A History of the Jewish People in the Time of Jesus Christ.* Edinburgh, 1897.

Silver, A. H. *Messianic Speculation in Israel.* New York, 1927.

Moore, G. F. *Judaism in the First Century of the Christian Era.* Harvard University Press, 1927.

Mathews, Shailer. *History of N.T. Times in Palestine.* Rev. ed. New York, 1921.

Lightly, W. *Jewish Sects and Parties in the Time of Christ.* London, 1925.

M. L. Margolis, and A. Marx. *A History of the Jewish People,* Philadelphia, 1927.

Harris, M. H. *A Thousand Years of Jewish History.* 7th rev. ed. New York, 1920.

Abrahams, I. *Jewish Life in the Middle Ages.* Philadelphia, 1906.

————. *History of the Mediaeval Jews.* New York, 1916.

————. *Judaism.* London, 1910.

Abelson, J. *Jewish Mysticism and the Future of Palestine.* New York, 1919.

Friedländer, M. *The Jewish Religion.* London, 1900.

Drummond, J. *Philo Judaeus.* London, 1888.

Montefiore, C. G. *Judaism and Saint Paul.* London, 1914.

Rosenau, W. *Jewish Ceremonial Institutions and Customs.* Baltimore, 1903.

Kohler, K. *Jewish Theology Systematically and Historically Considered.* New York, 1918.

Fullerton, K. "Zionism," *Harvard Theological Review,* X, 313–35.

Jastrow, M., Jr. *Zionism.* New York, 1919.

Gottheil, R. J. H. *Zionism.* Philadelphia, 1914.

Bevan, E. R., and Singer, C. (eds.). *The Legacy of Israel.* Oxford, 1927.

Ginsberg, Louis. *The Legends of the Jews.* 6 vols. Philadelphia, 1909–20.

Oesterley, W. O. E., and Box, G. H. *Religion and Worship of the Synagogue.* New York, 1907.

MOHAMMEDANISM

The Qur'an, translated by E. H. Palmer (Oxford, 1880), being Vols. IV and IX in the *Sacred Books of the East* edited by F. Max Müller; translated by J. M. Rodwell ("Everyman's Library").

Gilman, A. *The Saracens.* New York and London, 1887.

Lane-Poole, S. *The Moors in Spain.* New York and London, 1891.

Lane-Poole, S. *The Speeches and Table-Talk of the Prophet Mohammed*. London, 1905.

Ali, Ameer. *A Short History of the Saracens*. London, 1899.

Hurgronje, C. Snouck. *Mohammedanism*. New York: G. P. Putnam's Sons, 1913.

Muir, Sir William. *Mahomet and Islam*. London, 1895.

Bevan, A. A. "Mahomet and Islam," *Cambridge Medieval History*, II, 302–8). New York: Macmillan Co., 1913.

Margoliouth, D. S. *Mohammed and the Rise of Islam* in the "Heroes of the Nations" series.

———. *Mohammedanism*, in the "Home University Library."

———. *The Early Development of Mohammedanism* in the "Hibbert Lectures." New York, 1914.

Macdonald, D. B. *Muslim Theology, Jurisprudence and Constitutional Theory*. New York, 1903.

———. *The Religious Attitude and Life in Islam*. Chicago: The University of Chicago Press, 1909.

———. *Aspects of Islam*. New York, 1911.

———. "The Life of Al-Ghazali," *Journal of the American Oriental Society*, XX, 71–132. New Haven, 1899.

Nicholson, R. A. *The Mystics of Islam*. London, 1914.

Bliss, F. J. *The Religions of Modern Syria and Palestine*, chaps. iv–vi. New York, 1912.

Blair, J. C. *The Sources of Islam*. Madras, 1925.

Arnold, Sir T. W. *The Caliphate*. Oxford: Clarenden Press, 1924.

Barton, J. L. *The Christian Approach to Islam*. Boston, 1918.

Zwemer, S. M. *A Moslem Seeker after God*. New York and Chicago: Fleming H. Revell Co., 1920.

ZOROASTRIANISM

Jackson, A. V. W. *Zoroaster, the Prophet of Ancient Iran*. London and New York, 1901.

———. "Zoroastrianism," in the *Jewish Encyclopedia*, XII.

Müller, F. Max. *The Sacred Books of the East*, Vols. IV, V, XXIII, XXXI, and XLVII.

Moulton, J. H. *Early Zoroastrianism*. London, 1913.

———. *The Treasure of the Magi*. London, 1917.

Moore, G. F. "Zoroastrianism," *Harvard Theological Review*, V, 180–226.

Kapadia, S. A. *The Teachings of Zoroaster and the Philosophy of the Parsi Religion.* London, 1913.

Jackson, A. V. W., and Gray, L. H. "The Religion of the Achaemenian Kings," *Journal of the American Oriental Society*, XXI, 160–84.

Dhalla, M. N. *The Nyaishes, or Zoroastrian Litanies.* New York, 1908.

———. *Zoroastrian Theology.* New York, 1914.

———. *Zoroastrian Civilization from the Earliest Times to the Downfall of the Last Zoroastrian Empire, 651 A.D.* New York and Oxford, 1922.

Mistri, R. H. *Zoroaster and Zoroastrianism.* Bombay, 1906.

Moulton, J. H. "The Zoroastrian Conception of a Future Life," *Journal of Transactions of the Victoria Institute*, XLVII, 233–52. London, 1915.

Carnoy, A. J. "Iranian Mythology" in Gray's *Mythology of All Races*, Vol. VI. Boston, 1917.

Buch, M. A. *Zoroastrian Ethics.* Baroda, 1919.

Paury, J. D. C. *The Zoroastrian Doctrine of a Future Life.* New York, 1926.

RELIGION OF THE VEDAS

Grassman, Herman. *Rig-Veda uebersetzt.* 2 vols. Leipzig, 1877.

Deussen, Paul. *Sechzig Upanishads des Veda.* Leipzig, 1897.

Müller, F. Max. *Sacred Books of the East*, Vols. I, XV, XXXII, XLII, XLVI.

Lanman, C. R. Whitney's *Atharva-Veda Samhita.* 2 vols. 1905.

Macdonell, A. A. *A History of Sanskrit Literature.* New York, 1900.

———. "Vedic Mythology" in *Grundriss der indo-irenischen Philologie.*

———. *India's Past: A Survey of Her Literatures, Religions, Languages, and Antiquities.* Oxford, 1927.

Griswold, H. D. *The Religion of the Rig Veda.* Oxford, 1924.

Hopkins, E. W. *The Ethics of India.* New Haven, Conn., 1924.

Farquhar, J. N. *Outline of the Religious Literature of India.* 1920.

Hume, R. E. *The Thirteen Principal Upanishads.* Oxford, 1921.

Bloomfield, M. *The Religion of the Veda.* New York, 1908.

Hoernle, A. F. R., and Stark, H. A. *History of India.* Cuttack, 1904.

Hopkins, E. Washburn. *The Religions of India.* Boston, 1895.

Keith, A. B. "Indian Mythology," in Gray's *Mythology of All Races,* VI, 15-102. Boston, 1917.

BUDDHISM

Müller, F. Max. *Sacred Books of the East,* Vols. X, XI, XIII, XVII, XIX, XX, XXI, XXXV, XXXVI, and XLIX.

Warren, Henry C. *Buddhism in Translations.* Cambridge, 1896.

Smith, V. A. *Asoka the Buddhist Emperor of India.* Oxford, 1901.

———. *Early History of India Including Alexander's Campaigns.* Oxford, 1914.

Macphail, J. M. *Asoka.* Calcutta and Oxford, 1926.

Moorkerji, R. *Harsha.* Oxford, 1926.

Cunningham, A. *The Ancient Geography of India.* London, 1871.

Beal, S. *A Catena of Buddhist Scriptures in China.* London, 1871.

———. *Abstract of Four Lectures on Buddhist Literature in China.* London, 1882.

Saunders, K. J. *Gotama Buddha.* New York, 1920.

Brewster, E. H. *The Life of Gotama, the Buddha.* London, 1926.

Rockhill, W. W. *The Life of the Buddha and the Early History of His Orders Derived from Tibetan Works,* etc. London, 1884.

Grimblot, M. P. *Sept suttas pâlis.* Paris, 1876.

Neumann, K. E. *Reden Gotamo Buddho's.* 4 vols. Leipzig, 1896-1905.

Fausböll, W. *The Dhammapada.* London, 1900.

Copleston, R. S. *Buddhism.* London, 1892.

Davids, T. W. Rhys. *Buddhism.* London, 1903.

———. *Buddhist India.* New York, 1903.

Edmunds, A. J. *Buddhist and Christian Gospels,* 4th ed. Philadelphia, 1908.

Davids, Mrs. Rhys. *Buddhism*, in the "Home University Library."

———. *A Buddhist Manual of Psychological Ethics*. London, 1900.

Hopkins, E. W. *The Religions of India*. Boston, 1895.

Keith, A. B. "Indian Mythology," in Gray's *Mythology of All Races*, VI, 187–219. Boston, 1917.

———. *Buddhist Philosophy*. Oxford, 1923.

Suzuki, D. T. *Outline of Mahāyāna Buddhism*. London, 1907.

McGovern, W. M. *Introduction to Mahāyāna Buddhism*. London, 1922.

Law, B. C. *Heaven and Hell in Buddhist Perspective*. Calcutta and Simla, 1925.

King, Mrs. Louis. *We Tibetans*. London, 1926.

Waddell, L. A. *The Buddhism at Tibet*. London, 1895.

Legge, James. *A Record of Buddhistic Kingdoms* (The Travels of Fa Hien). Oxford, 1886.

Saunders, K. J. *Epochs of Buddhist History*. Chicago, 1924.

Beal, Samuel. *The Life of Huien-Tsang by the Shaman Hwui Li*. London, 1911.

Tachibana, S. *The Ethics of Buddhism*. Oxford, 1926.

Pratt, James B. *The Pilgrimage of Buddhism*. New York, 1928.

JAINISM

Jacobi, H., in Müller's *Sacred Books of the East*, Vols. XXII and XLV.

———. "Jainism" in Hastings' *Encyclopaedia of Religion and Ethics*, VII.

Hopkins, E. W. *The Religions of India*.

Stevenson, Mrs. S. *The Heart of Jainism*. Oxford University Press, 1915.

Keith, A. B. "Indian Mythology," in Gray's *Mythology of All Races*, VI, 220–29. Boston, 1917.

Guérinot, A. *La Religion Djaina*. Paris, 1926.

Jain, C. R. *The Key of Knowledge*. Arrah, 1920.

HINDUISM

Müller, F. Max. *The Sacred Books of the East*, Vols. II, VII, VIII, and XXXIV.

Basu, B. D., (ed.). *The Sacred Books of the Hindus* (translated by various Sanskrit scholars). Allahabad.

Barth, A. *The Religions of India.* London, 1882.

Hopkins, E. W. *The Ordinances of Manu.* London, 1884.

——. *The Great Epic of India.* New York, 1901.

——. *The Religions of India.* Boston, 1895.

Monier-Williams. *Brahmanism and Hinduism,* 4th ed. London, 1891.

Oman, J. C. *Indian Epics, the Ramayana and Mahābhārata.* London, 1906.

——. *The Mystics, Ascetics and Saints of India.* London, 1905.

——. *Cults, Customs, and Superstitions of India.* London, 1908.

Dutt, R. C. *Mahābhārata the Epic of Ancient India Condensed into English Verse.* London, 1899.

Arnold, Sir Edwin. *The Song Celestial, or the Bhagavad-Gītā.* Boston, 1909. (Arnold's translation conveys poetic feeling; that in *Sacred Books of the East,* Vol. VIII, gives the original with literal fidelity.)

Hastings, James. *Encyclopaedia of Religion and Ethics,* II, the articles "Arya Samaj," "Bhagavad-Gita," "Bhakti-Marga," "Brahman," "Brahmanism," and "Brahma Samaj," by different authors. New York, 1910.

Macnicol, N. *Indian Theism.* Oxford University Press, 1915.

Elmore, W. T. *Dravidian Gods in Modern Hinduism.* Hamilton, N.Y., 1915.

Advanced Text Book of Hindu Religion and Ethics. Benares, 1904.

The World's Eternal Religion (The Bharat Dharma Syndicate). Benares, 1924.

Radhakrishnan, S. *The Hindu View of Life.* London: Macmillan Co., 1927.

Macauliffe, M. A. *The Sikh Religion.* 6 vols. Oxford, 1909.

Monahan, F. J. *Early History of Bengal.* Oxford, 1925.

Woods, J. H. *The Yoga System of Patanjali.* Cambridge, Mass., 1913. ("Harvard Oriental Series.")

Rolland, R. *Mahatma Ghandi.* Paris: Stock, 1924.

Farquhar, J. N. *Modern Religious Movements in India*. New York, 1924.

Müller, F. Max. *The Six Systems of Indian Philosophy*. New York, 1899.

Das Gupta, S. *History of Indian Philosophy*. 3 vols. London, 1922——.

——. *Yoga as Philosophy and Religion*. London, 1924.

Radhakrishnan, S. *Indian Philosophy*. 2 vols. London, 1922——.

Doke, Joseph. *M. K. Gandhi, an Indian Patriot in South Africa*. London, 1909.

Gray, R. M., and Parekh, M. C. *Mahatma Gandhi*. New York, 1925.

Keith, A. B. "Indian Mythology," in Gray's *Mythology of All Races*, VI, 103–86; 230–50. Boston, 1917.

Eliot, Sir Charles. *Hinduism and Buddhism*. 3 vols. London, 1921.

Carpenter, J. E. *Theism in Mediaeval India*. London, 1921.

Parker, R. J. *Sadhu Sundar Singh*. New York, 1920.

Pratt, James B. *India and Its Faiths*. Boston, 1915.

Macnicol, Nicol. *The Making of Modern India*. Oxford, 1924.

Singh, Sadhu Sundar. *Visions of the Spiritual World*. New York, 1927.

Stevenson, Mrs. Sinclair. *The Rites of the Twice-Born*. Oxford, 1920.

Streeter, B. H., and Appasamy, A. J. *The Message of Sadhu Sundar Singh*. London, 1921.

McKenzie, J. *Hindu Ethics*. Oxford, 1922.

Oltramare, P. *Histoire des Idées theosophique dans l'Inde*. Vol. I, *La Théosophique bramanique*. Paris, 1907. Vol. II, *La Théosophique bouddhique*. 1923.

Walter, H. A. *The Ahmadiya Movement*. Oxford, 1918.

RELIGIONS OF CHINA

Gowen, H. H., and Hall, J. W. *Outline History of China*. New York, 1926.

Hirth, F. *The Ancient History of China*. New York, 1911.

Giles, H. A. *A History of Chinese Literature*. New York, 1924. New ed. London, 1927.

Müller, F. Max. *Sacred Books of the East*, Vols. III, XVI, XIX, XXVII, XXVIII, XXXIX, and XL (translations by Legge of Chinese Canonical Books and Life of Buddha).

Wilson, E. *Chinese Literature* (translations of the *Analects* of Confucius, the *Shi-King*, and the sayings of Mencius). New York, 1900.

De Groot, J. J. M. *The Religious Systems of China*. 6 vols. Leyden, 1892–1910.

———. *Sectarianism and Religious Persecution in China*. 2 vols. Amsterdam, 1903–4.

———. *The Religion of the Chinese*. New York, 1910.

———. *Religion in China*. New York, 1912.

Ross, T. *The Original Religion of China*, 1918.

Legge, James. *The Religions of China*. New York, 1881.

Douglas, R. K. *Confucianism and Taoism*. London, 1900.

Giles, H. A. *The Civilization of the Chinese*. London, 1911.

———. *China and the Chinese*. New York, 1902.

———. *Chinese Poetry in English Verse*. London, 1898.

———. *Confucianism and Its Rivals*. New York, 1915.

Soothill, W. E. *The Three Religions of China*. New ed. London, 1924.

Hodous, L. *Buddhism and Buddhists in China*. New York, 1924.

Monroe, Paul. *China, a Nation in Evolution*. New York, 1927.

Wieger, Léon, S. J. *Histoire des Croyances religieuses en Chine*. Hien-Hien, 1922.

Henke, F. G. *The Philosophy of Wang Yang Ming*. Chicago, 1916.

Skrine, C. P. *Chinese Central Asia*. Boston, 1926.

Bruce, J. P., (trans.). *The Philosophy of Human Nature. Chu Hsi*. London, 1922.

Bishop, Isabella B. *Corea and Her Neighbors*. New York, 1894.

Lyall, L. A. *The Sayings of Confucius*, 2d ed. London, 1925.

Williams, E. T. *China Yesterday and Today*, 4th ed. New York, 1929.

Foake, A. *The World Conception of the Chinese*. London, 1925.

O'Neill, F. W. S. *The Quest for God in China*. New York, 1925.

Parker, E. H. *China and Religion*. New York, 1905.

Kudo, T. *The Ethics of Confucius*. Tokyo, 1904.

Cave, Sidney. *Living Religions of the East.* New York, 1922.

Reichelt, K. L. *Truth and Tradition in Chinese Buddhism.* Shanghai, 1927.

Lew, T. T. and others. *China Today through Chinese Eyes.* New York, 1922.

Johnston, R. F. *Buddhist China.* London, 1913.

RELIGIONS OF JAPAN

Asakawa, K. "Japan," in H. C. Lodge, *The History of the Nations,* Vol. VII. Philadelphia, 1906.

Brinkley, F. *A History of the Japanese People.* London, 1915.

Nitobe, I. O. *Bushido, the Soul of Japan,* 19th ed. Tokyo, 1913.

———. *The Japanese Nation.* New York, 1912.

Armstrong, R. C. *Light from the East: Studies in Confucianism.* Toronto, 1914.

Aston, W. G. *A History of Japanese Literature.* London, 1899.

———. *Shinto (the Way of the Gods).* London, 1905.

———. *Shinto, the Ancient Religion of Japan.* London, 1907.

Griffis, W. E. *The Religions of Japan.* New York, 1895.

Gowen, H. H. *An Outline History of Japan.* New York, 1928.

Kato, Genchi. *A Study of Shinto, the Religion of the Japanese Nation.* Tokyo, 1926.

Reischauer, A. K. *Studies in Japanese Buddhism.* New York, 1925.

Suzuki, D. T. *Essays in Zen Buddhism.* London, 1927.

Anesaki, M. *Nichiren, a Buddhist Prophet.* New York, 1916.

Satow, E. M. "The Revival of Pure Shinto." *Transactions of the Asiatic Society of Japan,* III. Appendix.

Knox, G. W. *The Development of Religion in Japan.* New York, 1907.

Ashida, K. "Japan," in Hastings' *Encyclopaedia of Religion and Ethics,* VII.

Lloyd, A., *The Creed of Half Japan, Historical Sketches in Japanese Buddhism.* London, 1911.

Kaempfer, M. E. *History of Japan,* I, II, III.

Holtom, D. C. *The Political Philosophy of Modern Shinto.* Chicago, 1922.

RELIGION OF GREECE

Wright, Wilmer Cave. *A Short History of Greek Literature.* New York, 1907.

Farnell, L. R. *The Cults of the Greek States.* 5 vols. Oxford, 1896–1909.

——. *The Higher Aspects of Greek Religion.* New York, 1912.

——. "Greek Religion," in Hastings' *Encyclopaedia of Religion and Ethics.*

Fairbanks, Arthur. *Handbook of Greek Religion.* New York, 1910.

Nilsson, M. P. *The Minoan-Mycaenean Religion.* Oxford, 1927.

——. *A History of Greek Religion.* Oxford, 1925.

Glotz, G. *The Aegean Civilization.* New York, 1925.

Harrison, Jane E. *Prolegomena to the Study of Greek Religion,* 2d ed. Cambridge, 1908.

——. *Themis, a Study of the Social Origins of Greek Religion.* Cambridge, 1912.

Murray, Gilbert. *Five Stages of Greek Religion.* New York, 1925.

Rouse, W. H. D. *Greek Votive Offerings.* Cambridge, 1902.

Moore, Clifford H. *The Religious Thought of the Greeks.* Cambridge, 1916.

Campbell, Lewis. *Religion in Greek Literature.* London, 1898.

Harrison, Jane E. *The Religion of Ancient Greece.* London, 1905.

More, Paul E. *The Religion of Plato.* Princeton, 1921.

Davis, Gladys M. W. *The Asiatic Dionysos.* London, 1914.

Zielinski, T. *The Religion of Ancient Greece.* Oxford, 1926.

Nock, A. D., translator and editor. *Sallustius Philosophus.* Cambridge, 1926.

RELIGION OF ROME

Wissowa, George. *Religion und Kultus der Römer,* 2te Aufl. München, 1912.

Fowler, W. Warde. *The Religious Experience of the Roman People.* London, 1911.

——. *Roman Ideas of Deity in the Last Century before the Christian Era.* London, 1914.

Carter, Jesse B. *The Religion of Numa and Other Essays on the Religion of Ancient Rome.* New York, 1906.

———. *The Religious Life of Ancient Rome.* Boston, 1911.

Cumont, F. *The Oriental Religions in Roman Paganism.* Chicago, 1911.

———. *The Mysteries of Mithra.* Chicago, 1903.

———. *Astrology and Religion among the Greeks and Romans.* New York, 1912.

———. *After Life in Roman Paganism.* New Haven: Yale University Press, 1922.

Glover, T. R. *The Conflict of Religions in the Early Roman Empire.* London, 1909.

Herbig, G. "Etruscan Religion" in Hastings' *Encyclopaedia of Religion and Ethics*, V, 532–40.

Wenley, R. M. "Cynics," in Hastings' *Encyclopaedia of Religion and Ethics*, IV, 378–83.

Halliday, W. R. *Lectures on the History of Religion from Numa to Augustus.* University Press of Liverpool, 1922.

RELIGION OF THE CELTS

Rhys, Sir John. *Lectures on the Origin and Growth of Religion as Illustrated by Celtic Heathendom.* 3d ed. London, 1898.

———. *Celtic Folk-lore.* 2 vols. Oxford, 1901.

———. *Celtic Britain.* London, 1908.

MacCulloch, J. A. *The Religion of the Ancient Celts.* Edinburgh, 1911.

———. "Celts," in Hastings' *Encyclopaedia of Religion and Ethics.*

MacLagan, R. C. *Scottish Myths.* Edinburgh, 1882.

Nutt, A. *Cúchulainn, the Irish Achilles.* London, 1900.

———. *Ossian and the Ossianic Literature.* London, 1899.

John, I. B. *The Mabinogion.* London, 1901.

Ripley, W. Z. *The Races of Europe*, pp. 124–28. New York, 1899.

RELIGION OF THE TEUTONS

Gummere, F. B. *Germanic Origins.* New York, 1892.

Chantepie de la Saussaye, F. D. *The Religion of the Teutons.* Boston, 1902.

Rydberg, V. *Teutonic Mythology.* Translated by R. B. Anderson, London, 1889.

Ludlow, J. M. *Popular Epics of the Middle Ages.* 2 vols. London and Cambridge, 1865.

Horton, A., and Bell, E. *The Lay of the Nibelungs.* London, 1898.

Shumway, D. B. *The Nibelungenlied.* Boston, 1909.

Shaw, C. B. *Frithiof's Saga.* New York, 1925.

Helm, Karl. *Altgermanische Religionsgeschichte.* Heidelberg, 1913.

Amour, M. *The Fall of the Nibelungs.* London, 1897.

Cottle, A. S. *Icelandic Poetry or the Edda of Saemund.* Bristol, 1797.

Brodeur, A. G. *The Prose Edda by Snorri Sturluson.* New York, 1916.

Bugge, S. *The Home of the Eddic Poems.* Translated by W. H. Schofield, London, 1899.

Larned, A. *Tales from the Norse Grandmother (The Elder Edda).* New York, 1881.

Faraday, W. *The Edda: The Divine Mythology of the North.* London, 1902.

CHRISTIANITY

Burton and Mathews. *The Life of Christ,* New ed. Chicago: The University of Chicago Press, 1928.

Holtzmann, Oscar. *The Life of Jesus.* London, 1904.

Case, S. J. *The Historicity of Jesus.* Chicago: The University of Chicago Press, 1912.

——. *The Evolution of Christianity.* Chicago, 1914.

——. *Jesus.* Chicago, 1927.

Glover, T. R. *The Jesus of History.* New York, 1917.

——. *Paul of Tarsus.* New York, 1925.

Barton, G. A. *The Heart of the Christian Message,* 2d ed. New York, 1912.

——. *Jesus of Nazareth, a Biography.* New York, 1922.

——. *Studies in New Testament Christianity.* Philadelphia, 1928.

Bosworth, E. A. *The Life and Teaching of Jesus.* New York, 1925.

Klausner, J. *Jesus of Nazareth.* New York, 1925.

Bacon, B. W. *The Story of Jesus.* New York, 1927.

Warschauer, J. *Historical Life of Christ.* London, 1927.

Sabatier, A. *The Apostle Paul.* New York, 1893.

Bruce, A. B. *St. Paul's Conception of Christianity.* New York, 1894.

Stevens, G. B. *Pauline Theology.* New York, 1892.

———. *Johannine Theology.* New York, 1894.

Wood, C. T. *The Life, Letters and Religion of St. Paul.* Edinburgh, 1925.

Foakes-Jackson, F. J. *St. Paul.* New York, 1926.

Kennedy, H. A. A. *St. Paul and the Mystery Religions.* London, 1913.

Morgan, W. *The Religion and Theology of Paul.* Edinburgh, 1917.

Easton, B. S. *The Gospel before the Gospels.* New York, 1928.

Merrill, E. T. *Essays in Early Christian History.* New York, 1924.

McGiffert, A. C. *Protestant Thought before Kant.* New York, 1911.

———. *The God of the Early Christians.* New York, 1924.

———. *The Rise of Modern Religious Ideas.* New York, 1915.

Zenos, A. C. *The Plastic Age of the Gospel.* New York, 1927.

Streeter, H. B. *The Four Gospels.* New York, 1925.

———. *Reality.* New York, 1926.

Rawlinson, E. J. *The New Testament Doctrine of Christ.* London, 1926.

Scott, E. F. *The Fourth Gospel.* Edinburgh, 1906.

Walker, W. *History of the Christian Church.* New York, 1918.

Fisher, G. P. *History of Christian Doctrine.* New York, 1896.

Rainey, R. *The Ancient Catholic Church.* New York, 1902.

Adeney, W. F. *The Greek and Eastern Churches.* New York, 1908.

Workman, H. B. *Christian Thought to the Reformation.* New York, 1911.

Allen, A. V. G. *The Continuity of Christian Thought.* Boston, 1884.

Allen, A. V. G. *Christian Institutions.* New York, 1897.

Briggs, C. A. *Theological Symbolics.* New York, 1914.

Hatch, E. *The Organization of the Early Christian Churches.* London, 1892.

Lindsay, T. M. *The Church and the Ministry in the Early Centuries.* New York, 1902.

——. *A History of the Reformation.* 2 vols. New York, 1906–7.

Jones, R. M. *Studies in Mystical Religion.* London, 1909.

——. *Spiritual Reformers of the Sixteenth and Seventeenth Centuries.* London, 1914.

——. *New Studies in Mystical Religion.* New York, 1927.

Moore, E. C. *Protestant Thought since Kant.* New York, 1912.

Clarke, W. N. *Outlines of Christian Theology,* 15th ed. New York, 1907.

——. *The Use of Scripture in Theology.* New York, 1905.

Orr, J. *The Ritschlian Theology and the Evangelical Faith.* 2d ed. New York, 1898(?).

Ward, W. H. *What I Believe and Why.* New York, 1915.

Caird, John. *The Fundamental Ideas of Christianity.* 2 vols. Glasgow, 1899.

Gordon, G. A. *Ultimate Conceptions of the Faith.* Boston, 1903.

Wieman, H. N. *The Wrestle of Religion with Truth.* New York, 1927.

Smith, G. B. *Current Christian Thinking.* Chicago, 1928.

APPENDIX II

TOPICS FOR FURTHER STUDY, CLASSROOM DISCUSSION, OR ASSIGNED PAPERS

CHAPTER I

1. The Function of Mythology in Religion.
2. The Extent and Significance of the Belief in Immortality.
3. The Rise of the Belief in Pantheons and Departmental Gods.
4. Different Theories of Sacrifice.
5. The Place of Prayer in Early Religions.
6. The Conceptions of Sin in Early Religions.
7. The Nature of Salvation in Early Religions.
8. The Nature of Priesthoods in Early Religions.
9. The Characteristic Features of the Religion of the Primitive Hamites and Semites.

CHAPTER II

1. The Relation of Babylonian Views of the Supernatural to Those of Primitive Men.
2. Are There Traces of Totemism in Babylonia?
3. At What Period Did Astrology Develop in Babylonia?
4. How Do Babylonian Hymns Compare with Hebrew Psalms?
5. The Nature of the Babylonian Conception of Sin.
6. To What Extent Did Babylonian Religion Influence Morals?

CHAPTER III

1. The Relation of Egyptian Animal-Worship to Totemism.
2. The Various Theories Concerning the Cult of Osiris.
3. The Nature of the Egyptian Social Conscience and Ethics and the Relation of These to the Economic and Political Life of the Country.

381

4. The Relation of the Egyptian Conceptions of the Life after Death to Egyptian Ethics.

5. What Conception of Sin and Atonement Did the Egyptians Hold?

CHAPTER IV

1. Was Yahweh Originally Akin to Other Semitic Gods?

2. The Relation of Israel's Early Religious Development to Her Social Development.

3. Modern Views of the Messianic Hope in Pre-exilic Times.

4. The Influence of the Assyrian and Babylonian Wars on Israel's Religion.

5. Modern Views of the "Servant of Yahweh" in Second Isaiah.

6. The Contrast between the Prophets and the Law.

CHAPTER V

1. The Composition of the Psalter.

2. The Religious Point of View of the "Wisdom" Books.

3. The Nature and Function of the Apocalyptic Books.

4. The Rise of the Pharisees and Their Religious Influence.

5. Philo and Judaeo-Greek Philosophy.

6. Jewish Literature in the Middle Ages.

7. Jewish Scholars in the Middle Ages.

8. Jewish Influence in Modern Life.

CHAPTER VI

1. Comparison of Mohammed with the Hebrew Prophets.

2. The Ethics of the Koran.

3. The Mohammedan Tests of the Genuineness of a Tradition.

4. The Life of Al-Ghazali.

5. Ibn Khaldun's Metaphysics.

6. Islamic Mysticism.

7. The Druses and Babists.

8. Has Mohammedanism Contributed Any Great Truth to the World's Stock of Religious Knowledge?

CHAPTER VII

1. The Relation of Iranian Heathenism to the Vedic Religion.

2. The Ethics of Zoroastrianism.

3. The Ritual of Later Zoroastrianism (Vendidad, Yashts, and Pahlavi Texts).

4. The Zoroastrian Conception of the Last Things.

5. A Comparison of Zoroastrianism and Judaism.

CHAPTER VIII

1. The Nature of the Hymns Addressed to Indra.

2. The Nature of the Hymns Addressed to Varuna.

3. The Mixture of Priestcraft and Nature-Worship in the Veda.

4. The Influence of Racial Fusion and the Climate of India on the Upanishads.

5. The Contrast between the Philosophy of the Upanishads and Christianity.

CHAPTER IX

1. The Relation of Buddha's Conception of the World to That of the Upanishads.

2. A Comparison of Buddhist and Christian Ethical Teaching.

3. A Comparison of the Buddhist and Christian Scriptures.

4. A Comparison of Buddhism and Jainism.

5. A Comparison of Modern Buddhism with Primitive Buddhism.

CHAPTER X

1. The Relation of the Sankhya-Yoga Philosophies to Buddhism.

2. The Influence of Buddhism and Jainism upon the Development of the Vishnu-Religion.

3. The Differences and Resemblances of the Vishnu- and Çiva-Religion.

4. A Comparison of the Bhagavad-Gita with the New Testament.

5. A Comparison of the Vedanta Philosophy with That of Spinoza.

6. A Comparison of Ram Mohan Ray, Founder of the Brahma Samaj, with Martin Luther.

CHAPTER XI

1. The Chinese Conception of the Supernatural.

2. Chinese Divination.

3. To What Extent Is Confucianism a Religion?

4. The Mysticism of Lao-tze and Kwang-tze.

5. The History of Buddhism in China.

6. Chinese Popular Religion Today.

7. A Comparison of the Chinese Religious Temperament with the Semitic and Indian.

CHAPTER XII

1. A Comparison of the Chinese and Japanese Conceptions of the Divine.

2. A Comparison of the Reception Accorded Buddhism in the Sixth Century and That Accorded Western Culture in the Nineteenth.

3. The Causes That Produced Bushido.

4. The Differences between Confucianism in China and in Japan.

5. Catholic Christianity in Japan in the Middle Ages.

CHAPTER XIII

1. The Extent of the Influence of Aegean Civilization on the Religion of Greece.

2. The Growth of Greek Mythology.

3. The Relation of the Development of Greek Religion to the Expanding Life of the Nation.

4. A Comparison of Greek Philosophical Monotheism with Hebrew Monotheism.

5. A Comparison of Greek Religious Philosophy with the Religious Philosophies of India.

6. A Comparison of Greek Religious Philosophy with That of China.

7. The Influence of Greek Philosophy upon Judaism.

CHAPTER XIV

1. A Comparison of Roman Family Religion with the Earliest Forms of Other Indo-European Religions.

2. A Comparison of Early Roman Religion with Early Japanese Religion.

3. Etruscan Religion and Its Influence upon Rome.

4. The Influence of Imperialism on the Religion of Rome.

5. The Organization of Emperor-Worship.

6. The Birth and Development of Individualism in Roman Religion.

7. Oriental Influences in the Religion of the Empire.

CHAPTER XV

1. The Ethnographic Problem of the Celtic Race.

2. The Origin of the Druids.

3. Traces of Matriarchy among the Celts.

4. The Nature and Functions of the Irish God Lug.

5. The Celtic Elysium in Irish Poetry.

6. Mythical Elements in Teutonic Heroic Sagas.

7. The Nature and Form of Teutonic Temples in Germany, Scandanavia, and Iceland.

8. The Norse World-Tree Yggdrasil.

9. Teutonic Cosmogony.

10. Survivals of Celtic and Norse Religion in European Christianity.

CHAPTER XVI

1. The Nature of Gnosticism and Its Influence on Christianity.

2. The Influence of the Mystery-Religions upon Christianity.

3. The Influence of Greek Thought on Christianity.

4. The Influence of the Decian Persecution upon Christian Thought.

5. The Rise of Manichaeism, Its Nature, and Its Influence on Christianity.

6. The Influence of Roman Imperial Ideals upon the Church.

7. The Causes of the Reformation.

8. The Influence of the Philosophy of Locke on Christianity.

9. The Influence of the Philosophy of Kant on Christianity.

10. The Mystic Elements in Christianity.

11. The Influence of Modern Science on Christianity.

12. The Rise of Modern Missions.

13. The New Theology.

APPENDIX III

OUTLINE OF A BOOK TO BE WRITTEN BY THE STUDENT

CHAPTER I

1. Evidence for the Psychological Unity of the Race.
2. The Place of Ritual in Early Religions.
3. The Function of Myths in Early Religions.

CHAPTER II

1. The Prevalence of Animism.
2. The Conceptions of the Soul Entertained by Early Men.
3. Diffusion of the Belief in Transmigration of the Soul.
4. Conceptions of the Life after Death.

CHAPTER III

1. The Development of Gods.
2. Their Connection with Specific Localities.
3. Effects of Social and Economic Conditions upon the Ideas Entertained of Them.
4. Fetishism and Idols.

CHAPTER IV

1. Totemism.
2. Taboo.
3. Sacrifice.

CHAPTER V

1. Early Ideas of Sin, Atonement, and Righteousness.

CHAPTER VI

1. The Babylonian Conception of the Supernatural, and Man's Relation to It, Including Sin, Sickness, Atonement, and Healing.
2. The Influence of Religion on Morals.

386

CHAPTER XVI

1. Ancient Iran, Its People, and Religion.
2. Zoroaster, His Preparation for His Work.
3. His Prophetic Career.
4. Zoroastrianism under the Achaemenians.
5. Under the Greeks and Parthians.
6. Under the Sassanians.
7. Since the Mohammedan Conquest.

CHAPTER XVII

1. Zoroaster's Doctrine of God and Angels.
2. Angra Mainyu and Demons in Zoroastrianism.
3. The Doctrine of Man in Zoroastrianism.
4. Zoroastrian Ethics.
5. Zoroastrian Ritual and Priesthood.
6. The Zoroastrian Eschatology.
7. The Development from the Founder to the Later Religion.

CHAPTER XVIII

1. The Land and Climate of India.
2. The People of the Vedas and Their Social Organization.
3. The Strata of the Vedic Literature.
4. The Gods of the Rig-Veda.
5. The Ritual of the Rig-Veda.
6. The Vedic Conception of Salvation.

CHAPTER XIX

1. The Demonology and Magic of the Atharva-Veda.
2. The Development of Thought in the Brahmanas.
3. The Philosophy of the Upanishads.

CHAPTER XX

1. The Life of Vardhamana, the Founder of Jainism.
2. The Jain Conception of the Universe and Salvation.
3. The Rules of the Jain Order.
4. The Later Development of Jainism.

[1] See "Etruscan Religion" in Hastings' *Encyclopaedia of Religion and Ethics*, V, 532–540.

4. The Broadening Influence of Greek Philosophy upon Christianity.

5. The Development of the Idea of the Church in the West.

6. The Christological Controversies.

7. The Later History of the Eastern Churches.

CHAPTER XXXVI

1. The Rise of the Papacy.

2. The Theology of Augustine.

3. The Rise of Scholasticism.

4. The Closing of the Bible to the Laity.

5. The Christian Saints of the Middle Ages, St. Bernard, St. Francis of Assisi, etc.

CHAPTER XXXVII

1. Causes Leading to the Reformation.

2. The Work of Luther and Zwingli.

3. The Work of Calvin.

4. Minor Sects, Mennonites, Schwenkfelders, Anabaptists, Socinians, etc.

5. The Reformation in England and Scotland.

6. The Seventeenth-Century Christianity.

CHAPTER XXXVIII

1. Christian Thought and Life in the Eighteenth Century.

2. The Revival of Interest in the Nineteenth Century.

3. Christian Missions in the Nineteenth Century.

4. The Influence of Hegel on Christianity.

5. The Tractarian Movement.

6. Reactionary Movements in the Church of Rome.

7. The Influence of Expanding Knowledge on Christianity.

CHAPTER XXXIX

1. The Difference between Gods and Other Animistic Spirits.

2. Savage Conceptions of Gods as to Functions, Shrines, and Ethics.

3. Pantheons and the Feeling for the Unity of the World.

4. Evidences That There Was a New Epoch in the Spiritual Development of Man between 800 and 400 B.C.

5. The Religion of Pantheism.

6. Religions of Salvation by Self.

7. The Various Forms of Mahayana Buddhism.

8. The Religious Value of Monotheism, as Shown (a) in Judaism, (b) in Zoroastrianism, (c) in Islam, (d) in Christianity.

9. The Most Satisfactory Form of Monotheism as Shown by Its Fruits.

INDEX

INDEX

Aaron, 62
Abbaside caliphate, 103 f.
Abelard, 328
Abelson, J., 367
Abrahams, I, 96, 366, 367
Abu Hanifa, 91, 107
Abydos, Egyptian city, 37, 40
Achaemenian dynasty, 119, 127 f., 130
Acock, F. E., 363
Acts of the Apostles, 316
Açvins, 146
Adapa, 29
Adda, Babylonian storm-god, 23, 25
Addis, W. E., 75, 78, 365
Adeney, W. F., 379
Aegean civilization, 243
Aeschylus, 242, 254 f.
Aesculapius, 272
Aeshma Daeva, 133
Agade, Babylonian city, 20, 22, 23
Agathias, 131
Agni, fire-god, 122, 138, 145, 184
Ahab, 65
Ahmad ibn Hanbal, 108
Ahriman, 133, 134, 135. See also Angra Mainyu
Ahura, 121
Ahura Mazda, 121, 123 f., 125 f., 128, 130, 133, 135
Ajatasatru, 169
Akiba, Rabbi, 88
Akkad, 24
Al-Ashari, 112
Al-Bokhari, 106
Alexander the Great, 81, 131, 169

Al-Ghazali, 112 ff.
Ali, Ameer, 367
Ali, fourth caliph, 102 f.
Allen, A. V. G., 379
Al-Mohads, 115
Al-Moravides, 115
Altars, Hebrew, 65; Indian, 178
Alu-ellu, 19
Amen (Amon), Egyptian god, 36, 37, 47, 50 f.
Amesha Spentas, 133, 134
Amitabha, 220
Amorites, 23
Amos, 66, 67, 332
Amour, M., 378
Amurru (Amorites), 23
Anâhita, 129, 133
Analects of Confucius, 201, 211
Anath, Syrian deity, 49
Anaxagoras, 253
Anaximander, 253
Anaximenes, 253
Anesaki, M., 375
Anglo-Saxons, 304 f.
Angra Mainyu; 126, 130, 133, 134, 135
Animal worship, 37
Animism, 6 f., 336 f.
Anselm, 327 f.
Antiochus IV, 83
Anu, god, 22, 25, 27
Āpastamba, 178, 184, 185
Aphrodite, 242, 247
Apis bulls, 49
Apocalypses, 83
Apocalyptic literature, 83

397

[PRINTED IN U.S.A.]